S C H "Sammy" Davis

My Lifetime
in Motorsport

To Jimmy Jackson
With best wishes

Peter Whitehead

Dedication

To Michael Worthington-Williams,
who was more than brave to trust me with the original manuscript.

Peter Heilbron, Reigate, June 2007

The Editor: an Appreciation

Whilst this book is self-evidently about Sammy Davis it would never have come to publication without the indefatigable effort and persistence of Peter Heilbron. It was Peter who saw the possibilities in Sammy's badly typed "manuscript", deciphered it, and laboriously put it onto his computer so that it could be further worked upon. He also recognised the historic value of the Log Book, transcribed it, and turned it into the coherent entity that it now is. Peter also contacted people who could shed light on matters that Sammy did not always make clear, chased hither and thither to find illustrations and additional information, and although he graciously acknowledges the help of others, without his unremitting determination to see the project through to its conclusion the efforts of all those who helped would have been in vain.

I regard it as a privilege to have been in some way associated with this project and am pleased to be allowed to record here my admiration and appreciation for what Peter has been able to do.

Malcolm Jeal, Easterton, June 2007

S C H "Sammy" Davis

Sammy's pen-name "Casque" evolved from a remark to "Caput", L V Head of The Autocar. *"My crash helmet was the dead spit and image of a steel casque, one belonging to a Britain (sic) who fought in Caesar's army, now in the British Museum."*

My Lifetime in Motorsport

His Final Autobiography with Log Book for 1913-14

Compiled and edited by Peter Heilbron
Assisted by Malcolm Jeal

Herridge & Sons

Published 2007 by Herridge & Sons Ltd
Lower Forda, Shebbear,
Beaworthy, Devon EX21 5SY

Copyright © Colin Davis 2007
Edited and compiled by Peter Heilbron

Designed by Ray Leaning,
Muse Fine Art & Design Ltd

ISBN 978-1-906133-02-3
Printed in China

Editor's Acknowledgements

Malcolm Jeal, without whose help this book would never have
been completed

Derek Grossmark, to whom special thanks for much advice, and for
his time and patience scanning documents and pictures for illustrations

Jean Heilbron, for much help with deciphering the log book, and
for her patience and forbearance throughout

Duncan Ferguson and Colin Davis. See Introduction, Foreword
and Epilogue

Bryan Goodman Pictures
David Burgess-Wise and Aston Martin Owners Club
David Hales
David Rolfe, Hon Archivist and Bentley Drivers Club
Donald Cowbourne
Geoff Morris and Lt Col A J "Tiny" Ayers, Sunbeam Motorcycle Club
Hervé Guyomard, Automobile Club de l'Ouest, Le Mans
Ian Wagstaff & Marcus Chambers
John Pulford, Curator of Collections, Brooklands Museum
Kenneth Ball, Autobooks Ltd
Manx National Heritage, Isle of Man
Mark Morris
National Motor Museum
Neill Bruce, Automobile Photo Library
Robert Orlan
Ron Clarke
Steven Cropley, Editor-in-Chief, Autocar

Illustrations

Every effort has been made to trace the copyright of photographs
and illustrations. If as a result any copyright has not been acknowledged the Editor offers his sincere apologies.

Contents

Foreword

Isn't Sammy wonderful... How do you follow that – with a question mark or an exclamation mark?!

The choice was a sort of family game. Often, memorably often, some usually car-crazy visitor to the house would end enthusiastically praising my father. The word "wonderful" came up frequently. He was called "Sammy" by virtually everyone except my mother and family who preferred Sydney. I was happily saddled with "Pa", a compromise between the overly deferential and today's first name familiarity by children towards their parents.

Sammy respected both ancient and modern. His acute interest in history was nicely balanced by a love for young people. He lived in times of extraordinary changes. He witnessed and indeed played his own part in bringing some of them about, such as car ownership for everyone. He loved the sheer joy of driving on the often empty and open road in Britain and France, as one was privileged to know it for some two-thirds of the twentieth century. I well remember him in his mid-eighties looking at a solid traffic jam in Guildford, one of his favourite towns, and saying "Well we won – but where we go from here I don't know". He excelled as a communicator. He listened as well as spoke to the young and enthusiastic, and whether someone was re-building an old car or wanting his advice on how to start motor racing, they would be given as straight forward and sincere suggestions as possible.

As Jack Lemmon remarks at the end of Billy Wilder's film *Some Like it Hot* – "nobody's perfect".

Every now and again somebody managed to annoy Sammy; I know that on one occasion I did, and I can only describe his temper as formidable. There was the Welsh warrior side to him as well as the artistic, chivalrous and sporting. These varying facets of his nature had one thing in common – they were perfectly genuine. I have seldom, if ever, come across anyone who was less interested in putting on an act to impress others. If there was an exception it was in his tendency to feign indifference to the charms of attractive women, claiming in the occasional conversation with me that he was "far too old for that sort of thing". He wasn't.

Sammy had a wonderful sense of humour. This, if anything, increased over the years. If there was one sombre burden which he carried for most of his long life, it was memories of the First World War. He resolutely refused to discuss it in any detail; it was too painful. During the war Sammy lost both his brothers and almost every one of his close school friends. But humour was part of his personality and it emerged in just about everything he did. There was delightful absurdity in many of his cartoons. There was the typically British idiom of carefully choosing an understatement to achieve emphasis in his writing. There was wit in his conversation. He appreciated humour in others and much enjoyed the books of W W Jacobs and P G Woodhouse.

Over the years, I have often thought that it was a pity that Sammy did not reveal more of himself in his previous recollections. This has now been remedied by Peter Heilbron with the appearance of this book. I am most grateful to him for his long and hard work and his consistent enthusiasm in preparing the manuscript for publication. I would also like to thank Charles and Ed Herridge for being the last vital link in the chain and becoming the publishers. Enjoy it.

Colin Davis, Capetown, RSA,
June 2007

Editor's Introduction

I was on the point of leaving my golf club one day when a familiar voice said, "Peter, I have some papers relating to Sammy Davis which I think you might like to look at." I was somewhat surprised, but then recalled my fellow member Duncan Ferguson knew the Davis family, particularly Sammy's son Colin. Soon after, Duncan confronted me with a tea chest full of papers and various photographic albums, rescued by Peter Wilson, a test pilot friend of Sammy's, after the tragic fire in which he died in 1981. The papers then found their way to Graham Dutton Forshaw, who later handed them over to Sammy's grandson, Paul.

In an ideal world it would have been nice if all the contents of the chest had found their way to The Veteran Car Club's library. I fought hard to achieve this, particularly in view of Sammy being one of the founders of the Club, but to no avail. Deep down I had to reluctantly agree with Duncan that other marque clubs could lay claim to some of the remaining Davis albums including Alvis, Aston Martin, Bentley Drivers, Daimler, Riley and Sunbeam. In any event, and as will be seen, the VCC has gained greatly, thanks to Colin Davis and with Duncan Ferguson's kind assistance.

Apart from photographic material there is an electric table clock (still in going order) presented to Sammy from his "Friends at Dorset House" dated January 10th 1950, no doubt celebrating Sammy's connection with Iliffe Publications for forty years; his City of Coventry driving licence issued in 1906, renewed annually through 1909; and an original Official Programme for the *Daily Sketch* Run to Brighton, Sunday 13 November 1927. In addition, there was a somewhat scruffy little black notebook, full of hand-written notes pertaining to motoring activities entitled *Log Book continued*, S C H Davis. Underneath, 1912 had been altered to 1913, the contents starting on 1 July of that year and finishing on 10 July 1914.

There was some difficulty at first deciphering the log, not only on account of the handwriting but, strange as it may seem, because it only appeared to be a motoring diary, recording excursions with friends as well as odd rallies, trials and visits to Brooklands, which, being Sammy, wasn't surprising. It was only after some research, and the mention of Ludlow Clayden, the then Editor of *The Automobile Engineer*, that the penny dropped. This was not only a diary but also a running record of Sammy's driving tests of various cars for his journal immediately before World War I. Sadly we shall probably never learn when he first started writing the log, but at least we have a fascinating background to vehicle testing at that time. The cars Sammy drove were obviously thrust upon him, mainly small ones, and reading between the lines most of them suffered from one fault or another: however it was motorcycling that loomed large in his life at that time. He rode his 2hp Douglas all over the place, even in France and of course at Brooklands.

It was then that events took a somewhat bizarre turn. On acquiring the Davis papers I felt it might be worth casting back to *VCC Gazette* Vol. XIII No 157, March/April 1981, which contained many tributes to Sammy following his death. At that time Mike Worthington-Williams was the Editor, so I decided to contact him to ask if he could fill me in on various points as I knew that he had got to know Sammy and his second wife Susie quite well. As our discussion progressed Mike told me he that had acquired a typewritten manuscript from Sammy in the form of an autobiography, but that it was full of alterations and scratchings out – he also murmured something about Valhalla! It appeared Sammy had approached the publishers Batsford with the manuscript in the late 1960s but they wanted a sizeable sum up front, money which Sammy simply did not have. In any case so much had already been written about him and life had moved on, so the timing was perhaps inappropriate. In addition, he had already written two autobiographies, *Motor Racing* in 1932 and *A Racing Motorist* in 1949, some of which was based on his first book. Armed with the Log Book it seemed to me that with the further passage of time it would at least be worthwhile to peruse the manuscript, which Mike then very kindly lent to me. At the same time he said he had various other items which had belonged to Sammy and which he would consider making over to the VCC, including Sammy's spectacles, a watercolour paintbox, two slide rules and a typewriter. (With the other items already acquired I was beginning to envisage a mini Sammy Davis museum with or without his beret – qv Hillstead.)

In reading the manuscript I came across much that had been previously published but there was also further material that had not, and it seemed (to me at any rate) a good story, so I decided to take the plunge and started transcribing.

Though I have come to learn a little more about the stature of the man, I quickly realised that because he wrote so much I would not be able to cope with all his many and diverse outpourings, as his name appears so often in motorsport books and periodicals – fascinating for research but very time consuming. My own interest in motoring history relates more to veteran than vintage. Thus, when confronted with myriad articles and reviews published in *The Autocar* for over 40 years after World War 1, many under the pen name "Casque", I nearly gave up.

In tackling the log first, I was fast coming to the conclusion that Sammy was a dyslectic. However, when I started reading the manuscript I was spared any further doubts in that direction because he admitted he could not spell. He added, "My handwriting needed an interpreter, being otherwise indecipherable". My wife, Jean, reluctantly found herself in that position, trying to umpire on a multitude of letters and words, but in the end there were only a few that defeated us. It is interesting to think therefore that his editorial staff must have taken infinite pains to correct his mistakes; this also applied to his books. Often his syntax was quaint, to say the least, and so many sentences started with conjunctives. Naturally it was made easier for him when everything was published by Iliffe. On the other hand, *Atalanta*, his book on lady racing drivers published by Foulis, was not in the same mould. Nevertheless, Sammy's racing and other exploits when transferred to paper are exciting to read, and at times also very funny. The humour carried itself over to his cartoons, of which there were a large number through the years. He actually preferred to call them sketches, as portrayed by *Casque's Sketch Book* and its successor *More Sketches by Casque*. In his first book, *Motor Racing*,

there was a little sketch at the end of every chapter, a few of which are now included in this book. Although he attended the Slade School of Art, Sammy was never going to be a great artist (seeing Gordon Crosby's early work must have convinced him of that) but he certainly produced quality mechanical drawings; his oils and watercolours were amateur by comparison. Where on earth did he find the time to juggle it all? His energy must have been prodigious, for it must be remembered that between the two World Wars he was writing for *The Autocar* every week, testing cars, frequently racing and also serving on various club committees.

Life to Sammy was one huge schoolboy adventure. You would have thought the dreadful First World War would have changed his attitude, but he was still wanting to pop off guns again when the second one came round. Yet it is his driving, read through his words, that remains uppermost; you even get a whiff of it out of a bare-bones logbook. The original book manuscript contained a quantity of repetitious text, varying in degree and some of it running to pages. This was carefully revised and the contents remain basically unaltered. I hope that in so doing I have not inadvertently dulled anything the author wrote in his inimitable way.

Of all the comments made about Sammy by authors and journalists that I have thus far read, there is one that I feel was particularly poignant. It came from the pen of Arthur Hillstead in his book *Fifty Years With Motor Cars*, published by Faber & Faber in 1960 when Sammy was still alive. Hillstead spent many years with W O selling

Bentleys and this is what he wrote:

"S C H Davis is best known for his amazing exploits on old No 7 in partnership with Benjafield. The race being, of course, that fantastic affair at Le Mans in 1927 when the entire Bentley team was involved in a multiple crash, yet Davis managed to extricate No 7 and eventually drive his battered mount to victory.

"As already stated, I first met Sammy at the Humber works during the 1914-18 war, but it was not until 1919 that I came to know him really well. At that time, had I not been aware that he was Sports Editor of *The Autocar* and a tremendous racing enthusiast, I should have imagined him to be a devout member of some religious sect. The bowler hat sitting erect upon a noble brow; the Sherlock Holmes pipe (often very insanitary); the winged collar; black overcoat; similar shaded trousers; clerical shoes and rolled umbrella, collectively painted a picture of bland benevolence in no way related to the roar of open exhausts and the stench of Castrol R. How true it is that one can never judge the quality of a cigar by the picture on the box.

"The longest run I had with Sammy was over the whole London-Exeter Trial's course, completed within twelve hours, on a 3-litre Bentley whose bad behaviour was unbelievable. Judging from this, and seeing him perform on a variety of mounts both at home and abroad, I should describe him as a driver of precision. At Le Mans, for instance, his corner work was set to a pattern which seldom varied. It was just as though he had a fixed mark for every operation, which – provided one makes allowances for the progressive wear of brakes – is just as it should be. But Sammy carried it further than that. Having safely negotiated Mulsanne and once more changed into top, he appeared also to have a mark which prompted a sudden burst of Valkyrian song. To use his own words when writing up a trip on the prototype Bentley, '...there comes an irresistible desire to burst into some wild war song, even greater than the immortal song of Roland – in defiance of the demons that howl invisible without...'

"Sammy had so many successes, both at home and abroad, that I could not begin to enumerate them; he also held the Brooklands badge for having attained a speed of 120mph on the track. Apart from actual racing and record breaking, he has been responsible for much organization in the world of competition and still serves on several committees.

"I am not at all certain of the exact date when he acquired his famous beret, nor have I been able to discover whether the original survived until the wearing of helmets became compulsory. I like to think it did, and is today a cherished possession spending its old age in a glass cage; tattered, no doubt; inevitably stained with oil and perhaps a little moth-eaten in places. But, nevertheless, a symbol of that golden age which will live in memory for all time. So be it."

Peter Heilbron, Reigate, July 2007

Chapter One

Childhood under Victoria and Edward

That our odd family bequeathed to me certain advantages, I agree. My beautiful and beloved mother, Georgina Maud Fielding, a pioneer cyclist, was the daughter of the well-known artist, Arthur Boyd Houghton (1836-1875). A B H was a real character, full of fun, enjoying life to the hilt and entirely devoted to his wife, who was not only extremely ornamental but could run him, his household and any business with an efficiency quite miraculous in Victorian times. To me the interesting part of all this is that grandfather's black and white illustrations have great freedom and atmosphere (as for example in Dalziel's edition of *The Arabian Nights*) though his oil painting tends to be pre-Raphaelite. But it is easy to forget that one has to do what one's clients want the way they want it.

Anyhow, grandfather, who had lost an eye when very young owing to unwise experiments with a toy cannon, enlivened St John's Wood by summoning beer from the local pub by blowing a coach horn out of the studio window, and cheerful tricks of like nature. Grandmother, by the way, was the sister of another famous character, Captain Gronow, whose reminiscences remain one of the best sources of information about Georgian times. He was one of the real dandies and decided he preferred to be with his regiment for Waterloo rather than on guard at St James' Palace, and he got away with that without adverse comment from anyone. Gronow seems a strange name for a Welshman, but Welsh he was, from Ash Hall, Glamorgan. One can only think that the surname was chosen at random, the same as all those Celts when surnames become necessary.

The more we understood about our ancestors the more intriguing life became, partly because it created a desire to be like them and partly because something of theirs influenced our thought and behaviour as we grew up. And there seemed to be no end to the close relatives who had been involved in history one way or another.

Grandfather Houghton had a heavily side-whiskered brother who was a

General during the Indian Mutiny and its aftermath, yet attained the friendship of, and retained the liking for, the inhabitants of India. Great-grandfather on that side was a naval captain, also heavily whiskered, and extremely pugnacious. Father, Edwin Davis, was a fine horseman and whip, so much in love with my mother that nothing else really mattered to him. He possessed a natural taste in clothes that made him almost a dandy. His father Edwin ran away with Miss Sarah Latham and made her my wonderful grandmother, to the white-hot fury of his exceedingly Welsh father, who cut him off for ever with a penny and actually sent along that coin as a token. Great-grandfather, you see, was a real Celtic autocrat with a wild temper and a notion that no son of his might do anything without parental permission. But grandfather was equally obstinate and, ably assisted by his wife, who was an autocrat in her own right, did something which must have brought his parent near to apoplexy. He started a shop – a *shop*, mind you! Moreover that shop in Hull prospered exceedingly. At a guess I would say that great-grandfather can be heard all over Valhalla still going on about the subject.

We had a magnificent time with the grandparents in their big comfortable home, Wolferton, at Kirk Ella near Hull, a house which has been with me in spirit all my life. Grannie survived her husband for many years and though a Victorian had nothing of what people call "Victorian" about her except her immense dignity. Come Sunday we children, sister Evelyn, brothers Hugh and Cyril, had lunch with her, in state, but with instructions that we were to return to our part of the house when the meal was finished as "Grannie will have her nap". Grannie would then ensconce herself in an enormous armchair with a huge Bible on her lap, and a parlour maid would pour out for her a glass of

Grannie Sarah (née Latham) Davis.

home-made elderberry wine. When we were small we used to regard Grannie with great awe, but it did seem to us that the stately old lady was a mite odd at tea time. I was nineteen before I found out why. Not only was Wilkie Collin's book *The Woman in White* concealed within that Bible but the elderberry wine was ninety-nine percent pure alcohol. She gave me some and it nearly blew my head off. It was at that age too that I discovered a new Grannie I had never suspected and was considerably taken aback. One of her tales seems to me the all-time record of tact and politeness.

Grandfather Edwin was in the occasional habit of going to London on some business or other. Usually when he returned one or other of the staff would unpack his bag. For no explicable reason Grannie did this for him on one occasion. In the bag she found a highly ornamental set of feminine panties. Edwin being at the shop she took the brougham into Hull and there purchased a complete outfit of the very latest thing in fashionable clothes. To the panties she then pinned the bill and left the exhibit on Edwin's dressing table. From that day on nothing was said, the bill was paid at once and life continued with the utmost cheerfulness. This tale from a much loved woman of over eighty could never be forgotten especially when you remembered the very naughty smile with which she told it.

Another thing I learned was that Edwin had serenaded her from a boat on the moat of her old house when they were courting. I remembered suddenly how very attractive she must have been when young and that age had done nothing to alter the attractiveness when once you thought of her as a woman rather than as one's grandmother. All this talk of the family is not unreasonable when you remember that some of my relatives' qualities, and no doubt their failings, were permanent ingredients in the strange chemical composition which was me.

Looking back along the years to those days of childhood emphasizes the difficulty of making sure what you remember and what was told to you years after the event. Certainly it was a very carefree time even if memory evokes moments when the world seemed a very hard, unfriendly place. That, of course, was due to discovering that however completely one worked out an explanation for some delinquency or failure to do what one should, grown-ups possessed a seemingly diabolical power enabling them to find loopholes in that plan and get at the truth by instinct.

We had no financial troubles, never in fact thought about money, though pocket money never sufficed. Once I do remember a financial crisis, but that was caused by a rule making us deposit some of our money in a small cash-box to teach us to save. This being resented, one of my brothers and I had an inspiration. If we buttered the blade of a table knife, then inserted the blade through the slot for the money and turned the safe upside down, we could extract the money coin by coin. This we did and lived happily on the result for weeks, even the tremendous trouble resulting from the discovery of our method of financial increment being worth all the subsequent pain. The only fly in the ointment was the unbearably dignified and almost perpetual criticism from our sister about the matter; her grievance being that we had extracted her money as well but not given her any, to which it was difficult to find a watertight answer.

As a whole, though, we presented a united front to all and sundry, each helping the other. Dealing with three, then four, then five of us was more than any Victorian nurse could achieve. Governesses had no better luck until a certain Miss Chivers – immediately altered to Miss Mischievous – took charge, and she for some unknown reason actually taught us a great deal. We had been six but Dorothy died as a baby before we really knew she was there, while Beryl developed a very bad abscess behind one ear, spent all her time in hospital and died quite young. During Beryl's rare appearances we were rather frightened by her heavily bandaged head but did find her pathetically friendly and pleasant. Mind you, none of us realised she was seriously ill until one day it occurred to us that we had not seen her for a long time. Mother said she had died and we talked this over upstairs, still without realising what it meant save that we felt very sorry. In fact we had no knowledge of birth, death, or even pain, any more than we had of life.

Of the family there then remained my sister Evelyn, who had inherited the family's feminine charm in full measure together with two very blue eyes which she could use with very great effect, my

Hornbrook House prep school, Chislehurst, Kent, with Sammy Davis standing second from right and in need of a haircut. Malcolm Campbell sits cross-legged second from left.

brother Cyril and at a later date, another brother, Hugh Courtney. Together we had chicken pox, in the holidays of all times, and we enjoyed the world, none of us caring much for "education" as practised in the schools of the period. Since I had a mania for drawing and painting it was assumed I was to be the "artist", and this helped since adverse school reports were excused on that account.

My preparatory school was, I admit, pleasant, since it was run at Hornbrook House, Chislehurst, by a tall friendly Head named Fisher, who seemed to understand small boys. It was there that I met a smallish, freckled youth named Malcolm Campbell, though I had no idea our paths would cross and run together in the far future and I thought him very Scottish, especially with pocket money. Then the assistant master, whose name I simply cannot recall, interested us to an extraordinary degree in theatricals. Being extremely shy I simply could not imagine myself standing on a stage and saying anything to an audience, nor apparently could he, but he actually persuaded me to be made up as one of the soldiers at the

court which tried Shylock in *The Merchant of Venice*. I enjoyed it, although my realism when I had to eject Shylock after the verdict did produce criticism as much from the victim as from the producer. Incidentally, this master rose to great fame as the best organiser of those enormous pageants which were the thing at the commencement of the twentieth century. *The Miracle*, for example, achieved greatness with an acquaintance of mine in the chief role.

I admit that my learning lagged at school but one drawing I did of the Holy Ghost was kept and shown by the Head after I had been well beaten for lack of religious appreciation. I never quite understood that until I was very much older. More bother arose from ingenuity. I had been told to write out one hundred times "I must do what I am told". Writing being a thing I disliked, and being anxious to get away to the cricket match even if late, I bound three pens together so as to write three lines successively. The result I presented to the Head. He stared at it for longer than I liked. Said he: "Boy, bring me the pen with which you wrote

Studio portrait of Sidney Charles Houghton Davis.

that the pre-school period did not have. There was the annual journey to Yorkshire by train – no corridor carriages and no lavatories. It was a great adventure though we generally arrived at Wolferton tired out; what my mother went through passes understanding. Christmas time was especially exciting, with hounds meeting on the lawn. It was a real treat for us, great big wonderful horses and the stirring sound of hunting horns. There was certain to be fun with uncle George, my father's barrister brother, who was rather small. He found gripping a horse with his knees a trifle difficult and fell off quite often, not that this worried him in the least or weakened his enthusiasm; my father on the other hand was a fine horseman. Uncle George was something of a hero for me because he had coxed the Cambridge boat three times, twice to victory and once for that 1877 dead-heat which has resulted in so much controversy even to this day. Trophies of his prowess were all over Wolferton: rudders, photos, fox brushes, and the like. Moreover he was good for half a crown or even half a sovereign any time.

Of course sleep was difficult on Christmas Eve, but we had all mastered the art of pretending to be well away when the door opened and our parents tiptoed in, whispering, to pile things on the table at the end of the bed. There followed, after a tactical interval, a crawl down to that table and much exploring of the pile by touch, to try and discover whether we had received certain presents we had hoped for. And the Christmas lunch, believe me, was something out of this world. Even I had enough to eat. Soup, enormous helpings of turkey with vegetables galore, Christmas pudding in abundance, mince pies, cream, second helpings and slices of magnificent ham to fill any gaps. We were even allowed a glass of

this". I did, asserting at the same time, though timidly, "Please sir, I did not know there was a rule against this". After a painful interlude it was explained to me that using one's brain to make work easier was good, but any action must be thought out fully beforehand, that being what a brain was for. In this case I did well to think of the treble pen device, but failed to remember that with it extreme care was necessary or any fault would be repeated and thus instantly obvious, therefore the scheme was a failure. Curious thing is, that lesson had a very great and permanent effect on me.

Holidays now had much more meaning, bringing a sense of freedom some very exciting liquid called port in order ceremoniously to drink our grandmother's health, all standing, which the old lady received with enormous upright dignity never to be forgotten. Mind you, this was after church in our best Sunday clothes, which was all very well for Evelyn who liked these things, but which Cyril and I disliked intensely because our Sunday boots hurt so. Best part of the whole business was the bell-ringing, since the operators were friends of ours on the quiet and their skill seemed out of this world, especially when they stopped the bell upside down. Second came hymn singing, which somehow roused wild and stirring feelings not, I realise, connected with Christianity. All the rest tended to be boring unless we could carry on a private war with others of our age, without being discovered, with a pea-shooter or small catapult.

As far as I was concerned I took God for granted as an Englishman, with a huge white beard and a rather unfair ability not only to know what one was doing at any time, but what one was thinking as well. Once or twice when involved in trouble I had a vague idea there was something to be said for the Devil.

One Christmas Cyril and I came up against life inexplicable. We had as usual crept along the corridor from our room to the head of the big staircase in order to listen to the grown-ups at dinner and catch a glimpse of grannie and my mother in their full evening dress, complete with jewellery, and seeming to us like something from fairyland. Well, on this occasion there seemed to be more noise than usual and that not of the right kind, more like large dogs growling. Then the dining room door flew open and two male figures in full dress rolled out punching and kicking, the air being full of words we had never heard before but stored for ever after. Scarcely had we taken all this in when out came grannie, a quite different and terrifying grannie, who beat the combatants hard with an ebony cane saying: "George, Frank, stop it at once! It is disgraceful, go to your rooms immediately and do not let me see you until you are sober. This was very frightening, for never had we seen grown-ups behave like this. Someone, we thought, would be killed, as we legged it along the corridor to regain our room before the combatants came up the stairs. We were so frightened we locked the bedroom door. But at breakfast the next day everyone seemed to be quite calm, as usual, everyone that is save the uncles who did not appear until after lunch. It was very many years before I found out from grannie what the rumpus was about. It was, she said, "A disagreement about Gladstone". The violent aftermath was due to neither of the men "being able to hold their liquor like gentlemen".

If I remember rightly it was at this same Christmastide that I got into trouble. We had, as usual, been taken to the magnificent Christmas party given by the Wilsons at Tranby Croft[1], the party of all parties. Towards the end a grown-up, probably Muriel Wilson, offered me a simply wonderful piece of Christmas cake thickly iced, the only remaining piece on the plate. This I accepted eagerly. Just as I was about to take it, along came another grown-up with one of those horrible little long-haired small girls for whom I had no use at all. She said, "Dear, will you have a bit of cake?" Before I could say a word the little beast said "Yes please"

---

1. Sammy recalled encountering the Prince of Wales (Edward VII) there. See Bibliography *A Racing Motorist*, p212 and took the cake. I grabbed at the cake, she held on. We punched and scratched, rolling on the floor. I was removed with vigour by some huge male person and sent home in disgrace, still boiling with just rage. It was my bit of cake and I still maintain it was even today. Of course I had to apologise, but not to that brat, and it struck me as odd at the time that the grown-up who received my apology kept hiding her face behind a handkerchief. Mind you, my apology was for bad manners, *not* for trying to take that bit of cake. I made that quite clear. Life is very interesting. Years and years after this incident ought to have been forgotten it came up again. I happened to be the officer in charge of a military works. Very high Authority came down to inspect the unit. At the end Authority thanked me very pleasantly indeed. Then, a pause and, "Have you stopped scratching girls faces yet?" Damn but it *was* my piece of cake.

I suppose we must have been quite a handful all those years ago. From one of our favourite places, the V roof of the cow shed in the paddock field, we succeeded in sliding Evelyn on to the back of a cow. But she rode that bony animal round the field for all that. I had cronies, Barquiths, Eggingtons and the like, the younger males that is, with whom to go hunting with bow and arrow or weave illicit huts of branches and ferns on other people's property, a business in which we were aided by very friendly local inhabitants with noose-like rough beards. Grannie's gardener, Firth, in particular taught us wonderful country lore. To this very day I value the memory of those friendships and the kindness of that world.

There was a miller with an intriguing windmill which provided Kirk Ella's bread. Marshall, I think the name was, and his wife would give me wonderful cakes while he would take infinite trouble to explain mill machinery to a small and grubby boy. The large red-faced cook also provided delicacies if I ventured into what seemed a mysteriously huge stone-walled kitchen almost underground. The herdsman, the man in charge of the Eggington's prize cattle, told me that bulls turned red before they charged, the result being I had no fear of these great horned monsters, though I kept a wary eye on their colour.

Always I felt at ease with these people as distinct from other grown-ups of what is now called a different "level", one of the stupidest terms ever created. And there was no suggestion of an act put on for the son of some "gentry". I had my head clouted time and again for carelessness or neglect of proper precautions. These were not "serfs", they were sturdily independent and had been ever since their Norse ancestors landed, or their Celtic ancestors refused to knuckle down to the invaders. Nor was there any attempt to patronize them, to act Lord of the Manor. That would have met stonewall resistance, for neither wealth nor rank, education nor position counted, but only that you did honestly the best you could for all and were judged accordingly.

Not long ago I went back to Kirk Ella. It had changed and Hull seemed much nearer, but the old house was every bit as friendly as ever, though it had been reduced in size and much of its land had gone. The new owners, the Bladons, were friendly too in just the old way. Most interesting of all, the visit did not evoke the ghosts of the long dead but, as it were, their very selves happily reviving the wonderful days of youth.

Then one fine day father told me that I had finished with preparatory school and was to be admitted to Westminster. How that happened I don't know as I thought I had made one big mess of the entry exam some time before, but beyond doubt it meant that I was growing up, and that seemed to change one's point of view about the world in general. There followed a solemn interview with a man whom I can never forget, the Head of Westminster, Gunnion Rutherford. One glance at him was sufficient to make me certain this was somebody quite different from anyone I had met beforehand. The long gown, the small white tabs at the collar and the tasselled mortarboard were awe-inspiring in themselves. But that was nothing to the man's face, sallow maybe, but with all the character of an eagle, an eagle with universal knowledge almost ranking with, but after, God.

Although I was shy to the point of timidity, that man put me sufficiently at ease to talk, or rather to answer questions, therefore to understand that for this ancient school I had to change all my ideas of life. All my time at Westminster that awe of "Gunnie" remained, and in very few intervals afterwards he opened to me a world almost too marvellous to contemplate. I was not in any sense a scholar and never attained even mild success at lessons, maths particularly. I must have been the bane of all the masters under whom I sat. Only at art and football could I achieve anything. Yet Gunnie, a world famous Greek scholar, a man of infinite learning, made me understand more about life than ever anyone had before. His chats alone about history were enthralling, not dead history but the very life and purpose of nations. Further, the necessity for remembering that conflict may arise not from one people who are wrong and another who are right, but from each side being right from different points of view. Why he took so much trouble with a very small, very untidy, very timid youngster, I will never know. Publicly of course he

was a man of stern character, enforcing the regulations and punishing inefficiency. He offered no favours and publicly I was "handed" by him with a very unpleasant birch for offences committed. But it was those few private talks which made all the difference, creating a debt I can never repay.

Mind you, the school itself had an effect, the ancient grey stones of the Abbey and its cloisters, particularly Little Cloisters, which was the most peacefully calming place I have ever known. Then the armorial bearings of famous old Westminsters had an effect, all this immensely aided by the Abbey itself. For here to me was history, not the dullness of a technical book on the subject, but history as it really was. Odd as it may seem for a small boy, I liked to sit in the Abbey in or near the chapel of Henry VII and think about the kings and queens buried there. From this a new thought was born. These men had come as conquerors or gone forth to conquer. In their time some had been sure they had conquered England. Yet in sober fact England, or rather Britain, had just quietly absorbed them and their followers, though it took hundreds of years, so that their very descendants of today were integral with Britain, more Britons than the Briton. I even became accustomed to walking about in public in a short Eton jacket and top hat, a thing I could never have thought possible, and fought any of the younger plebs who dared to mock.

Scared at first by tales I had heard or read, I did not look forward to being a boarder in Rigaud's house with pleasure. Yet I soon found that bullying did not exist, that the monitors were quite normal people and that the little odd things which seemed ridiculous but were traditional had genuine meaning. Rumour too made the Play Supper, the ceremonial supper after the scholars have enacted their Greek play, horrible to contemplate, particularly because I heard that everyone had to sing a solo, which was quite an impossibility for me. It must have been my one effort at *Clementine* during the initial trials of possible singers, before monitors, that did the trick, for I was never asked to sing from that day on.

Holidays at all events were every bit as good as before, at the London house in Earls Court's quiet backwater Philbeach Gardens, especially as we had all taken to cycling in a big way. My machine, a Beeston Humber, took me over miles of Britain to my infinite contentment and vastly increased my knowledge. For example, I used to cycle from London to Kirk Ella very comfortably, enjoying such company as I met at rests for meals by the roadside including several genuine gypsies and road menders of an older school. The cycle was, as I now know, grossly overloaded, yet it carried me well all those miles on the road. Ipswich trips were frequent too, since I could stay with my big uncle Arthur Wood, go with him on his doctor's rounds in the high dogcart astern a fine fast horse, and be well looked after by all his patients' families. His wife was my mother's sister and they had two fine brats, Vivian and Cecil. Vivian blotted his copybook early on. Being strapped to the seat of the dogcart to accompany his father, he remained safe and secure when the horse fell down on a wet road and his father performed a neat parabola, ending head first on the recumbent horse. At that Vivian, crowing with glee, said, "Do it again, daddy, do it again," and was very upset at the resultant cuff he received. By making every mistake known to cyclists I learned much roadcraft the hard way and was very thankful for the lesson.

The real high spot in family life occurred when we were all taken to reserved seats to watch Queen Victoria's Diamond Jubilee procession, – in 1897 if memory serves aright. Truly this was a magnificent and moving spectacle, with column upon column of troops in review order, and the glittering crowd of other reigning monarchs and celebrities. I can still remember the impression made by the Germans in silver spiked helmets which looked far more warlike and exciting than the helmets of other armies. Leading one section was the tallest man in the British army, Ames, an officer in the Lifeguards and just the right person for ceremonial of this type. But all this fantastically coloured glitter, all these Kings, Emperors, Princes and their like, were as nothing to the effect of the Old Lady herself. She really was a Queen, not an official mouthpiece for political decisions, a Queen to annoy whom was much more than the most popular Premier, or the most honest communist – yes we had them too – could do and survive. There she was, a tiny but highly dignified figure bowing majestically, assisted, I was told, by a mechanical device, and looking every inch a Queen.

Never before or since have I seen a spectacle to equal that procession, even with the help of highly skilled producers, for the whole spirit of the thing was marvellous, and this Nation as a Nation would have it so of their own free will without preliminary propaganda. Moreover, that evening sundry relatives arrived home by hansom cab still in parade uniform with swords. Certainly it was a day not to be compared with any other. Now I have read all about Victoria, about how difficult she could be and what a hotch-potch of bits and pieces she considered the right ornaments for that time; as also, the autocratic ways of the aristocracy "grinding the faces of the poor". All I can say is that it was not in the least like that, not in any way. That the women looked every bit as delightful in those clothes which now seem so odd, and that far from grinding anyone's face the "poor" were looked after as a duty, though I never found one of the people now referred to as the "proletariat" who did not consider himself anyone's equal and able to earn his own way in the world. Of course there were pubs with sanded floors and men or women who drank themselves paralytic with gin or other mixtures of alcohol. There were organ grinders with monkeys, and navvies whose language was vividly bloody but, by and large, they were no worse or better than people in other generations. As I write, much the same is being said about teenagers' habits with equal injustice.

Second high spot of the Jubilee was the illuminations, which seemed to me splendid beyond compare. Our house was dressed with flags, an occasion when I learned that the National Flag is not the Union Jack but the Union Flag, and which way up it was flown. That night we lit hundreds of small candles in little coloured glass bowls, every householder vying with neighbours to produce the best show. The clusters of flags increased an interest in heraldry which the emblazoned shields in Westminster Abbey had originated, a subject which intrigues me still.

There was other unexpected entertainment. For example there was a church in Philbeach Gardens in which, according to whispered rumour, they actually used incense and other "Popish" practices. One fine Sunday afternoon there arrived a curious fanatic named Kensit with a band of odd-looking companions intent on creating a near riot of protest. This the police, with the utmost good humour and no religious bias, dealt with, bundling some of the "protestants" into a Black Maria. It was all free entertainment of the best type, though none of us under-

stood one thing about the cause. My uncle, the General, became quite purple in the face about it though, and delighted us by demanding that the Police use the utmost severity in suppressing the "riot". To this a large and comfortable looking sergeant replied, "Don't you worry, sir. we'll move them on in ten minutes", which with perfect equanimity they did.

I suppose that we were a naturally adventurous family, with bias towards any fighting. Certainly we devoured all the adventure books we could get hold of, Henty being a favourite. So it may not seem surprising that one day Evelyn set out for the Imperial Court of the Czar of all the Russias with some night clothes in a bag, one banana and two-and-sixpence in ready money. Alas, she got no further than Earls Court station because the clerk in the booking office, who had no imagination, was unable to produce a ticket for St Petersburg or even understand where that city was.

From 1899 onwards so many things changed that my life was a whirl of excitement. Every relative, it seemed, was off to the war in South Africa, mostly in the Border Regiment. Of course I wanted to go too, father approving though with some humour. But try as I did, and much as I increased my age, all I met with was more humour and several gifts of chocolate, with promises I could be taken on later. That I could shoot did not seem to make the difference I thought it should, because I really could shoot, though I say so myself.

Mind you, reading relatives' letters and listening to other members of the service who had not yet gone out gave me an idea of the war which did not mate with that illustrated in weekly papers by Caton Woodville: horsemen charging at high speed, infantry doing marvellous things in a hail of bullets. In fact some of the generals seemed to know nothing about war and to expect attacks modelled on Waterloo tactics, if the conversation of one's elders meant anything. Consequently I never took to the fashion of wearing small buttonhole badges of famous war leaders which became a craze. Nor did I quite understand the extraordinary behaviour of the public when Mafeking was later on relieved after siege. I had been taught that war was a serious business requiring immense thought and almost superhuman wariness.

To make things more exciting my father took me in 1900 to see the start of the 1000-Miles Trial for the new automobiles. I was interested in these vehicles from their very beginning, therefore disliked intensely some elderly visitors who seemed certain the Devil was in these things and they were to be hindered at all costs. If the Government would not see that, they must be banned altogether from the public roads. I lost both a birthday present and another for Christmas for being rude to my Houghton aunt on the subject when she carried anti-motoring to extreme limits. Further to increase my enthusiasm, a French friend of my mother not only arrived on one of these new cars late in November 1900 but took me for a ride on it down Cromwell Road, and actually allowed me to hold the steering tiller from the passenger's seat for quite two hundred yards. That ride, on what I thought was a Benz but am now convinced was a Peugeot, was not a certificate allowing me to call myself a "motorist", but it felt like that for several years. From then on I haunted the Science Museum, wherein a friendly curator taught me how a gas engine worked, and I read every paper I could get my hands on if it dealt with automobiles. Naturally I thought, heaven help me, that I knew almost everything about automobiles. Judge therefore of the catastrophe when I

offered to assist a man whose De Dion tricycle was in trouble. Said he, "Do you know anything about these things?" Unwisely I answered, "Yes". Holding up the sparking plug he asked, "Which is the earth wire?" Never having heard of such a thing I had to admit ignorance. Very rudely he said, "You know nothing". I remembered this for years – it was an awful day. But it did me a power of good for all that.

Then, in 1901, the great Queen died, and after watching her coffin proceed slowly between lines of troops with arms reversed, even I thought an era had ended, for I could not imagine any other person like her, nor that life would ever be the same. This again was to be a memory which never faded and which became more vivid, more sorrowful, every time depression made me recall the past.

To mark the occasion, as it were, my father asked me to see him, which was not usual, and when I did so in some fear, he told me kindly that the days of boyhood were gone and that I was to go to the Slade School of Art after the next term at Westminster. He added something I have never forgotten. "Remember," said he, "you are now about to face life as it really is. Remember, too, this is not your home. Your home will be the one you make for yourself with, I hope, a wife. That is why I insisted that you conform with my ideas while you were here, for this is my home. In your own home alone can you have the freedom to do what seems to you best. Your mother and I will help you in any way we can, whatever advice you may want, whatever troubles you may have to face." The phrase "this is not your home" had recurred from time to time when we were all very young, and though I did not quite understand it, yet it seemed to explain why I had to conform with certain unwritten rules with which I was not so sure I agreed. Now it took on a much deeper and more personal meaning. This was indeed a milestone in life, to be thought about with unusual solemnity for weeks. For a while I even thought I ought not to play with toys any longer, and that was secretly disturbing since I treasured the yacht I sailed on Kensington's Round Pond, and even more the large army of Mr Britain's lead soldiers with which I had fought battles innumerable. It may seem amusing that those soldiers are with me still, at eighty, so you may guess the result of those deliberations.

Westminster seemed different during that final term. Maybe it was that a tail-coat had superseded the short jacket of a junior, possibly it was a sense that I was almost a man. Then there were doubts bordering on fears. At school I knew the routine, the etiquette, and in that little replica of the world outside I had friends with whom to discuss everything and form opinions. Would the world outside be anything like this? It seemed like returning to the "new boy" days which I disliked so much, but on a much larger scale. So the finale was anything but joyful. Armed with a birch and cane as souvenirs, I left reluctantly – very reluctantly. How much I owed to my masters I did not know until years had passed, but even then I felt I owed them something. Gunnion Rutherford (I could not think of the new Head, Gow, in the same way), Mike, with the long moustache so easy to caricature, Huckle, who tended to de-wax his ear with an immense pencil when worried, old Failes, housemaster of Rigaud's, Nall, Tanner and the rest including Kneen, the art master, who had taken immense pains with me and with whom I had painted landscapes during the holidays. My career was anything but distinguished but at least I had been first in drawing every single year, which was all the more satisfactory in that you could only be given the actual prize once. So it was fun to be first while the second bloke was given the prize. How I would enjoy talking it all over with those masters now and learning what they really thought of the disreputable small boy they taught.

Chapter Two

Entry to
the World

So, loaded with portfolio and large board I departed for the Slade, but first there were some curious preliminaries. Father and Mother seemed to be strangely secretive. Several times I seemed to interrupt low-toned conversations between them which I suspected concerned me. Then I was summoned by father again. All this conspiratorial business concerned *Sex*! Now sex was something which I had never considered, having too much to do every minute of the day. True that at the age of six I had exchanged rings from crackers with one Hilda Giles during an Ipswich party, vowing eternal fidelity. That had just lasted about a week, serious disagreement about some chocolates causing trouble, while neither of us was at all sure what happened next. Then a man whose face I did not like and who had a clerical type collar kept pressing my knee when we were alone in a District Line railway carriage. Instinctively warning bells sounded and I secretly unclasped a serviceable knife in my pocket with no clear idea what I was to do with it. The

damned man would accompany me from Earls Court station to near home, repeatedly promising a wonderful party if I would go with him after leaving my top hat at home. This I had promised to do, but as soon as the front door closed I rushed to father and told him what had happened. Father only paused to pick up a fine large stick, then dashed out. Never have I seen anyone run quite so fast as the bloke with the clerical collar, but no explanation of the incident was offered.

There had also been an unfortunate occasion when the son of a clergyman told me how babies were made when we were "up fields" at Westminster. Now it may seem odd but I had no notion of any anatomical differences of importance between girls and boys. As I have said, I was fully engaged with more interesting things, so what he said sounded nonsense. For his pains he then received a perfect peach of a black eye, plus instructions never to try to tell me ridiculous lies again – thus is truth received by the young. But on the way home I thought there might be some substance of truth in his extraordinary tale. So, without stopping to think, I burst into the drawing room, where my mother had an "at home" in full swing, and blurted out, "Mother, how are babies made?" Never have I been ejected more quickly. The peculiar thing was that I could have sworn I heard peals of laughter from behind the door.

There was nothing of instructional interest in the Rigaud dormitory, and such boys as told "dirty jokes" were of a type beneath notice anyway. So father's talk was a surprise – not that I could see it had anything to do with me apart from the notion that I did not like the whole business. Included was advice about "loose" women, whoever they might be, the peculiarities possible among art students, overmuch ill-advised drink, and the fact that I would see a naked woman as a model. Of course we had a certain amount of talk around the subject, when something which happened automatically to me convinced me that I was seriously ill in a way difficult to explain, but that was only the shadowy introduction to the subject.

Well, the Slade was fine, one master, Tonks, successfully bullying me into far better methods of drawing and painting, ably assisted by Willie Russell, though less forcefully, and by occasional lectures from the Principal, Brown. To my surprise there was none of this "new boy" stuff. I was accepted as a responsible being, and we worked like Trojans without overmuch notice of time. Moreover there was none of this "wild artist" business, though one man did wear a sombrero, corduroy pants and a large flowery tie. Trouble with ribald medical students there might be, but all of it was good-natured. The years passed happily enough, aided by occasional parties in Soho which opened up a new avenue of interest.

The South African war came to an end, all relatives returning with wonderful tales of adventure and a few bullet holes. More wonderfully still, the parents arranged in 1903 that I went to Paris and saw the start of a real big car race, the Paris to Madrid. That was a marvellous experience. No sleep the night before, the run out to Versailles, the crowds of wildly enthusiastic cyclists with coloured paper lanterns instead of proper lamps on their machines, the dramatic roar of nearly open exhausts, and the struggle through the crowd to get some view of the racing cars – never could that be forgotten. I even recognised my hero de Knyff, and from that day a friendship with the French commenced which has remained unaltered to this day. You can imagine my dismay when the terrible casualties of the last race in the heroic age appeared, duly exaggerated in the London papers. I did not learn until much later that it was all due to the thick dust, the fact that people crowded on to the road itself the better to view the cars, and the enormous number of cars which started. This was ample food for every anti-motorist then alive, and they made the most of it. Even experts, they pointed out, could not control these devilish machines. Why else, they asserted, could drivers like Marcel Renault, Stead, Barrow and Mark Mayhew have such appalling crashes? How else could one account for the hundreds of dead?[1] It was an extraordinarily bad time for all enthusiasts about motoring, as in fact for all who motored.

But once more there dawned a determination somehow or other to get into this racing game, though there did not seem the slightest chance I could ever attain that ideal. Years before at West-

1. Total fatalities were actually 7.

minster I remembered sitting in a window of Rigaud's with my nose pressed against the window glass and my whole being, in imagination, driving one of the cars in a big French road race, similar to the ones described in the paper I had just read. Very vividly my imagination worked then.

Well, in spite of this distraction the work at the Slade passed, without distinction it is true, but replete with interest and knowledge gained. Incidentally, my first sight of a naked woman model produced no thrill. Instead, I was fascinated by the shadow under one breast, the colour of the shadow being almost unattainable in paint, while it surprised me that she seemed a much darker colour than I had expected. The enjoyment of life, among people who were very different from any I had met before, was that we were all were struggling with our work, which could drive one near to despair one moment, produce extreme elation the next, yet never attain the result one had imagined. Every moment of every day we learned something more, only to find there was more to be learned, while the vivid discussions which raged from to time, and Tonks's rude criticism, did everyone a world of good. But as the years passed a niggling doubt became more insistent: could one live on the proceeds of one's work? In moments of depression that doubt became greater, and if other students' talk was anything to go by the chances of success seemed slim. Certainly I knew I had not the courage to live in the traditional garret, probably on eggs, despite the urge to paint and paint and go on painting. Somehow or other it was essential to earn a living, for though father was generous in the extreme and mother encouraging, one could not subsist on them for a lifetime. As the problem grew in importance another side of life seemed to become

more attractive.

At Westminster I had acquired two particular friends, an Australian, Roy Geddes and a large, fat, amiable enthusiast called Bowes Scott. Together we had tackled all and sundry problems, together we had left to face the world, but still with the bond between us being motoring. Some years before I had acquired a Werner motorcycle from an owner who never wanted to see it again. That machine burst into flames on the Hammersmith Road before I even had time to master its temperament. Then a large solicitor friend of the family, Fisher, had allowed me to drive a 3hp Benz on one splendid and memorable day – real driving this time. At Ipswich I always accompanied my doctor uncle on his new Argyll motorcar, learning a packet as a result, while yet another acquaintance had allowed me to drive his big Wolseley down the Mall, though this was far from a success as I could not master double-declutching when changing to a lower gear. Useful as these adventures might be for impressing other people, none of them permitted me to call myself a driver and that irked. Well, the "godlets" took pity.

An engineer friend of "Fatty" Bowes Scott, who must have been out of his mind, actually lent, yes lent, his 1904 surface-carburettor Rex motorcycle to us. The family had moved to a flat off the Finchley Road by now, so we could learn to ride on the almost traffic free roads round Hampstead. True, the engineer took the Rex back after he discovered that we had taken the engine down to see how it worked, but he could not take back the experience gained despite the notable fuss resulting.

Three incidents with that Rex still stand out in memory. Normally we started it by pedalling hard until nearly exhausted, then letting go the exhaust valve lifter hoping that the engine would fire. One day we saw a man push his motorcycle briskly, then start the engine and mount with careful negligence from one of the pedals as the machine got under way. This struck us as the cat's whiskers. We tossed up to decide who should be the first to try the new method. Fatty won, but he seemed none too anxious to commence. Urged on by our pungent criticism, at long last he took hold of the handlebars and began to trot. The trot became a run and the run increased to quite exciting speed. Then he released the exhaust valve control and the engine started, but he had forgotten to set the throttle control for slow running. Never had we seen our robust friend run so fast as the engine accelerated cheerfully. Then he leaped wildly for the pedal, missed it, and the machine fell over on top of him. Appalled at the probable damage to our beloved machine we rushed to the spot, picked it up and examined it carefully. The pedals were quite bent and there was paint off the fuel tank. Seething with rage, Roy and I began to wheel the Rex home, ignoring completely Fatty's piteous plea that he had scraped his leg until it bled and torn his trousers. After all, the repair to the Rex was going to cost all of a pound, while his leg would mend, free, gratis, and for nothing, and he had another pair of trousers. However, there was no denying Fatty's luck was out for the moment. Not three weeks later he was in a trailer behind the Rex, a trailer we had actually bought, and as I enjoyed controlling the machine I had an idea there was some unusual noise coming from somewhere – there was. The basket part of the trailer had broken its front attachment, revolved round the axle, and Fatty was now lying on his back with only the basketwork between him and the road, yelling blue murder for help. The third episode generated a certain reluctant sympathy with the victim of all this.

I was riding the Rex on a wet day along a woodblock road and trying to control bad belt slip the while. I approached a rank on which there was a line of hansom cabs. One cab wheeled suddenly off the rank across the Rex. I braked hard, slid the motorcycle sideways, went down with a crash and continued sliding right under the belly of the horse. That blasted animal merely sneezed, but I had trouble with the cabbies, all of whom asserted it was my fault. I managed to repair the Rex before either Roy or Fatty knew of the incident.

Wonderful times we had with that bike all the same, though by far the greatest experience of these early "puppy" days occurred much earlier than this. Walking along the Finchley Road one day I came across a *real* racing car, a Mercédès with just two bucket seats. Moreover, it was emitting great clouds of steam. The sole occupant, a friendly looking man, asked me,

Sammy on a 3½hp Rex, probably a single-speed sportsman mount, 1909-10.

"Is there any water round here?" Was there not. In a matter of seconds, all shyness forgotten, I had borrowed a pail of water from an astonished house-holder. Then came the great moment. The Mercédès driver asked, "Would you like a ride, boy?" Would I not! All the way to Barnet I sat supremely happy on the floorboards, mechanic fashion, enjoying every second.

All this created a problem which worried me considerably. I longed to be an artist, yes, but I also longed to have as much to do as possible with these new cars, and the two desires were in direct conflict. I thought it out day and night for a week before I decided that earning money to live as I wanted would be unlikely with art, whereas there was a much better prospect with cars.

It took another week to summon enough courage to tell my father and mother. Both agreed immediately, with an alacrity which seemed to prove that they too had been worrying over the same problem. Father was particularly pleased and went to see friends of his the very next day, friends concerned with the motor industry. That resulted in a quite frightening interview with the Chairman of the Daimler Motor Co., Sir Edward Manville, a most intimidating person in a magnificent office with wood panels on the walls and every sign of wealth. It must have been my natural impertinence, which could not be diminished by extreme shyness, or something of the kind, but after saying, "Now, youngster, will you work?", a suggestion easily answered, he accepted me as an apprentice and all was well.[1]

So it was that, trying hard to conceal that I was scared stiff and clutching a pair of overalls unnecessarily patched to suggest experience, a small youth was conducted to the foreman of the

---

1. The Daimler factory, a former cotton-spinning mill, was in Coventry. It was christened the Motor Mills when Daimler bought the works in 1896

Despatch rider S C H Davis on army manoeuvres with a 3½hp Rex, 1909-10.

Daimler erecting shop (where the cars were assembled) to start a new life. Again the godlets must have looked after me. Never before had the subsequent experience been so enjoyable, despite my abysmal ignorance and the fact I must have been a fine big nuisance to all the men in the shop. Foreman Wormald was a character never to be forgotten. A little on the stout side, a man who stood no nonsense and knew his job from A to Z, he was certainly formidable. But for no reason that I can think of he took it upon himself to look after me, vigorously perhaps, but quite definitely. Then I remain eternally grateful to Ben Newal, the charge-hand of the gang to which I was allotted, for he took endless trouble to teach me the business once he understood I wanted to work.

I was at first highly suspicious of the gang to which I was attached, having been fed with stories about youngsters being sent to get a "toe punch" from the blacksmith or given a centre punch of lead to temper, but none of these things happened. Instead, the whole lot of them were not only friendly, making good jokes about my strange accent and pretending to believe I must have an endless supply of money, but helpful to a degree I never thought could be possible. Tommy Gelsthorpe, my immediate instructor, a thinnish red-haired bloke with a fine vocabulary of vivid language, taught me how to chip [fine fettle] by handing over a large cold-chisel and hammer and patching the many subsequent abrasions with "newskin". By general consent and after a stunned silence for consideration of my many names, it was decided that I was Charlie. Afterwards I found this was a compliment; it was all very

From left to right: Roy Geddes(?) on a motorcycle with a Blackburn engine (note the outside flywheel); presumably "Fatty" Bowes Scott on a Triumph; Nina Baxter on a drop-framed Rex, registered DU 2749; Sammy on a similar Rex, believed to be his second. The picture was taken in the yard of the premises where the Daimler premium apprentices stayed. Was this "The Croft", Nicholas Street?

Seated on a single-speed 3½hp TT Triumph is Geoffrey Smith, who later became Editorial Director of The Autocar.

wonderful, very interesting.

We, that is the gang, built some of the Herkomer Trophy (originated by the famous artist) cars for a long distance trial among the Alps, and the even more intriguing cars for the Kaiserpreis race in Germany, a race of over 290 miles for "touring" cars. As always, the competing cars bore no resemblance to anything we sold for "touring", they were just dyed-in-the-wool racing machines with huge 150x112mm 4-cylinder engines, chain drive and two bucket seats on a short chassis. Immense care was taken during their erection, every component was checked and rechecked, while the rivalry between the three gangs, each of which had one of these cars, was friendly but fierce. Exceedingly proud too was I that I was allowed to fit the chains, help line up the engine and gearbox, bolt the steering in position and put on, but not fit, the brake bands.

Order was that apprentices were not to work overtime, but it was easy to get round that and much more fun than attending the "school" evening class for

theoretical instruction by that very patient man Morgan – incidentally I was given the job of teaching him to drive. Well, our cars were not a success, much to our annoyance. The Kaiserpreis race had to be divided into qualifying races to select the cars which were to compete in the actual event, too many entries having been received to allow all to start at once. Our drivers, the envy of all who passionately wanted to drive in races, were that vigorous head of the running shed, Bush, with two of his men, Hodierne and Ison. Alas, Bush had trouble on the first lap of the eliminating race, as did Hodierne, and although Ison qualified, he got no further than the first lap of the actual race.

This was in 1907, and the only consolation was that a rival who was beginning to challenge our superiority in this country, the Napier, had just the same bad luck. Out of all this experience came one curious piece of knowledge. I had heard from time to time vague assertions about "these terrible Trade Unions". They, it seemed, corrupted the "working man" and made planned production impossible with niggling strikes and refusal to do real work. This had worried me largely because I had accumulated many friends who were working men and found them just the same as other people. Now personal contact with these men confirmed my opinion in full measure. The next factor was that I found those men who were not Trade Unionists were definitely less skilled, unpopular therefore because their work was below standard. The next discovery was that employers sometimes tended to set the rate for the job by the result from the most skilful workman, thereby handicapping those of average skill. Furthermore the Union official (we had no shop steward in those days) seemed to me to be a very reasonable being, if you remembered his job was to look after his members in every possible way. There was of course a communist or so in the shop but he was regarded as a standing joke. Even to my knowledge his arguments were far from convincing, though one of them would refer to me as "that bleeding young aristocrat bastard". His criticism resulted in one of my friends retorting, "Lay off Charlie, he's learning and wants to work, which is a bloody sight more than you do".

Taking it all in all I was very sorry indeed when my time in the erecting shop was up and I was moved to the machine shop in the old main mill, though there too I learned a packet and found work extremely interesting. True I was afraid of Needle, the foreman, because he could be extremely sarcastic even when he was imparting some sound information. When the men went on short time or there was trouble of any kind, I was despatched to a queer, dark cubby-hole to help the millwrights, a job of surpassing interest. The tobacco chewing fitters of that section seemed able to tackle any job from repairing a big machine to clearing a suds pipe, with pipe repairing and roof mending into the bargain.

The subsequent white-collar jobs in the drawing office and the even more fascinating purchasing department under Procter vastly improved my general education. I had some knowledge of the mysteries of "purchasing" in the days I was in the erecting shop, because this department occasionally wanted some new accessory or component tested on a car and I was then sent to collect the thing. Now, as I said, I was extremely proud of my overalls looking "workmanlike", and regarded oil and grease as natural accessories to the job. The purchasing department was largely run by a tall, exceedingly efficient girl called Molly Swain, and

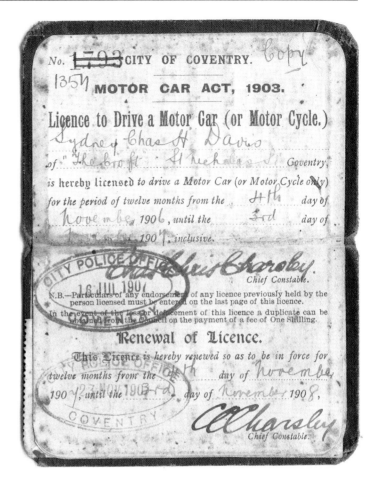

City of Coventry Driver's Licence No. 1354 issued in the name of Sydney Chas H Davis by City of Coventry Police, and commencing 4 November 1906. It would appear that Sammy mislaid his original licence as it was reissued on 18 July 1907 and then continued, with renewals, until 3 November 1909. His address was The Croft, Nicholas Street. He was living at 1 Ellys Road, close by, in1910.

The 6hp Wolseley owned by E B Wood of Daimler, with Sammy out for a spin with Nina Baxter, 1909-10.

driving through the narrow entry to the slope leading up to our garage and broke one of the steering arms, which I had to replace that very day at all costs.

Together Wood and I used to drive over to Stourport to see two attractive girls, Madeline and Nina Baxter, which led to quite an exciting result. Nina's brother Felix had a Rex motorcycle and had ridden in the 1910 Tourist Trophy race, therefore he was the local hero. Enthusiasm for motorcycling was rampant, as you can imagine. Nina and I decided we would rather have two motorcycles than one car, and two motorcycles it was, chiefly, I must admit, through her financial aid. The two machines were Rexes purchased from the works with the help of Dick Lord, the second machine being specially built with a dropped frame for Nina.

We had a wonderful time with those motorcycles and I even reached a stage nearer my ambition by competing in the Coventry and Warwickshire Club's Coventry-Holyhead trial, the high spot of that club's year, in the process getting to know Muriel Hinde, who certainly could ride. More exciting still, I rode with great energy and no skill in the Newnham hill climb. The result, when I think of it nowadays, seems to suggest a certain mental storm, temporary it may be true, but devastating none the less. I seem to remember riding everywhere as though I was practising for a race, taking bends at far too high a speed, not always on the left side, and doing things to make the exhaust highly noisy by increasing the compression and also removing all the baffles on the silencer. I must have been the biggest nuisance in the neighbourhood. Certainly I was lucky to survive, for the way I rode asked for trouble until the phase passed, with more experience and sense coming to my rescue. Total effect from the practical point of view was two summonses for exceeding the

she took exception to what she called "this horribly dirty little boy". To mark her disapproval she would refer to me as Little Black Sambo, a phrase from a children's book of that name. Some years later we became firm friends, so Little Black Sambo became "Sammy" and has remained so for all time. Bless her, Molly taught me more about life than I ever realised at the time, for which I am eternally grateful.

There were other very important things. Among the scientists at Daimler was a large man called E B Wood, and in the drawing office a pleasant youth called F Gordon Crosby. Wood owned a 6hp Wolseley and as we became firm friends we not only drove this little car all over England but did all the necessary repairs ourselves. The repairs were essential as the healthy single cylinder engine tended to pull the chassis to pieces. The inverted tooth chain driving the gearbox chewed pieces out of the clutch withdrawal fork, while the first speed was in no way man enough for its job. Very vividly I remember the occasion when I made a mistake when

10mph speed limit in a built-up area, one of which cost money, though in the other a friendly magistrate accepted my plea, I can't think why, that I had a fly in my eye.

Amusing to turn over the diary of those times noting the strange variety of machines handled: Quadrant, Singer, Triumph, FN, De Havilland and Antelope motorcycles, including a 6hp Rex; then Vulcan, Humber, Argyll, Richard-Brasier, Oldsmobile and various types of Daimler cars – not a bad bag for that age.

Then Nina and I became engaged with the blessing of her most attractive mother, and life took on yet another phase. Supremely happy we were for years until things seemed somehow to go wrong. Looking back, I can see that there was too much motorcycle and too little idea of what life, let alone marriage, was about, on my part. You must remember, though, I was a gormless youth, obsessed by mechanism and very much to blame for the final break in relations.

With Gordon Crosby I soon established a friendship which was to last for very many years. Together we painted and drew whenever opportunity occurred, argued for hours about various techniques and enjoyed ourselves to the hilt. At the time, Gordon was in the drawing office so there was little chance of developing in full his painting, for which he was to become so famous, but the germ of that idea was born at Daimlers. Outside my regular duties I could draw cartoons for the advertising department under Fleming (who, by the way, created the famous Daimler "D" in its nameplate) - cartoons aimed at S F Edge, the exclusive agent for our rival, Napiers

Then another friend acquired at this time was Montagu Tombs, a dandy

compared with most of us, a highly skilled craftsman and with the firm of Lotis[1]. In particular he wore a blue corduroy coat which gave him an unfair advantage with girlfriends and was probably why, subsequently, he married the most attractive of all the women telegraphists at the GPO.

It may seem ridiculous, but now I was in an office there was one thing which made me long to be back in the "shops". Instead of getting up at 5am I could now stop abed until 8am. But promptly at 5 every weekday I could hear first a few, then many, then a continuous patter of footsteps – the workmen going to the shops for a 6 o'clock start. I had a very strong temptation to get up and join them. The sound of those footsteps remains in my memory down to this very day.

A cartoon by Sammy entitled "A Nightmare". The result of celebrating in too convivial a fashion the commencement of another New Year. It appeared in Motor Cycling *of 3 January 1910.*

1. Coventry manufacturer of cars, taxis and vans, 1908-1912

Chapter Three

Journalism

One day Crosby suddenly told me that he had been offered a job as an artist-illustrator on a paper called *The Autocar*. We discussed the thing thoroughly, and after balancing the future in a drawing office against the joys of a much freer life doing real drawing, taking into consideration the very material fact that the salary offered was far better in the new job, we decided that it would be wise for him to accept. A month or so afterwards I suddenly received a letter offering me the job of illustrator on a new paper about to be published called *The Automobile Engineer*. The possibilities of such a job came about after sundry rather mysterious conversations with a long, lanky and bespectacled friend called Arthur Clayden[1], a man you would think was born to be a scientist. It was extremely difficult to decide what to do despite the previous discussion with Crosby, for journalism did not seem to offer anything like the possibilities that a job at Daimlers did.

In my own opinion I was a work-with-the-hands-bloke and not an office wallah. But the salary tempted me as much as it had Crosby, and another factor needed consideration. Something seemed to have happened to the Daimler Company, something difficult to explain for it was as though Britain's premier car firm had lost its way. Even to me, despite prejudice, our cars looked old fashioned.

During 1908 it had been decided to use a new type of engine employing unfamiliar sleeve valves, designed by an American, Charles Yale Knight. The prototype as demonstrated by him was indeed the most silent car so far, and that was something. Even the chassis was wrapped all over with felt and other materials to eliminate noise, and only tyres with a silent tread were used. Well, this engine was taken over by the drawing office so all seemed fine for the moment. But it was no length of time before teething troubles developed, especially in freezing weather.

1. Son of the Principal of Exeter College. See Bibliography, *The Art of Gordon Crosby*, p14

For one thing the engines were very hard to start from cold, which had of course to be done by hand using the starting handle. A little bother with the oil feed caused sleeves to seize, which was expensive to rectify, and then it proved difficult to eliminate the very smoky exhaust. To add to the worry, the firm of Napier, with its six-cylinder engines, had quickly acquired a very high reputation, especially for cars in the luxury class for which Daimler had been famous, and the Rolls-Royce Silver Ghost was beginning to pose another challenge. It did not take much analysis to see that Daimler was going to face a difficult period.

You must remember that the actual staff of any manufacturing works is prone to severely criticise that firm's products because they generally know more about the defects and troubles of the car produced than of the sales appeal, over-rating the value of rival cars; that is unless the morale of the employees is kept at high level. I was not to know that Daimler would over-come all these obstacles and continue happily for years to come. The future of the firm did not look too rosy to me in 1910 so I took the problem to Molly Swain, who said with no hesitation, "Take it". I did.

Thus after a number of years I returned to London to work in an office in Queens Street and live in excellent "digs" in Bloomsbury. It was a strange and most interesting existence, quite different from any I had had before. Arthur Clayden was Editor and I was the dogs-body who did copious line drawings of this or that peculiar mechanism, and I enjoyed it. What shook my ideas considerably was to learn that a paper could only exist on the revenue from its advertisers, yet the text must not be influenced by this fact, at least not much.

We mixed with the famous, with men whose names had been mentioned almost with awe as designers of the world's best cars, and found them very interesting indeed and very human. I took a special liking to Lawrence Pomeroy of Vauxhall and Louis Coatalen of Sunbeam, both of whom tempered high technical knowledge with humour and, in a way, extravagance. Herbert Austin seemed difficult of approach but very well worth listening to indeed, and was an enthusiast of the deepest dye. Frederick Lanchester was even more difficult, equally he did not seem to have wit so much as humour mixed with sarcasm, and a dislike of being corrected in any way.

The next shattering surprise was the day Arthur strolled into my office, took a bunch of drawings, paused on his way out, then said, " I want you to write the description of the new so-and-so chassis – get busy". Write?! What did the man think I was? I had never written anything in my life except letters. I could not spell, while my handwriting needed an interpreter, being otherwise indecipherable. Hell's bells, the thing he asked was impossible. But gradually an idea formed, born of a natural guile which might be called by worse names. If I read a description of a new chassis written by someone else, then used that as a basis, possibly I might produce something which served. I can still remember the labour, the constant reference to dictionaries, the difficulty of disguising the source of inspiration, but it served. Funniest part of it all was that the author of the original went out of his way to say it was good. It wasn't, it was awful, but somehow or other the thing interested me. So I sat up late at night reading all I could about writing as an art, which not only inflamed my curiosity but developed a sudden deter-mination to do the thing properly at any cost. It just shows you how easily fate may cast a die, for I have been writing ever since.

Emmie Kate, wife of Arthur Clayden with whom Sammy lodged. She is seated in the Pilot depicted in the Log Book and may well have been "Aunt" who was mentioned many times in it.

We were a very happy family in every sense of the phrase. Before very long I was living with the Claydens in an oldish house alongside Richmond Park. Arthur's wife Emmie Kate was one of the most wonderful women it has ever been my good fortune to meet. Not only did she run the household but somehow or other she seemed to control everyone she met, making life far more interesting and exciting. I do not think Arthur realised how much his wife influenced his career or created a friendly atmosphere, which was invaluable. Her parties gradually included the heads and engineers of almost every British firm and no few Americans, all of whom had the time of their lives and enjoyed the resulting relaxation. Many a time, in a room crowded with the "great", clouded by tobacco smoke, problems of all kinds, not always technical, were discussed until the early hours of the morning, Emmie's latest babe happily asleep the while in a basket behind the piano. More atmosphere was lent by the presence of junior members of the stage, remarkably free from inhibitions by the way.

Arthur incidentally had most curious eyesight. One August afternoon we were all out in a new type of car and were having it refuelled at a garage. Now Arthur could not see anything thin and vertical unless he turned his head until his eyes were in a vertical line. He reversed and the tail of the car came up against a flagpole. For some five minutes he proceeded to reverse up the pole, the tail of the car rising inches up it every time, but nothing would make him believe the pole existed. Earlier still he had taken Emmie in a highly pregnant state for a ride in a trailer behind his motorcycle. Cornering not being his strong point, Emmie was thrown out, a fact he failed to notice for a mile or so and then only because he could get no answer to his conversation. Meantime, friendly people had rushed out of a cottage and provided Emmie with a chair and brandy, though it would take more than a fall from a trailer to upset her equanimity. When Arthur returned all he remarked was, "Why didn't you say something?"

Naturally also, all of us went to the Paris Show for *The Automobile Engineer*. The French Show of those days was a far more joyous affair than it is now. Many an evening therefore was spent with French friends at the Moulin Rouge, which still possessed a little of the atmosphere created by that magnificent artist Count Toulouse-Lautrec. All this was education on the grand scale, particularly as the feminine company included many of the dancers after their turn had been concluded; what they had to say about the world in general was profoundly interesting.

On another occasion, which has become legend, all three of us went to the 1914 French Grand Prix race in a friction-disc driven Pilot car. The race was at Lyon, so near to Italy that the temptation to go and see that country was irresistible, though we ought to have returned to

England forthwith. Result was that on the way home a moment was reached when we had just enough money to go on to the Channel port, hungry, or stop at a good hotel, have a good meal and wire for some more money. Naturally we stopped and had the evening of our lives. The then Managing Director of Iliffe [publishers of *The Automobile Engineer*] always swore that the telegram we sent him read, "Dear Firm, are we still with you? If so, send ten pounds".

It may be as well to mention here that my excellent father, infuriated by my naïve priggishness and my total failure to understand what the world was about, had, much earlier on, arranged for me to see a friend of a friend of his in Paris, if you know what I mean. This to me was a dreadful ordeal since I had heard vaguely about these naughty little ladies and was both frightened of them and sorry they had to do this "dreadful" thing. The result, as you will imagine, was shattering. Not only was I thrown out as entirely unsatisfactory but my sympathy was entirely rejected. Never had I felt so outcast. However, the lady in question relented, I was allowed to return, given a long and most interesting lecture which changed all my ideas in one fell swoop, instructed never, *never* again to ask "How much?", then provided with a supper and enjoyment which I have remembered for the rest of my life. So I now enjoyed the company the "Mill" provided on terms of equality, and with sex just one of those things. Incidentally, Emmie Kate, being challenged one night to take a turn with the dancers, not only accepted but was frantically applauded by our French friends.

Mind you we worked (difficult as this may seem to believe) and we worked hard, though there were times when it seemed impossible the magazine would go to press on time. I moreover managed one step towards the racing I still desired above all else. With a new and exciting little Douglas motorcycle I enjoyed a number of races at the Brooklands track and learned a packet, since my desire for more speed outran my knowledge by quite a bit. Fast the machine certainly was, especially after the piston skirts had been made to resemble Mechlin [Belgian] lace, but progressive increases in compression resulted in violent pre-ignition on the last lap. That taught me all about sparking plugs and their funny little ways and what our principal plug firm KLG could do once they were interested.

Naturally the main advantage of this new job in "Journalism" was that you came in contact with the very latest ideas, and every new design, which in turn brought personal contact with all the chief men in the industry. Clayden even decided to design a car of his own, which, though it could not be built for financial reasons, was entirely fascinating but not part of our legitimate work on the magazine. One great advantage of being on the staff of an engineering magazine was attendance at the Institute of Automobile Engineers debates, because that brought contact with the top men in the design world, and highly humorous they could be. Lawrence Pomeroy for instance delighted in harrying Fred Lanchester, who tended to be dictatorial; Pomeroy's method being to contradict some assertion with a backing of complicated mathematics, to check which was impossible during the discussion. Such rapier thrusts agin the slow broadsword sweep was highly appreciated by the informed audience, as may be imagined.

The engineering folk of those times had humour in abundance. Louis Coatalen was forbidden to go further with an expensive experiment involving a six-cylinder engine, but during one of the Directors' official inspections they found that same engine still under test. Outraged, they summoned Louis. He came, solemnly counted the cylinders with one finger outstretched: "One, two, three, four, five, six. Why, so 'e have". And that was all the Directors ever got from the spritely Frenchman. Naturally friendships developed from all this which were to last, and from those came adventures not even contemplated, thus proving that friendship is the most important thing in the world provided it is genuine. Very much will be done if someone likes you, which otherwise would be considered solely from the business angle. Gradually I got to know a wide section of the industry's chief men, varying in type according to the factory they were in and the sort of car for which they were responsible; every single one with marked character and more interest in something new than in what we now call production.

At Brooklands too one moved among the famous, gradually getting to know people who had been almost legend before. René Thomas, for example, a big, square and delightfully French mechanic from the "heroic" age of racing, who drove with abandon yet stayed on track or road. Then there were the Guinnesses, Kenelm and elder brother Algy. Ken drove with great seriousness in the Sunbeam team time after time, could be extraordinarily regular lap after lap if the car was going as it should, and suffered badly from pre-start nerves. Algy was the direct opposite as he did not know what nerves were. Any car he drove, and it was usually a Darracq, had to stand up to maximum. Every curve was taken flamboyantly, so Algy's progress resembled that of a scalded cat flat out, his line a mite longer than the official lap distance. In the Grand Prix section of the Ardennes race in 1907 Algy was second, point three of a mile dividing him from first. In the 1908 "Four Inch"' race – the figure

refers to the cylinder bore *not* the race distance(!) – exactly the same time difference divided his car from that of the winner and in both races he was sensational. I was told that during the evening after the "Four Inch" in the Isle of Man, Algy almost succeeded in driving his car through the front door of the hotel housing the officials, the car's bonnet being decorated with Algy's temporary girl friends. And because it shows what I mean about the man, an incident many years later may serve.

My ancient vehicle [1897 Léon Bollée] had broken its valve-operating gear in the RAC Veteran Car Run to Brighton. If we pushed the twelve miles to the finish we could arrive in time, if we repaired the damage the delay would be too great – so we pushed. Now the regulations stated, "Cars must not be towed by a horse or vehicle or transported in a vehicle". Algy was the RAC Steward whose business it was to make sure the regs were obeyed. "But", said he, "It says 'towed'. Now if I put the front buffer of my Bentley against the rear of your car I can 'push' it." Never before had I heard the Steward of the meeting trying to find holes in the regs, but we thought it was a shade tricky so did not accept his offer.

You may judge that drivers of that time derived any amount of humour from every incident in racing, but then they had no financial difficulties. Meantime there was plenty of experience to gain in Trials especially when the small car arrived on the scene. By that time it had become a little difficult to be sure what paper we were on, though *The Automobile Engineer* remained our principal business. Both Arthur and I were briefed for work on *The Autocar* almost as much as on the engineering paper, while the advent of a new magazine, *The Light Car*, provided even more work. All this was made more exciting by the humorous feud which arose and reached fever heat between Iliffe and the rival Temple Press, who brought out *The Cyclecar*, which called everything we called a "light car" a "cycle car" whenever it could. Since an accurate dividing line could not be determined, even by the authorities, you can imagine the food thereby provided for journalistic enterprise. That all this tended to my advantage can be judged, since the higher command of the papers already considered that I could be detailed for any job entailing considerable discomfort; result was a splendid adventure.

A well-known driver, H R Pope, announced that he would beat the Blue Train or something of that type from London to Turin driving an Itala motorcar.[1] Since official observation by the RAC was impossible he asked *The Autocar* to tackle the job, and *The Autocar* was me. Well, the car turned out to be not a normal Itala but one of their Grand Prix racers to which a four-seater body had been attached somehow or other. An Italian mechanic was to travel with us, not altogether to his liking, and Pope announced that he would drive the whole way single-handed. Since he was an extremely burly, almost gorilla type with bulging muscles, this seemed fairly reasonable, except to raise a doubt whether this run was to advertise the car or the driver. We waited at Victoria station until the train guard blew his whistle and then set off at a frightening speed for Dover, taking absolutely no notice of such things as speed limits or, apparently, the rules of the road.

I cannot be blamed for feeling this was not my cup of tea before we arrived at Dover. Obviously some influence had been at work, for never in my life have I seen a car taken on board so

quickly or a ship get under way at such speed. The run in France was better; for one thing the roads were much more suitable for the full speed of the car. Secondly, there was less traffic, and thirdly, the French liked this kind of thing. So we reached the Italian border in a wonderfully short time, having had only two dicey moments, one with a cow, the other with a level-crossing gate and its guardians. Dust there was in volume, so all of us were coated with the stuff, and all of us were a mite tired into the bargain. Mind you, the huge fuel tank which had been fitted proved its worth, since the number of stops to refill was reduced to a minimum. We had a certain amount of incident of minor character, such as missing a tree trunk by about two inches and turning completely round four times when the brakes had to be applied at full power, but that is all part of the game.

Hair-raising is not a description sufficiently expressive to use about our descent of the Italian mountain roads, during which it was best to shut one's eyes and pray; a proceeding which I was glad to note the Italian mechanic joined with fervour. But he did not seem too certain of Pope's skills anyhow, as he gave me his wife's address "in case", as he said. Believe it or not, the car arrived at Turin railway station in 23 hours and 36 minutes from Victoria, beating the train handsomely.[2] Final memory of that trip was Pope's language at our dinner with the Itala people, the cause being the necessity for removal of numerous special sticky bandages he wore round each forearm, all of them being equivalent to Sellotape – Pope was unusually hairy.

As to the Trials with the new "light" cars my principal memories concern one during which the car [a Pilot] boiled like a steam engine nearly all

1. Pope was the English Agent.
2. See Log Book, July 19th/20th 1913. and *The Autocar*, July 26th, 1913

the way to Land's End. In the worst part of Salisbury Plain the car's friction gear[1] gave up the ghost during the return journey, causing my navigator and I to take the whole blamed thing to pieces and practically make a new drive, a process which took hours. Soon after that the engine went sick, reviving partially about ten miles from Staines. Just as we felt we could finish a tyre went flat. Tired as we were this seemed the last straw, but we managed to patch a nail puncture and crawl into Staines hours after everyone else, but we had finished.

Trials high spot was the RAC Small Car six day affair centred around Harrogate, a very official business intended to select the most reliable type of car and with "observers" on each machine to record everything that went wrong. Curious, but the weaker one's car, the more certainly it appeared we were allotted the heaviest observer. From the start it was obvious that the Cummicar I drove was *not* one of the most reliable cars in the trial; in fact my observer had to borrow more recording sheets before two days had passed. Then the engine gave up altogether, having seized at least one piston, on Sutton Bank[2]. The immense despondency thereby caused was however lessened because the driver of the little Pilot fell ill and piteous pleading allowed me to take his place.

On the third day the friction gear began to slip, and on the fourth the slip was almost continuous despite my secretly pouring sand on the discs. Water leaks developed in the radiator, while for good measure and horrible to relate, the engine sub-frame broke off at its front end. So the fourth day's run was a triumph of determination over machinery, especially when we were

faced by Sutton Bank once more. It was some consolation that Leno, [son of music-hall comedian Dan Leno] was in just as bad a pickle on that horrible gradient with a "baby" Peugeot. There was only one hope. We made our observers walk up, relieved of which great load the two wrecks of cars did climb the hill in clouds of steam. While Leno urged the observers to hurry, I managed quite a number of unrecorded repairs and we finished! True, those Godlike real motoring journalists, Thornton Rutter and Massac Buist, were very scathing about our cars, which did not help sales, but to finish was enough for us, and both of us treasured the small red buttonhole badge issued to all who drove in that trial.

My friend Leno was quite a character, as was his brother, who was called Gavin to avoid confusion. A year or two later these two became interested in an apparatus they had thought out for preserving fruit in tins. They erected this in the house cellar and on one memorable day fed it with twenty tins of fruit. In theory the tins would travel through the machine, be heated to extreme temperature, then delivered in style. The first tin emerged and Leno and his brother were congratulating themselves on success when the tin exploded. With sudden horror they realised that nineteen more tins were to come and nothing would stop them. For a matter of twenty minutes they crouched under a table while explosion after explosion projected masses of pulped fruit all over the place. It is said that their long-suffering wives had a great deal to say about the mess.

However, to return to cars. Two runs remain fixed in memory, both looney. In one, our old friend Pope decided an observer from *The Autocar* should be in

1. Pilot, see Log Book April 5th.
2. A notorious hill-climb, a mile long and rising 600 feet.

the Itala while he endeavoured to prove how cool the engine would keep by driving up and down Sutton Bank continuously. We made fifteen successive ascents in all, each one perilous in the extreme, and the car seemed no more "standard" than the one used to go to Turin[1]. Then Sheffield-Simplex, who built a six-cylinder car they thought would rival Rolls-Royce or Napier, decided to attempt a Land's End to John O'Groats run in top gear accompanied by an observer from *The Autocar*. We actually succeeded, though the multi-plate clutch was as near white-hot as metal could be in the process and, be it said, the top gear ratio seemed remarkably low.

Incidentally, it may amuse to list the cars driven during these years since some of them have been long forgotten. They were La Ponette, Sirron, Banner, Adams, Fafnir, Regal, Flanders, Mitchell, Germain, Unic, Decauville, Calthorpe, Mathis, Belsize, Turner, Averies, Ronteix, Straker-Squire, Crespelle and La Licorne[2] – apart that is from the really well known makes, and every kind of motorcycle

Life was very joyous though, and full of adventure. Much centred around Brooklands track of course, since all the drivers and mechanics and material supplier representatives were people enthusiastic beyond belief about everything concerning racing or cars generally. The friendships thus created led to tests of racing cars or runs with their driver. For example, Hornstead, who possessed a huge racing Benz which was one of the stars of the track, took me round several times, each more exciting than the last. An all-pervading humour increased the enjoyment. Kingston-upon-Thames at that time had

a 10mph speed limit along the riverfront road. Nearly all the Brooklands cars went to the track along this road so naturally a police trap was set at once. It was our habit then to crawl along as soon as the first timekeeper was spotted, then open up and pass the second one at speed, waving to the uniformed constable, who always waved back. The whole affair was conducted on the most friendly lines. But Superintendent Beck had a sense of humour too, and one day he set a second trap just beyond the one we knew – result, a series of summonses. We had to give him an unofficial dinner as a sign of appreciation for his tactics.

In 1912 the track authorities had arranged accommodation and facilities for the new flying machines, with highly exciting results. In preparation for a flight with one of the "birdcage" biplanes it was usual to sleep the night in the bunks provided within the aircraft sheds, because only in the early morning was the wind down to a minimum. It was not of course true that no machine went up if a blade of grass moved, but that is what sceptics suggested. Biplanes were the rule, monoplanes being suspect on account of the weak appearance of the wings unbraced by stout timber. Many an hour was spent with friends who allowed one to try handling a flying machine, always provided no one was found out.

On one occasion I was with Tommy Sopwith[3] in a rather unusual machine called a Coventry Ordnance biplane, which had a rotary engine driving the airscrew through a chain. It was a remarkably hot day but that did not altogether explain what seemed to be a strange number of large flying insects going past our ears with a snapping

1. See Log Book Aug 19th 1913.
2. Many of these vehicles feature in the Log Book.
3. The founder of Sopwith Aviation Co., of Sopwith Camel fame.

noise. As much depended on hearing any odd noise and making sure what it was, it was decided to land. It was just as well we did for the snaps were not caused by insects, but by broken pieces of the rollers for the chain links, all of these having seized.

Another amusing occasion only indirectly concerned aircraft. In the shed was a delightful small bear kept as a pet. Ooley, as he was named, also had a sense of humour. It was his habit occasionally to scramble up the ladder to a bunk, delve down beneath the blankets and go to sleep at the end of the bed. One day a visitor who did not know our ways had to stay the night. He undressed and got into the bed, then yelled the place down and shot out at very high speed complaining furiously that there was an animal in it. There was, it was Ooley. Another time Ooley made a mistake. He had a habit of scrambling up one's back and holding on with both paws round one's neck, a manoeuvre executed with surprising gentleness. Unfortunately he did this to a girl visitor who, alarmed by feeling something alive and strange on her back, then saw a bear's face looking over her shoulder. Promptly she had hysterics and so did the now terrified Ooley.

In spite of all these distractions we managed to get through a surprising amount of work for the various magazines. Indeed, the Claydens and I moved to Tiverton Mansion, Grays Inn Road, to be nearer the job. Here again, you could find the flat filled with every kind of interesting person of an evening, ruled over completely and thoroughly by Emmie Kate, who was equally at home with the chorus from Dalys or the Gaiety, engineers, editors, journalists, or artists. Montagu Tombs, who had also joined *The Autocar*, and Crosby were frequent guests.

During the visit of the American Society of Automobile Engineers Emmie really shone, so much so that there seemed to be a lunch or dinner especially for her almost every day. That nearly all these engineers were hospitality in itself, besides having an entirely new way of looking at automobile design problems, was extremely interesting, as you may imagine. Arthur was in fact hypnotised by the Americans almost at once, so that American influence seemed to come into everything he wrote, while they in turn were apparently most interested in some of his engine designs, all of which was to bear unexpected fruit.

Apart from all these excitements much had happened to the family circle. Fatty had gone off to India and Roy Geddes was engaged in mysterious doings with fruit imports on a large scale, with intervals when he developed an immense and rather difficult fervour for religion. Both father and mother were in India, busy with tea gardens and McCleod & Co of Calcutta. My beautiful sister Eve had married an altogether delightful, thoroughly temperamental Irishman, while Cyril, having had enough of the Navy, had gone to Canada, and the youngest of us, Hugh, was now a grown man. Barring my most understanding mother, I do not think any of the family could understand what I did or how I did it, though our sincere friendship stood the test. So the wonderful world I knew came to 1914.

First inkling that all was not well came when Arthur, Emmie and I went over for the French Grand Prix at Lyon in July. The weather was wonderful and our friends from all the various countries were there. In some way I could meet the drivers and mechanics on even terms during that week of intense work before the race. Bill Guinness took me round the long circuit in the Indianapolis Sunbeam he used for practice instead of the car he was to drive in the race, and gave me a lecture on racing driving which was of the utmost value. Charles Faroux, greatest of French journalists, gave us lunch, largely, I feel certain, because he was naturally attracted to Emmie, and in the doing gave a wonderful exhibition of perfect manners and true appreciation of food and wine as only a Frenchman can.

For as long as I live I will remember that race before all others. The atmosphere seemed to be menacing, for one thing, and that was unusual, the cause being the presence of the German Mercedes team. There was no obvious rudeness between the Germans and the French, certainly not between the drivers concerned, but an almost icy politeness between the two nationalities which seemed strange. Then the race was fiercely national, not as before an affair between two rival teams, France being represented by the Peugeots. The race by the way was for 4½-litre unsupercharged cars and any form of special fuel was forbidden. Of the Peugeot team Georges Boillot was the acknowledged chief driver and eminently fitted for the task. Round this man there was, as it were, an atmosphere strongly reminiscent of the heroic age created by Dumas in his *Three Musketeers*, Georges being the equivalent of D'Artagnan. He carried himself with that swagger which was in no sense offensive, and he would have given all he had as champion of France. There was something stirring too in the difference between the cars of the rival teams, the Peugeots being big bluff machines, direct descendants of the great cars from the finest days of racing. The Mercedes were lower, looked lighter, had a shark-like character and engines much more of aircraft type than those of the French cars.

A huge crowd of many nationalities assembled for the start, all the more interested because in those days there was only one real race a year, the French Grand Prix, not as now with twenty Grand Prix to disperse the interest. Though short (by earlier standards), the circuit was a beauty, with a long straight switchbacking all the way from the right angle of Pont Rompu to the even sharper turn ominously nicknamed "*Le virage de la mort*". After the easily curved leg leading from the start at Sept Chemins to the curve at Givors, there followed corner after corner after corner' at each of which it was vital not to make a mistake, and so to Pont Rompu again and the comparative freedom of the straight. Totalling 23.3 miles it featured every kind of driving hazard as far as racing was concerned.

From the very start there were only two cars in the race that really interested the spectators: Boillot's blue Peugeot and the leading Mercedes handled by Lautenschlager. Though there were 470 miles to cover, Boillot drove at the Peugeot's full speed from the start, handling his car magnificently so that it was never overstressed yet was on the borderline all the time. Beyond doubt it was his finest drive, and he was further inspired by the obvious fact the enthusiastic crowd was with him to a man. The way he came round the *virage de la mort* and changed gear for the hairpin below that corner had drama in it, though the mechanism was moved as delicately as ever. Boillot led, but to those of us who watched two things were apparent. The Peugeot was not getting away from the three Mercedes, which came round lap after lap almost as regular as clockwork, and the German cars were being controlled scientifically from their pit, not by the craftsmanship of their drivers as were the Peugeots. As the race went on this became more and more apparent until I felt there was something remorseless in that formation of German cars. But still the Peugeot led, right up to the last laps of that long and vigorous race, still Boillot was as magnificent as ever, so that a French win seemed assured. And then – the Peugeot failed to come round to time. Instead, the pointed front of the white Mercedes appeared when every eye was glued to the *virage de la mort* up the hill. There was a sudden deadly silence, and then the German team came over the finishing line, one, two, three under the yellow flag of victory. Far away on the circuit the Peugeot was stationary with engine trouble. Boillot wept. I have never experienced a race with such drama, and curious as this may seem, the effect of that sudden German victory was not as pleasing as it should have been considering that Mercedes were the historic cars directly descended from those of the heroic age.

At home we were as merry and as happy as ever, perhaps because our present mode of life seemed secure, the future even more so; that was in July 1914. Came August, overshadowed by much talk of the worsening situation with Germany, a situation which, though this was almost impossible to believe, gradually became more serious to a point when it was just possible there might be a world conflict. Then, the August Brooklands Meeting on the 3rd, at which for once no one talked much about cars and the usual racing jokes were notably absent, for the unbelievable then happened – we were at war the next day.

Chapter Four

Through war to manhood

August 1914 can never be forgotten; for the moment the world seemed to have gone mad. Crowds sang with apparent glee, flags were waved and a curious hysteria gripped everyone. Now, the family history was full of war, so I was in some sort handicapped by prior knowledge of what it meant and was not so sure this was an occasion for celebration. I had heard a good deal about the German regular army, all tending to the belief it was a first class fighting force, not to be underestimated at any cost. This, curiously enough, begat a certain savage elation at the prospect of fighting them. That we might lose never crossed my mind, even if the war went on for years. Well, determined at last to get into the army off I went to Whitehall to see various friends and relatives. It was a most irritating process as what I wanted was to take a hand in the shooting, knowing that I could use a rifle effectively, having done so from infancy. Every darned "high authority" I saw tried to wheedle me into a commission on the engineering side on account, they said, of my excellent mechanical knowledge.

They kept on saying that at twenty-seven I was too old for use as a private soldier.

The result was extraordinary and unbelievable. Coming away from Whitehall I encountered a red-faced, sturdy bloke who asked if I would like to join the Royal Naval Air Service. In a flurry of excitement I accepted. Next day off I went to Sheerness and in no time at all found myself in blue, sleeping in a hammock and intrigued beyond measure by the Navy's languages and its ways. To cut a long story short, I was just doing fine in my own estimation when a friend of Emmie Kate's, a major of Marines, spotted this absurd object in blue. Before I could think, I found myself transferred to the RNAS armoured car division as a Chief Petty Officer. You should have seen the near apoplexy which afflicted the magnificent specimen of the real Naval Petty Officer (twenty years in the Navy) when he heard what had happened to one of his flock.

Before very long I was promoted even further to Sub-Lieutenant, and this resulted in an attack of "kittens" since I

A posed photo of Sub-Lieutenant S C H Davis. RNAS, 1914.

could not see how I could possibly afford commissioned rank, especially in a squadron commanded by the Duke of Westminster. Well, we got over to the war mighty quickly, so this problem solved itself. At that stage armoured cars were not able to function any more than the cavalry, but at least we had two assets, plenty of Maxim guns and three armoured lorries with small quick-firing guns, and both could be used with verve. Moreover I soon found myself in good company among friends and relatives.

So we came to Neuve Chapelle, May 9th and the first gas attacks [chlorine] at Ypres – affairs that can never be forgotten. Mind you, most of our time was spent staging quick bombardments of strong points with the guns of the armoured lorries. During the May 9th show, for example, we had two lorries among the ruins of a village on the Rue

de Bois firing most of the time, while on one occasion we were asked to cause grief and bad temper by suddenly making holes in a nasty little strong building used by the opposition partly for coffee breaks and partly for sniping. Unfortunately this entailed going out along a road between the opposing lines, which we did not relish over-much, but the local infantry were delighted with the result so we presumed the Boche were not. Trouble arose out of this with Naval procedure. To fire the guns on a broadside the opposing side armour had to be lowered to form a platform for the gun crew. Firing at maximum rate as in this instance, the floor became littered with expended cartridges. Naturally some of these fell overboard, and when their box was returned to the Naval store officer, Dunkirk, it was deficient of some empty cartridges. This resulted in my receiving a formal demand for the empties. Taking this to be red tape, I replied light-heartedly that the cartridges were not available. But the blasted official continued to demand the missing cartridges and even suggested I might have to pay for them. Temper rising, I replied that if he wanted the damned things they were at grid reference so-and-so and he could go and get them; at that the signals became really nasty. Bouncing with indignation I drove down to see the Naval Captain in charge at Dunkirk. Gravely he listened to my furious but polite complaint. Then he smiled and said, "My boy, the Navy is very old and wise, you do not know the correct language. Now I will write a signal and you will send it." The signal read that the cartridges had been "Lost overboard in heavy weather". Perfect peace followed.

More entertaining was the sudden awareness that camouflage was valu-able. The big lorries were painted in matt colours broadly banded to destroy the outline. But for work among ruined houses this did not suffice, so I had the joy of designing a canvas screen resembling a ruined house to be worn by the lorry in such circumstances. For good measure we painted the gun barrel strong white underneath, shading that into matt black on top, and it served admirably. An enthusiastic gunner who took great interest said we ought to have a stuffed dog sniffing at the "wall ruin" for a complete illusion. We had a bit of unexpected humour with the Rolls-Royce light armoured cars too. Since a puncture might have fatal results, the tyre tubes were filled with some special jelly-like substance in place of air. Fine, splendid, but after a long run the tyres became hot, the jelly melted, and then solidified only after the cars had stood in their emplacements. Driving that car afterwards with four uneven flats on the tyres was hell.

Before these smaller actions we usually went as near to our firing point as possible and then laid up. One night in pouring rain it seemed to me there was a practical house nearby. I explored it with caution and found a loft in which was a French farm-hand asleep, with his hat firmly on his head. So I took my fleabag inside and settled down to comfort and reading a book by the light of a small candle. Suddenly I thought the floor was moving all around. It was bugs, million upon million of bed bugs, the whole place was alive with them. But the Frenchman was immune, or so it seemed.

Brisk though these actions were, much of the time was definitely boring. I was lucky in that I could manage several days shooting with my cousin Vivian when the Border Regiment was in the line nearby. Extraordinary how impersonal sniping can be, especially if you have a good telescopic sight on a proved rifle and a nest or hole which your opposite number cannot find. It did not seem like shooting at a man but at a figure on a cross-hair mark, and a very small part of the figure at that. I know an instance when a sniper of ours had established "friendly" relations with his German opposite number, to such extent that they ceased to fire at each other but at any other unlucky target which offered. Come tea time a jam tin placed on a parapet gave the signal for an hour's lull. On another occasion a wounded German was brought into our trench line bandaged and, when I saw him, was having a cup of tea with his captors to underline the impersonal nature of modern war.

The fact of the matter is that you know quite well the other bloke feels the same as you, is scared before an action starts like you, is fiercely and savagely exalted when it is in full swing, and is doing his job the same as you. Interesting also, how difficult it is to realise someone else wants to kill you, a difficulty entirely due to over-civilisation. Strange too to note how easily one returns to natural man with an alert wariness all the time, and the ability to see instantly any very small movement which means danger. On occasions we had long and interesting discussions about all this, first of all agreeing that if there is war *both* sides are right, as taught by Gunnion Rutherford. It is the point of view which differs, a finding not at all popular with civilians. Secondly, fighting is natural to man and is in some ways the finest expression of manhood. Lastly, how odd it is that if you find a wounded enemy you seem bound to succour him in every way, which results in his being a prisoner, then exchanged for one of your men so that he can shoot at you again. Which brought up the matter of military etiquette, as exemplified by a wounded German officer who offered his sword to one of ours during the battle of Neuve Chapelle while all hell was loose. The Briton told him to hop it in terms which were quite rude; after all, what the blazes could one do with a sword? But the German put in an official protest in all solemnity about his wounded honour; it seems that the sword hilt should have been touched, then the weapon returned to him.

As time went on the heady exuberance caused by contact with life in the raw began to fade. Personally I became more and more despondent and we attacked with every preparation known to man. The "Dailies" claimed the result as a victory, yet when you came to think it over, all we had gained was a matter of eight or nine hundred yards. Easy to see that at this rate the war would last for a hundred years, which was depressing. And though unfair, there was no great enthusiasm for the high command. For instance, I had to visit a headquarters on some matter or other and found them dining in state with everything which would have been available in England in peace, and in a château the atmosphere of which was completely unwarlike. The only time I saw a high member of the command he was riding a horse, had a sword and was followed by a horseman carrying a banner. It was too much like Henty's books about the Crimea.

Then the loss of friend after friend and relative after relative began to tell, exaggerating death and biasing thought unfairly, which would not have happened if there had been any sign of movement from those infernal trenches. I still knew we were going to win and never challenged that belief, but I felt certain I would be dead before long. Mind you, the thing which made victory certain, even allowing for those occasional fits of gloom, was the

magnificent courage of the fighting troops, particularly those in regiments with long histories to sustain them and genuine discipline. Through mud and blood and every kind of hardship these men kept their sense of humour, to the bewilderment of all beholders. The jest that the German army knew the British were far too dangerous if you interrupted their tea was almost true. There were none of the psychological problems that writers of today make plays about, none of the dramatic patriotism favoured by American screen heroes. They did not like the job but they were not going to give up until it was finished – and by God they didn't. Easy to understand why, once they accepted the discipline, the Britons, the inhabitants of these islands, were so dangerous to annoy, from the time of Tenchbrai[1] onwards.

We did not have sufficient fighting and did have a deal too much waiting for the breakthrough which never occurred, same as the cavalry who seemed so absurd with their lances. To cap it all I had one leave in England to learn on one day that almost the whole family had gone: father; brother Hugh, shot down attacking a German squadron, apparently on his own in berserk mood; and Cyril, killed as a machine gunner in the salient at Ypres. Only mother and Evelyn were left. One cousin, Wood, had been killed in air combat, two nephews had gone, two uncles as well – it seemed impossible to believe. Afterwards, what with gas in the first gas attack and this and that, I was seriously ill and saw no more of the real war.

When I was fit for duty again there was more trouble. The board, assembled to pass me as fit, were no doubt excellent and helpful officers, but they infuriated me once again. One member

1. Alternatively Tinchbrai, battle won by Henry I in 1106 to conquer Normandy.

of the board asked me what I would like to do, I replied, "Fly". Instantly the President interposed, "But he is too old and he has special technical qualifications". Blast the technical qualifications! But the Navy is the Navy, so I found myself at Humber Coventry to look after Naval aircraft engines. Which was all the more extraordinary because at Humber was Walter Owen Bentley, whom I had known as a boy and at Brooklands, busily engaged in designing a new rotary engine to supersede the Clerget.

It was all most interesting. W O worked through a delightfully stubborn man, Burgess, who was the Humber car designer, and so every day had its moments. A rotary engine is a curiosity in any case, someone alleging that it ran by centrifugal force relieved by the cylinder explosions. Anyhow, the cylinders and crankcase went round with the airscrew while the crankshaft stayed put, so centrifugal force governed everything. We had the time of our lives with that engine, which really played its part in winning the war, though I would not have liked altogether to handle the fighter aircraft powered by it. I had the uneasy though unjustified idea that one day the fuselage would turn round the engine in mid-air instead of vice versa. Teething troubles had to be remedied as we proceeded, even if the works manager, Meeson, came near to apoplexy, or the managing director, Niblett, alleged the company was ruined. We always turned W O on to the official concerned, for no man can shake W O when he is certain of what he wants and intends to have it – not even a modern American production team.

Occasionally one or other of the Naval high command would come visiting, the problem then being to make W O even pretend to salute the galaxy of gold sleeve rings. Just to make

life easier the powers that be decided to make a hash they called the Royal Air Force out of the Royal Naval Air Service and the Royal Flying Corps. Excellent on paper that might have been, but it did the morale of both forces no good at all, for the RNAS was as fiercely proud of its individuality as was the RFC, and both with reason. For quite a time neither side would wear the new uniform so it was not a pleasant period.

It might have been partly the worry over this, or general worry, but at that point, and just when W O's latest much bigger engine was getting into production, I was carted off to hospital by the combined forces of highly placed friends in Harley Street. All of us in that hospital were surgical cases and were remarkably cheerful in the circumstances even though the quota of arms and legs did not correspond with the nominal roll. There were certain advantages in being so close to Harley Street, seeing that all famous surgeons are enthusiasts. For example, one genial celebrity came round and, distending our nostrils with a gentle thumb, asked, "Do you breathe better now"? The reply was naturally "Yes", whereupon almost all of us were removed to the theatre where he chipped away with what appeared to be a chisel aided by snipe-nose pliers. The result, though a mite bloody, was beneficial for about two months.

Well, my inside received a drastic but beneficial overhaul, though I was frightened stiff by being placed in a private room as a serious case when I knew that the last two occupants had gone from it in a box. Another interesting point was the gradual discovery of what had been done. Firstly I was shown a group of enormous gallstones, then it appeared my appendix had gone too, and finally it was revealed that my colon was now sewn to my diaphragm. That gave one plenty to think about, with resultant panic. Those stones had grown within me in a certain number of years and I expected to live on about the same number – barring accidents. Therefore the damned things would grow again and they hurt. In a considerable state of anxiety I asked the expert for information on this important subject, only to receive evasive answers such as, "They can't", which did not make sense to a mechanical mind. Only after fervent pressing for an answer did I get the right one, which was, "Oh well, we also removed your gall bladder".

There was another minor trouble. When I recovered from the anaesthetic I found a rubber tube sticking out of my stomach. This seemed intriguing so I followed it along and discovered that it led to a glass bottle under the bed. Not quite liking this I rang urgently for the nurse. It was some hours before I was pacified, largely because I had no notion a rubber tube could be used like this. When the tube was removed a lump remained round the hole which a nurse promptly began burning off with caustic. The row I made aroused our beloved Scottish Sister "Mac", who demanded why I was making all this noise. "The bloody thing hurts like hell, Sister." "Nonsense, Captain Davis". "But it does, Sister." "Alright then I will do it."

Armoured lorry 2AS retiring out of action in 1915, signed SHD. (The initial C was usually dropped). This is from the history of The Armoured Cars Division, with particular reference to No. 2 squadron.

And bless her she did, every morning, and I never even felt it. Thus was learned a most valuable lesson – if you suffer in silence you suffer, but if you raise hell they bring an expert and it doesn't hurt.

Months passed and then I was sent off to the convalescent hospital at Swanage in company with a friend, Lawrence Irving, grandson of the great man. Swanage was a tonic in itself, the place apparently having been decorated by Mr Mowlem, the government building contractor of note. We discovered all the lamp posts were second-hand from London. Alfred's defeat of the Danes was celebrated by a stone pillar on which were five Napoleonic cannon balls, and there was a wonderful steel-hard stone model of the earth on which visitors had tried to carve without avail. Of course we did things which were almost but not quite forbidden. For instance, Lawrence and I decided to go for a row on a really beautiful hot day. The better to enjoy the sunlight we stripped to the waist. It was easy enough to row out into Swanage bay but getting back was far more difficult. In fact there were moments when we were not so darned sure we could manage it. To cap it all we overdid the sunlight and were burned all over our backs, for which we got no sympathy but a hell of a talking-to from Sister. Another friend came out to a tea-shop one afternoon only to forget to bring back his crutches.

But there was no doubt that we were really fit by the time we were discharged at last, and, being fit, took an interest in the war once more; an interest the more exciting because at last the German line was broken and the end in sight. Then, almost as a shock, came the armistice and the end of it all, leaving one numb and unable quite to imagine how on earth one was to face civilian life once more.

Chapter Five

A Dream Comes True

The first wild excitement of peace having faded a little, many of us had the curious feeling that an unbridgeable gap separated those who had been in the war from those who had not. For some inexplicable reason it seemed quite impossible to get through the barrier; we were neither talking nor thinking in the same way. I went back to Iliffe to discuss with a high level executive about resuming my job. It was not as pleasant a meeting as I had envisaged. I was asked what I had done in the war and when I came to the part about development of the aircraft engines "High Authority" said, "Well, that's of some use to us anyhow". It took some hours before I could cool down enough to realise this sentence did not mean what it seemed but was a case of unfortunate phraseology, interpreted one way by me, another by the speaker. For one whole day, though, I thought of refusing to return to the firm. But the phase passed and sanity returned with a sense of humour for which I was afterwards

very glad indeed.

Mind you, much had changed. The paternal family affair of pre-war had gone to a large extent since the fatherly autocracy created by Walter Staner and Harry Swindley, Editor and London Editor respectively, had weakened as new and younger men came forward. Also there was now an urgency, a premium on new ideas and a sense of rivalry which was exciting. But most important of all was the fact that I had married during the war (with all the glamour of war, arch of swords, St George's Hanover Square and the rest) to Rosamund Pollard[1], sister of a Westminster friend of long standing. She was the daughter of that altogether loveable character "Old Joe" Pollard, Harley Street doctor who minced no words to his patients or his colleagues and was universally loved wherever he went.

In other respects life was becoming more and more full. Attention was concentrated on the small-engined car, mainly because that was the type most

---

1. Rosamund was twenty and Sammy thirty one; the wedding was on June 16th 1917.

Rosamund Pollard, driving at a young age.

people could afford, so development was most interesting to watch. My activities now centred more and more on the *Light Car* rather than *The Automobile Engineer*, mainly because that gave one far more opportunities to take a hand in the practical side, but also because Clayden had taken a job in the United States so he and Emmie Kate were far away. Unfortunately those predictions of before the war held good as something went wrong. Arthur and Emmie Kate parted, and that seemed to put an end to a life amusing beyond words, reminiscent in some ways of the Victorian and Edwardian existence.

In the hurly-burly of postwar years there was plenty to do, which prevented any tendency to brood on the past. All manufacturers of small cars were intent on proving their worth in Trials, of which the Motor Cycling Club's "Exeter", "Land's End" and "Edin-burgh" were the chief. Now the cars were not altogether reliable, so we never experienced a dull moment. For example, in the first "London-Exeter" after the war H C Lacey, who had been a constant companion during the war, and I, started bravely enough from Staines with all the other competing cars. Twenty miles short of Exeter the magneto contact-breaker spring broke which, as the magneto was not at all easy of access, caused much profanity and delay. Then the machine boiled like a tea-kettle in full blast every time we tackled a test hill. All the lamps went out and we had hell rigging up torches in their place, postponing repair until the breakfast stop in Exeter. On the return journey the top seam of the radiator succumbed to steam pressure and split, emitting more scalding water than Vesuvius. This meant we had to refill, drive at high speed until the water boiled, then refill and repeat the process time after time. Just as it seemed we might regain schedule a gear selector fork came loose. Super-human efforts by Lacey removed the gearbox lid so that we could prise one gear into position and then we had to drive like mad to keep up. Alas we overdid it and, arriving at a control too early, were disqualified. But we did finish at Staines for all that, and finishing was a "must" for both of us.

There was a strong team-spirit among those who drove works cars in the trials, but of course none of the elaborate service facilities now so obvious, or any of the financial assistance. What went wrong you repaired then and there with anything handy, including pieces of trees or even fences nearby. Works rank went for nothing. During one trial the navigator, a works mechanic, ex-Navy, was infuriated by the fact that the driver, who was Managing Director, would leave gear changes until the last moment on test

Sammy noted that this AC was prepared in 1914 for a 1½-litre "Tourist Trophy" race on the Isle of Man that the outbreak of war prevented taking place. An international cyclecar TT was planned for September 1914 and AC may have entered, but this car has the appearance of a post-war track racer. Sammy and Westall are seen in the car in the paddock at Brooklands.

hills. Driven to the end of his self control on one hill, he nudged his superior forcibly in the ribs and shouted for all to hear, "Change down, you bloody fool". All this taught you to think quickly. For instance the officials were sleepily setting up the timing post in the early hours of a winter morning at a control into which no competitor should enter before his scheduled time. Suddenly a sports car skidded round a curve and arrived. Seeing the crowd the driver asked, "What place is this?" Receiving the answer, "Yeovil", which was a checkpoint, he yelped "My God", and before anyone could take the car's competition number he was off in reverse out of sight.

Well, all this was great fun but it wasn't racing, which I felt as determined as ever to attain despite financial handicap. Also there was a small worrying cloud on the horizon, no

larger than a man's hand. Argue however skilfully you could, the fact remained that doing things is not really part of a journalist's job. Why "Authority" stood for my adventures I can't say, but though there was this undercurrent of disapproval it was very weak and half-hearted, thank heaven. Common sense though dictated that I should compete with as many makes of car as possible to avoid any suggestion that I favoured one or other, and this introduced complications, as you may imagine.

In September 1921 Selwyn Edge asked me to take a hand in an attack on Class records at Brooklands with one of his six-cylinder 2-litre ACs, a record lasting for two periods of twelve hours, therefore called the Double-Twelve. The memory of that exhilarating ride has never failed. A Noble, W G Brownsort of AC and

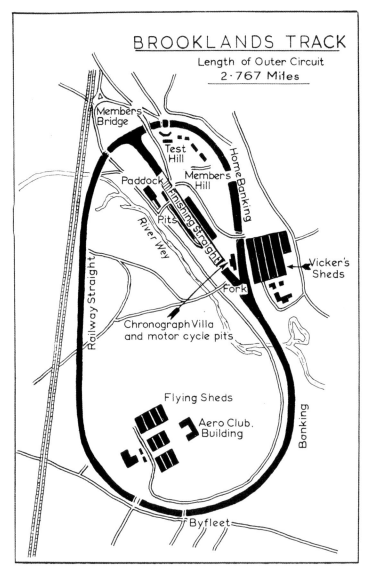

BROOKLANDS TRACK

Length of Outer Circuit
2·767 Miles

world to tyre wear if you failed to remember this.

Naturally a driver had to know at any time what the instruments were telling him, naturally also he had to note instantly any change in the signals given from the depot established at the track side for the mechanics and equipment. We did not have a silencer then, for the local residents had not succeeded in obtaining an injunction against noise from the track, so the exhaust was a full-throated roar – most inspiring even if deafening. All went to schedule for twelve hours so we amassed a nice parcel of intermediate records, much to Edge's satisfaction. Come nightfall and the car was locked away by the officials.

Arriving dismally early next day I was worried to find the track was covered by a thick autumnal mist, but we had to start all the same, with the mist obviously slowing the car. My spell was unpleasant. Even staring over the top of the tiny screen without goggles did not make it possible to see clearly enough, so you had to drive by instinct. Sometimes I thought we were going down the finishing straight instead of round the circumference, which was bad for the nerves, but by gradually increasing speed I was able at last to see the OK signal and that was an immense relief. Eventually the mist lifted and we could all enjoy ourselves. I was off duty having lunch when a message arrived from Edge telling me to return as I was to take the car for the 2-litre hour record as part of the main record attempt. Squeezing into the cockpit I was busy looking at the mechanics refilling and changing wheels when the man who was changing the sump oil said, "Blimey, what's this?" Then he got up holding the small end of a connecting rod. Ah well, it had been a wonderful time even if we did not get the aimed-at final record. In all we had

myself took spells at the wheel of that thin, single-seater streamlined car and enjoyed every second of it. People used to say there was no necessity for driving skill at Brooklands, and they were completely wrong. All the time you had to make sure the car was holding the record speed yet being given the smoothest run possible. That meant keeping to a line accurately on both bankings and, more important still, on the unbanked curve by the Vickers shed. It made all the difference in the

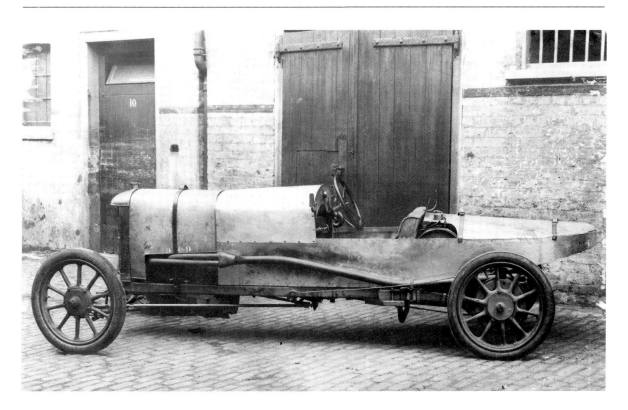

captured 18 records, most at over 70, which was a fast average in those days – all of us walked with the gods. The reason for a Double-Twelve record was that after Edge had opened Brooklands with a twenty-four hour record in 1907, any further runs at night were forbidden as a result of the uproar from local inhabitants.

Better still was to come in October that same year, when the new Junior Car Club boldly decided to organise a 200-mile race at the track despite the fact that every member of the committee was agog with fear that such impudence would stir the RAC to vigorous action, but as it happened the RAC proved benevolent. For this race Edge asked me to drive an AC of the official team. Never before has anyone lived with their racing car so much as we four, Davy, Brownsort, R J Munday and myself, all centred on three new-type cars designed by John Weller and totally different from their predecessors,

too different as it happened, for we had teething troubles galore. Moreover, the cars were completed so close to the day of the race that there was no time for careful and systematic testing. Fortunately two cars of normal design with Anzani engines were entered as well and one was to be driven by a friend of mine, Stead, whose tendency to disregard high authority was equal to my own, and who was a journalist of the Temple Press. My car was a bundle of trouble all the time. First it suffered from water leaking into the crankcase, then when that was botched up the clutch refused to hold. Mechanics worked all night before the race and we just got to the start in time, albeit there was no chance of testing the altered clutch.

On the starting line amidst the crowd of other cars, vast clouds of oily smoke made it difficult to see anything, much less the starting flag, but at a glimpse of its fall I let go. The car refused to move

Experimental AC racing car, probably in 1921.

– the damned clutch had failed to hold. Using vigorous language, I shut the throttle while my mechanic and I pulled lustily at the rear wheels until the car crept forward. Then the clutch held at last and we were off, quite well too as we actually held on to Bill Guinness's Talbot-Darracq, most favoured of all the cars to win. Alas, our joy was short-lived for on the fourth lap a cylinder cut out. At the pit we found that a valve was defective – actually a large piece had broken away from it – but in the mood my mechanic and I were in we were not going to stop for little things like that.

All afternoon we suffered, the car seemed to creep though it was faster than several others even then. The clutch slipped every time we went up on the home banking, and on four occasions the sliding joint for the clutch-shaft failed to retain the shaft. We were appalled to find that Munday's car had overturned in a ditch, that Davy's was stationary at the side of the circuit, but heartened that Stead, with the side-valve engined car, seemed to be going strong. So we finished, though everyone had packed up by the time we crossed the line, and Edge gave us his special congratulations for racing in the "right spirit". Quite different "spirit" was what we thought we needed after that!

Incidentally, I did have the pleasure of taking five other good Class records with an AC using Weller's new four-cylinder 1500cc engine which had driven us nearly crazy with valve trouble in the 200-mile race. All this was not only very good but the better because of friends made in circumstances when friendship is genuine. It was through such a friendship that the next very great adventure came.

Much better luck followed in an historic run in May 1922 with an Aston-Martin for records at Brooklands. The reason why for me this record stood out was that the whole thing was planned down to the last detail. The refills, wheel changes and control generally were exceptionally good on the day, and the three drivers, Kensington Moir, Clive Gallop and myself, were drilled into exactness before the run started. Great secret also was the schedule which was planned to make the 1500cc Aston-Martin the first ever light car to capture World records. To add to the fun an AC driven by Joyce and Day was running on the track simultaneously to capture the Double-Twelve record and such other 1500cc class records as could be beaten in the time, so we had direct competition.

Well, it was a great success, the Aston-Martin "Bunny" did its job splendidly. The refills were astonishingly quick and we took 10 World records besides 22 Class records in fine style. What caused us amusement was that when the AC stopped at 7pm the car's control could not imagine what in blazes we were still running for, but began to suspect a mystery. When it was announced that Aston had taken World records they had considerable difficulty in meeting Edge's ice-cold request to know why the AC control had not thought of this idea before-hand. Managing Directors of his calibre can be very difficult!

At Brooklands one of the striking characters (for which the track was noted) was Count Louis Zborowski, a man who delighted in driving a car with the largest possible available engine. Back in the heroic age of racing Zborowski's father had been famous as a driver of the first rank, usually devoted to Mercédès. During the 1903 climb up La Turbie hill down by Nice, which could be called one of the social events of racing, Zborowski drove a Mercédès with his usual verve. Then, as he shifted his grip on the steering

The 1924 French Grand Prix at Lyon saw Sammy in action as riding mechanic to Louis Zborowski in the Miller. The Count retired the car on lap 16 of the 35-lap race as the front axle was in a state of disarray.

wheel, the linked cuff of his right sleeve caught the throttle lever on the wheel and opened it wide, just when it had been shut. Uncontrollable, the car shot off the road to crash against the rock face on the corner. Zborowski was killed instantly and a tablet marks the spot on the hill today.[1]

Louis was not the conventional type of millionaire. Firstly, he was rich only at the beginning of each month because it seems that a cloaked man brought him a large bag of money from Spain the night before the month started. The family money seems to have originated when the first Polish Zborowski emigrated to New York, there to acquire land afterwards of immense value. During the latter part of any month Zborowski was as broke as any of us.

Very well then, Louis entered an American Miller car in the 1924 French Grand Prix, a 2-litre straight-eight with a magnificent engine in a not so good

chassis. He asked me to go with him as mechanic, the mechanic who rode in the car that is. Note how the godlets who look after me had done their stuff. At last I was to take part in the most famous of all races, lineal successor to the long-distance events on uncleared roads with which racing started. There were now other Grand Prix, it is true, but none had the prestige of this one, in which the most famous drivers of the time drove. It was almost beyond my wildest dreams. Over to Lyon we went, to find the city *en fête* as befitted the occasion, every café full, every house decorated, every shop displaying something connected with racing.

Louis was absolutely set on driving this time, mainly because his chance to compete in the 1921 race had been dismally lost through no fault of his own. For that race he was entered to drive one of the straight-eight engined cars produced by Sunbeam-Talbot-

1. This is the popular story, but modern analysis of the event does not support the cuff-throttle lever sequence. *The Racing Zborowskis*, 2002 Bibliography.

B M "Bunny" Marshall at the wheel of the Crossley-Bugatti with which he took 6th place in the 1922 1500cc Trophy race run in conjunction with the Tourist Trophy. The Bugattis took the team prize, the cars being painted lemon yellow rather than the French blue to emphasize the Crossley connection. Although Sammy did not participate, his clothing suggests that Marshall gave him a taste of the event over a practice lap. Munton, the mechanic, stands by the car.

Darracq combine under Coatalen. Although all the cars were the same, never had there been such a muddle. The Sunbeams and Talbots ran as British and the Darracq as French, but none of them was anything like ready. The evening before the race no one knew whether the cars would even start. Very late that afternoon Louis was allotted a Darracq still in shop grey. Almost by force Clive Gallop and I made him go to bed, then we painted the car blue by the light of oil lamps. After hours of checking the more important details of the chassis and engine, we found that all the shoes from the brake drums had been illicitly "borrowed" for another car.

Racing was like that, or could be, but Louis was having none of that nonsense this time. He was running his own car, prepared by his own mechanics, William and Len. Practice revealed defects, which were dealt with as required, but also that the car was faster than we had expected. Further, I revised my opinion of Zborowski's driving, which I had thought to be a mite wild but which proved definitely

ALGY

SPRAGUE BUCKLEY IRVINGE

MARSHALL BEDFORD DIVO

DUTOIT *MUNTON* *BILL* *DE HANE*

exciting but good. We took the car to the official inspection clean as a new pin, both of us wearing our Sunday best clothes as tradition dictated. We chatted with other drivers and mechanics, the great Nazzaro included, and later on we practiced refilling and changing wheels until we were tired out.

Bill Guinness, Dario Resta, De Hane Segrave, Bordino, Benoist, Campari and all turned up for a chat in the evening, the principal subject for discussion being the new Bugatti cars. Far more beautiful and quite different from any that Ettore's genius had produced before, they were therefore dark horses. We had fun too with one of Louis' great friends, a driver named Howey, who had a horror of eating frogs. They were therefore specially prepared for the

This picture was captioned "8.30 A.M. AT THE QUARTER BRIDGE, JUNE 1922". It was taken outside the hotel where a number of the teams stayed. Standing on extreme left, Marshall in dark coat, his mechanic Munton seated in middle. Algy Guinness is second in back row. Immaculate De Hane Segrave on right, his mechanic Du Toit seated on left. Drivers Bedford and Divo (The Autocar printed "A. Divot"!) in white linen jackets and trousers standing next to Marshall. Note the goggles on the bottle next to Du Toit. The race weather was foul. Presumably Sammy was there in the guise of journalist.

next lunch, in such fashion as to be indistinguishable from the most delicate chicken – these Howey enjoyed. Unfortunately another friend, unable to contain his amusement, asked him whether he knew what he had eaten, on hearing which Howey was immediately ill.

On the night before the race Louis

The following eight pictures show the diversity of Sammy's activities including reporting, speed trials, road testing and long-distance trials.

Above: Sammy in the passenger seat of a 1914 French Grand Prix Pic-Pic at Southend in 1920. A Vauxhall 30-98 is on the right.

W O at the wheel of the first Bentley, which Sammy road-tested in 1920 for The Autocar.

Sammy at the wheel of a Ruston Hornsby on the 1921 London-Exeter trial.

Record breaking at Brooklands with the Aston-Martin "Bunny" in 1922.

Sammy driving an air-cooled twin-cylinder ABC at Beggar's Roost, Devon during the 1923 London-Land's End trial.

At the top of the Brooklands Test Hill. Sammy is in the passenger seat, for a change, of this 1924-25 Talbot.

Removing chains at Whitesheet in Wiltshire on the 1924 London-Exeter trial. Sammy in beret.

Sammy lighting his usual pipe, not competing but probably reporting on a rally, standing at the side of a 1500cc Argyll tourer, 1924.

and I went off to a country house away from Lyon to make sure of a quiet night's rest. But Louis possessed that tremendous depth of melancholy which all Slavs seem to have in full measure. He could not sleep, his mind concentrating on the probability of death, the more so because the cars were to start in a mass all together for the first time, instead of one by one as usual. So we went for a walk under the myriad stars of a perfect night, and as we walked, chatted of mysteries normally concealed from everyone but oneself. When we returned we knew each other intimately, as few people however friendly can do. The morning dawned and, as the hot sun rose for a perfect day, somehow or other the fears of the night faded entirely; all seemed well in the world.

The start of the race seemed enormously exciting, mainly because we were not left behind as we had feared but were actually up among the fast cars, which was exhilarating, the tail-end not being a place either of us liked. Though busy keeping an eye open for cars approaching from the rear, and making sure the numerous gauges told the right story, there was still time to talk, which added interest. Louis actually succeeded in overtaking a Fiat, amazement at which feat led to our sliding wide on the next curve, hitting a sandbank and both getting a mouthful of sand. Best part of the fourteen-mile circuit was the long straight leg, on which the Miller could really get up to speed, a straight made up of those ups and downs which are called *Montagnes Russes*. That it ended in a sharp right-handed corner called *Le Virage de la Mort* was not so funny, for it seemed likely to live up to its horrible name.

The race went on and on: we noted Segrave's Sunbeam at its pit, Nazzaro's red Fiat having trouble by the roadside, Chassagne having hell changing a

Bugatti wheel and Viscaya's Bugatti in a ditch. Knowing that the brakes of his new cars would need adjustment by half distance, when the wheels would be changed because of tyre wear, Bugatti had provided the spare wheels with brake drums of slightly smaller internal diameter. Unfortunately the tyres gave trouble early, before the brake shoes wore, so the drivers had to file the brake linings before the wheels would go on. Another interesting incident was a view of a Fiat proceeding at high speed across a field, the driver having misjudged a fast turn and gone off the course. Marvellous as it seemed, we were getting along quite well and needless to add enjoying ourselves. But gradually it seemed that the Miller was not quite stable on the fast straight, as it appeared to snake more than it should. This we discussed and finally decided that the steering felt odd so we had better go to the pit and investigate. We arrived a mite too briskly, overshot and had to push back while being lectured excitably by the *commissaire* in charge of the pits – not that we cared.

Louis adjusted the brakes while I had a look-see at the steering. I found the large nut locking the worm thrust-bearing had come loose. The only way to get at the nut quickly was to cut a hole in the side of the body with a chisel, a not very nice process, leaving jagged aluminium which scratched, but I did get that nut tight again. Off we went then, now aware that Bordino had led with a Fiat but had been overtaken by one of the new Alfa Romeos driven by that cheerful little man Ascari, and by Divo with a French Delage. Two laps later our engine cut out and we found the lead from the coil to the distributor had come adrift so had to remake the connection. Then the brakes became feebler and feebler, much to Louis's annoyance. Result, we took an escape road at Givors causing the officials seated there on a patch of grass in the centre of a triangle of roads to leap for dear life, only to encounter Bordino's Fiat which had crashed, also owing to brake trouble.

The road was going to pieces too, the car leaping and bounding over very unpleasant potholes and being showered with stones from the rear tyres of any other car nearby. Fortunately we had wire guard screens which could be flicked up for such trouble. I had just told Louis that, judging by the behaviour of the manual air pump, with which I had to maintain air pressure in the fuel tank, we were getting near the refill point. I had given him a pair of clean goggles when the car began to snake more than ever and Louis said, "Steering's gone again". A glance satisfied me that the offending nut was still tight so I had a good look forward. The front shock absorber my side seemed to have broken away from the axle. This I told Louis, adding, "Take it to the pit". Louis's reply was to slide like blazes round *Le Virage de la Mort* and overshoot the pit once more. Once stopped, Louis began splashing the fuel from five-gallon cans into the fuel tank according to our drill while I went to see what had happened in front. I had the fright of my life: the shock absorbers had broken free all right, but so had the front axle, which was now retained to the springs by two badly bent bolts out of eight. We had completed nearly one lap like that and the axle ought to have come off at any moment. I spent a long time trying to extract the broken ends of the bolts from the axle pad, in which they had sheared flush with the pad, but it was no good; only a power drill could have done the job. Our Grand Prix was over but it had been a remarkable experience.

The finish of that long race was dramatic. With only twenty-eight miles left of the five hundred, Ascari was in sight of victory but the Alfa's engine was obviously sick. He and his mechanic stopped at the pit and changed all the plugs in record time but the engine refused to start. Finally the mechanic pushed the car, though he was exhausted, while Ascari tried to restart the engine. That failed and both men then wound the starting handle until they almost fell down with fatigue. Finally, they pushed and pushed towards the distance with almost every single soul in the huge crowd praying that the engine would respond. Then Campari with another Alfa and Divo with the Delage passed, to take first and second places, followed by Benoist, taking third. But all our sympathy was with those gallant two, Ascari and his mechanic, who had led for almost all the race but could not make their car even finish. It was a great race and one in which I was proud to have been involved.

Extraordinary when you come to think of it that the Miller, a car designed for the American brick-surfaced track at Indianapolis, should have managed to do so well in a road Grand Prix. Louis went on racing, always with fervour, until one fatal day at Monza when his Mercedes struck a patch of oil and crashed, fatally injuring its driver. That day for the first time he was reputedly wearing the cufflinks that his father had worn at La Turbie.

Chapter Six

By favour
of the godlets

From 1925 onwards the godlets provided interest and sheer joyousness, wonderful to remember, and altogether unexpected – the opportunity to race. The fulfilling of an ambition came so suddenly that I still wonder that it ever happened, and looking down the years it still seems a near miracle. Certainly it was a time so eventful that the memory of those days remains as vivid as ever.

The chance for real racing had originally come about when Louis Coatalen unexpectedly asked me to drive the big 350hp Sunbeam round Brooklands one day when nothing much was going on at the track. Now that Sunbeam was the envy of all. Huge, with its V12 18-litre engine in a narrow single-seater streamlined body, this car was always associated with Bill Guinness, who had broken the lap speed record with it time after time. It was a magnificent machine, animal in the sense that if it liked you all was well, and if it didn't, all hell would prevail. Well, from the moment we started I knew I liked this machine, and obviously it consented to like me for we put up quite a

respectable lap speed, and I had the drive of my life. It was also not without a humorous moment. I was coming fast from the Byfleet banking towards the Home banking and negotiating the one tricky unbanked curve on the circuit, passing only about a foot from the side of the Vickers aircraft shed, when a mechanic opened a door and stepped out onto the track. Never before or since have I seen a man retreat so rapidly in one record backwards leap – but he did!

The result of this drive was enough to make one feel one was walking with the gods, for I was offered a drive in the Sunbeam team for the twenty-four hour race at Le Mans, France. Always I had thought of road racing as ideal on a real road, super ideal if over very long distances. Here was the opportunity for just this very thing.

I went to Le Mans as the second driver to a most experienced Frenchman, Jean Chassagne, from the heroic age, who was also a first-class mechanic and just the man to show me how a car should be driven, and I learned a packet the right way. The team had two cars, both six-cylinder Sunbeams, the other machine being driven by De Hane Segrave and a great friend of mine, George Duller, a famous horse-racing jockey in extra measure. Many people alleged George was a horse by descent. All I know is that a horse would do anything George told it to and that he always commenced any sentence in what he swore was French by saying "*Allez*". As to the first, we actually saw him call a French officer's horse across the road to him while we were in France despite its rider's furious efforts to stop it. While as to the second, George once put all his baggage in a French taxi then turned to the driver and began "*Allez*", whereupon the driver naturally drove off and George had hell retrieving his baggage days after.

On landing in France with the Sunbeams, Chassagne said he was worried about our car's frame. Dead right he was too, for one side member cracked ten miles from Le Mans. Straight away the machine was driven to Paris for the frame to be reinforced by Sunbeam's partners Darracq. Pretty dismal I felt about that, as it meant there was now no car for practice. However, a Darracq arrived from Paris so that I could drive round the circuit day after day until every curve and turn was familiar. Official practice was a sketchy affair in those days, it being doubtful even whether the circuit was kept clear, but none of us minded that, except maybe a French driver who departed in style from the pits and did not come back. A friend of his went off to see why, to return laughing his head off. "Old so-and-so," he announced had "entered into a cow and there rested". He had too.

The circuit at Le Mans was quite different from the one so well known today though composed of some of the same roads. Firstly the road went straight on at what is now Dunlop Corner until it reached a very sharp hairpin turn, almost in Le Mans city. After that turn the road was uphill, then downhill, but as straight as a die all the way to Mulsanne. Next difference was that the circuit was very much narrower and the whole of it very dusty since dust-laying compound, or dustless material, was extremely expensive. Partly because there was no binding material the surface went to pieces after about fourteen hours, the road then resembling a seaside beach of big stones. In 1925 a trifling disagreement between the organisers and local land owners resulted in the pits being placed on the straight near the Café de l'Hippodrome.

At all events, Le Mans city is most inspiring to me, containing as it does a smattering of our history. The ancient town is still almost medieval and the cathedral has a character only extreme age can bring. I knew that Henry II of England had died after he set fire to the city he loved to prevent it falling into the hands of that loveable but eccentric fighting man, Richard Coeur de Lion, Le Mans being the home of our Angevin Kings.

There is something unusually friendly about those who control the races

Louis Coatalen (centre) gave Sammy his first chance to drive a powerful car, at Brooklands on the 14 April 1922. The experience behind the wheel of the Land Speed Record 350hp Sunbeam gave Sammy the feeling that he had "walked with the Gods". Sunbeam mechanic Bill Perkins (left) looked after the car.

Le Mans circuit,
1923-28.

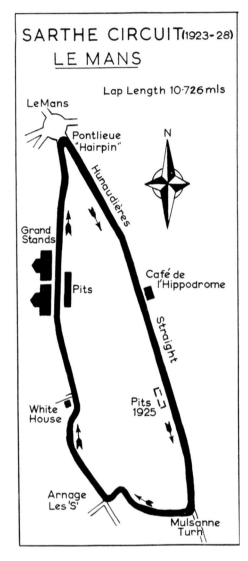

SARTHE CIRCUIT (1923-28)
LE MANS

Lap Length 10·726 mls

LeMans

Pontlieue
"Hairpin"

N

Hunaudières

Grand
Stands

Café de
l'Hippodrome

Pits

Straight

Pits
1925

White
House

Arnage
Les 'S'

Mulsanne
Turn

inspection before the race, presided over by Charles Faroux, we knew our opposition: two Ariès, three Lorraines, two Chenard-Walckers, three Diattos, two Bentleys, three Rolland-Pilains, three OMs, two Bignans, together with other less formidable rivals, making 49 starters in all.

The start was spectacular, the drivers running across to their cars, raising the hoods[1], and getting away as soon as the engines fired. Chassagne was among the first, I was pleased to see. Thereafter it was a fight all the way, with the Bentleys, Lorraines and Chenard-Walckers ever a threat. Segrave drove at almost full speed from the start, so I was not surprised that the car fell out before half time, though I was surprised that neither Coatalen nor Bertarione, the Italian responsible for the engine, did not signal the machine to slow.

When my spell came I was curiously confident I could keep to schedule, but as nervous as a cat on hot bricks that I would forget the refilling routine in front of Coatalen's critical eyes. You see, the driver, or one of the drivers, had to do the whole thing single-handed: refill, furl the hood, which had to be kept up for the first driver's spell, effect any adjustments or repairs, and change wheels if that was necessary. All of it had to accord with a plan or too much time would be wasted. Well, Jean came in, I took over and the refill went very well, the better because little Jean spoke quietly but clearly to me all the time about the state of the car, the rev-limit, the difficulties he had found, and advised me of such drivers who seemed more than usually troublesome to overtake. The subsequent spell was sheer heaven, the car ran splendidly, handled well and felt good. Naturally I did my best to give it the easiest possible run while holding the speed, and that took

there; for example the Clerk of the course, Georges Berthier, and the club President Jean Lelierre, were real friends to us all. It was quite unlike any other centre of racing in the world.

Our Sunbeam returned just a day before the race. Segrave's and Duller's had been there all the time so they had plenty of practice, although I thought, and Jean confirmed, that the car was used a shade too much for its health. After the traditional ceremony of

---

1. 1925 was the first occasion that the "Le Mans start" was used.

concentration; the joy of taking a curve or corner exactly right was as heartening as good wine. Especially was this so about the hairpin at Pontlieue, where an error of placing of no more than one foot would have resulted in the machine having to be reversed – a nightmare in the circumstances. It was immensely pleasing to encounter friends, particularly if their cars were going slower, for the friendliness between all drivers was very marked indeed in those days.

Something I was sorry to see had happened to the Bentleys, for I knew that Bertie Kensington Moir's car was out owing to a miscalculation of the fuel consumption since the cars could be refilled only after 20 laps or 200 miles had been covered on each tankful. Then a duel with "Sunshine" Clement on another Bentley ended when one of his carburettor float chambers broke away. There was trouble a plenty, an overturned Lorraine just before White House turn for example, and the wreck of a crashed Amilcar by the roadside.

Gradually the light faded and then I had a nasty shock, as switching on the headlights produced no light whatsoever. With that sinking feeling always caused by serious trouble I went to the pit, there to discover that the liquid [chloride] used to keep down dust had been thrown up by the rear wheels of other participants, to spread thickly all over my car's lamp glasses. This took time to remedy as the wire stone guards for the glasses were flush, so prevented a rag being used. A hastily borrowed syringe with water did the trick but in what seemed hours. There was another little thing I did not enjoy, namely that the throttle pedal did not always close immediately it was released. This bother was diagnosed, correctly as it happened, as the effect of the increasing amount of dust on the barrel-type carburettor throt-

tles. But the night run was as enjoyable as ever once I discovered that one could maintain daylight speed by keeping to the cut-off points which had served in the daytime, although I could not see accurately enough by the headlight beams at that speed.

All too soon that wonderful run ended as the "come in" signal showed at the pit when the car had covered its 214-mile spell. Imitating Jean, I told him as calmly as I could all about the headlights and the throttle and that the road surface after Mulsanne was breaking up. Then, as the Sunbeam went off in style, I trotted to the Weymann pit in which there were armchairs for rest and a nice selection of suitable refreshments. There too I met other drivers whose spells had ended, so we had a great time telling each other cheerful if optimistic lies about how well our cars were running. Somehow or other there seemed no need to sleep because all of this was so exciting that never a minute should be missed.

So it went on, spell after spell, each better than the last as far as I was concerned and each full of incident. I had a bad moment when the throttle stuck full open before the Mulsanne right angle but just managed to keep on the road. Another round and at that very same corner a small man with a bright red forked beard was dancing in the road waving his arms and shouting. The driver performing this equivalent of a Zulu war dance was Robert Sénéchal, who had slightly misjudged the turn and bent his machine [a Chenard-Walcker] beyond repair. In fact the circuit was now almost lined with cars whose run had ended. Racing of this type does put a phenomenal stress even on the best machinery.

The road was going to pieces so much that the stretch from Mulsanne was covered in stones, most of which were catapulted at one by the rear tyres of any car in close proximity. At all events I suddenly received a blow on the forehead which made me see stars in no uncertain fashion and nearly led to the car getting out of hand. Afterwards, the stone that hit me was found in the driving compartment and was inches long each side, so I was lucky the damage was slight. But the most difficult part of the drive was control of the throttles since now they would not close unless I could get a foot behind the pedal and pull like hell, which was no manner of joke as you will imagine. Each of us freed the throttles whenever we had a stop at the pit but at ten laps the damned things were jamming again.

We were going faster after daylight returned, not so much because we wished to, but because Coatalen had found out that we were very well up with the Chenards and Lorraines which were at the head of the race. He knew too that these teams were perilously near their limit so that it was a legitimate gamble that inspired one to greater effort. Then Chassagne came in unexpectedly, his face a picture of worry. Overtaking a difficult car Jean had been forced to take avoiding action by going onto the grass verge at full speed. In that grass was a nasty deep drainage ditch resulting in a very bent rear axle; but it would have taken more than a bent axle to stop us then, though both of us could not help wondering how long that useful piece of mechanism would last.

As he came in for the normal refill Jean said, "The car is second – keep it so", and that was the most inspiring instruction I had ever heard. Bent axle or none the car was to go faster; so faster it went and we gained, yes we gained. Waiting for my last spell I overheard Coatalen and Bertarione discussing the axle. They did not know I was there because of the partition in the pit separating us. They discussed it

in every way, took due note of the fact that the inner sides of the rear tyres were now rubbing on the body, and came to the conclusion that the axle might break at any moment, but it was worth the risk! Can't say I found that altogether encouraging, yet when I had the car's wheel again I ceased even to think about the axle.

With a matter of six laps to go I stopped deliberately at the pit to hand over to Jean, for he was the first driver and had had most of the work to do with the preparation of the car, so deserved that marvellous moment when the car comes over the finishing line for the last time in the twenty-four hours. Which, amid the loud cheering of the spectators who had followed the battle intently for the last four hours, was what Jean did. Believe it or not I had been the driver of a car which was second in one of the historic races of the time and it was my first road race too – verily the godlets had been benevolent. The winner was a Lorraine driven by de Courcelles and Rossignol for 1388 miles. The Sunbeam was only 45 miles behind. Third was another Lorraine, handled by Brisson and Stalter. Both deserved their success and, as I drank more champagne than was usual, so I thought did Jean and I.

The result of that race is curious to look back upon. Admittedly I felt as though I was walking with the gods, but I still hope no one else ever knew of that. Agreed, I had always thought secretly that if the opportunity occurred I could drive at the same speed as anyone else but stay on the road. Yet when the opportunity did occur I found myself nervous lest something unforeseen might happen, especially something mechanical that I could not diagnose immediately and correctly. Naturally the possibility I could get killed in a crash arose, but only a little on the night before, then rather more

Le Mans, 1925. Sammy and Jean Chassagne drove this 3-litre twin-cam Sunbeam to take second place in the 24-hour race. It was Sammy's first international road race and he is seen at a pit stop filling the oil tank.

just before the race started. There was also the odd feeling that one was separated altogether from all other human beings during the five minutes or so before the start, but I never was actually sick as quite a few drivers were. The big burly Frenchman, René Thomas once told me that even after all his races he still had the same feelings when facing the start of another.

The friends made during all this were of lasting quality. Lionel Martin was very Etonian, built for comfort rather than speed, magnificently just in judgement, requiring only that his drivers should do what they were told, and was responsible for the Aston-Martin resulting from his experience of the little Singer. Kensington Moir was another, with his most intriguing laugh, his enormous sense of humour even in adversity, and his excellent driving manners when racing. Afterwards, he was to be one of the best racing team controllers ever and a man of infinite tact. For instance, we had a driver at one time who would work hard at the wheel after the manner shown by actor drivers on the silver screen, see-sawing at the wheel rim – result, the car was entirely unstable, but what to do? Moir solved the trouble and a mechanic was instructed to appear to make an adjustment to the steering. Then Moir said to the erring driver, "You wait here and watch, I'll get old so-and-so to drive". So-and-so, duly briefed, came by at speed not moving the wheel even a fraction. Said Moir, "There you are, you see, he isn't moving the wheel even half an inch, just as should happen". From then on the erring driver was completely reformed and the car was steady. Clive Gallop, always called "Gallo", was almost more French than British and drove with a Gallic fire well worth watching. He was an expert in racing etiquette and a man on whom you could absolutely depend. There were many others from all countries.

Naturally there was superstition; there always is and has been from the days of the Circus Maximus. Some drivers wore trinkets and hell broke loose if these were missing. Others preferred a St Christopher badge, as did I, but never did I start in any competition without a feminine stocking round my neck – a used stocking of course and from a great friend naturally. One driver preferred a photo of his latest girlfriend pasted on the steering wheel boss, but covered with tissue paper until the race started, whereupon the paper was torn off. He said the photo was a marvellous inspiration. But there was an unfortunate day when he forgot to remove the photo after the car finished and all Hades burst into flame when his girlfriend of the moment found it was not hers. Mind you this superstition is, as a rule, protectively encouraging and not morbid, though I did know one driver some years later who was almost possessed by the certainty he would be killed – he was too.

Racing apart, everything went well. There were cars of all types to drive, and attendance at all the principal races was now much better for a feeling of having joined the "club". True, my old Editor Arthur's American experience had been extremely bad, and worse still his wife Emmie Kate had had to return to this country for good because things in the USA were impossible. But Arthur's loss was our gain after all, for Emmie Kate could still control all and sundry by sheer force of character.

Naturally there were some problems of conflict of interest as my activities outside writing increased; problems which concerned policy were therefore tricky. Obviously it was essential that I should not be thought to be connected with any one firm of manufacturers. Obviously also, anything I did in competition should benefit a British concern if possible. That as it happened coincided with my own view since I had an entirely national outlook about everything. However, most of the first-class racing cars were foreign in those

days and I was asked to drive one quite frequently. I think this vastly improved my ability to get out of an awkward corner without offending anyone, which is not as easy as it might seem.

Be that as it may, 1926 brought my first official drive in the Bentley team at Le Mans and was the curtain raiser to real excitement. Brought up to believe that the only real races were those from Paris to Berlin or Vienna along ordinary roads, I had a natural liking for this race as the nearest to the ideal, the more so in that the driver had to do all repairs himself. The cars were 3 Litres and very carefully prepared indeed, every detail being subject to full discussion. I was to drive with a friend, Dr J D Benjafield, the cheeriest of mortals, a very determined driver, a real team mate, thinking only of the car's success and in no way concerned with his own save that he loved every moment of a drive. For some unknown reason he could never remember which way a nut had to be turned to unscrew it and this led to his leg being pulled time after time, taken with great good humour. The other drivers were "Sunshine" Clement and George Duller, "Gallo", and "Scrap" Thistlethwayte. Part of the fun was a hunt to eliminate every wood-screw used on the machines, substituting a bolt for security, while the hoods were now held down by quick-acting clips and the carburettors had stronger "necks" as a result of the 1925 run. This time also there would be no mistake in fuel consumption figures.

It seemed to mean something that the Bentleys were housed at the Hotel Moderne, in sheds which had held the Renault before that car went out to win the first ever French Grand Prix in 1906. The team lorry arrived with chief mechanic Clark and "Caput", nickname for L V Head of *The Autocar*, who was to help me in race after race and was the very essence of enthusiasm. Between repeated test runs on the circuit we had coffee at the Café de l'Hippodrome of an early morning and as usual practical jokes abounded. Imitating Segrave's trick with a watch the year before, George Duller timed one of our cars at a near unbelievable speed for a lap, greatly to the excitement of a rival Peugeot driver, André Boillot, who did not know the watch was adjusted to run slow. Then the always cheerful Foresti poured a jug of cold water over a total stranger whom he mistook for his team mate Minoia, causing a first-class ruction. There was never a dull moment though all of us worked like beavers. At the team strategy conference it was decided we were up against five serious rivals, the three Lorraines and two big Peugeots with first-class drivers (apart from any unknowns amongst the other 36 entrants).

Well, we had a great race – Benjy and I found Number 7 was in fine fettle and going well. George had Number 8 right up among the Peugeots, so much so in fact that team control and his partner Clement became a little worried at the Bentley's speed, which was above that scheduled. During the night the screen of the leading Peugeot shattered, the frame having come adrift. Furiously the driver came into his pit and, tearing the ruins from the body, threw them away into the pit and set off once more, only to be stopped by the officials and told the screen must be put back according to the regs. Since the wreckage could not be reassembled a furious argument arose, ending in the car having to retire.

To complete the Peugeot misfortune the indomitable veteran, Louis Wagner with the second Peugeot was forced into a ditch by the driver of a smaller and slower entrant, which also as near as no matter upset de Courcelle's Lorraine. The Peugeot having returned to the road, all the drivers concerned adjourned to the pit and the row of a lifetime arose, bloodshed being avoided by a miracle. To cap

it all, when Wagner tried to restart, the engine refused to do so, despite the fact that the driver's language should have moved anything. Since the engine always had to be restarted with the starter every time a car came to the pit, another good car was out.

After eight o'clock in the morning the pace increased still further, since the leading bunch of cars were all close to each other. The Lorraines were first and second, our Number 9 third, another Lorraine fourth, Number 7 fifth with something in hand, while my old partner Jean Chassagne was gaining from the rear with an Ariès which was much faster than we had anticipated. Things were bound to happen and they did. Maybe it was the new steel used for the valves, or perhaps a shade too many revs, but we lost Number 9 and very soon after Number 8, both with incurable valve trouble.

Just as control was wondering whether it would pay to ensure a finish for our one car or take a risk and fight on, Benjy overtook the third Lorraine triumphantly, while our "intelligence" section reported that the second Lorraine seemed a little sick, though the leader was running as well as ever – so we determined to fight it out. Benjy came in and I took over for the last spell. There is something fiercely triumphant about a drive when you know that every fraction of a second must be saved yet the machine must be kept in one piece. Only trouble was that the brakes had become weaker and weaker, though Benjy had taken up some of the adjustment and I used the rest before I started on that last spell. After one "faster" signal from team control the comforting "OK" had appeared each lap and the engine of Number 7 was still magnificent. I overtook car after car, anxiously checking their numbers, but still no Lorraines appeared as welcome blobs in the far distance, and then I saw the second Lorraine at its pit. Simultaneously our signal read "flat out"!

Never had Number 7 gone so well. It was as though she knew that if we could cover one lap we could get ahead of our chief rival. But those damned brakes were dangerous, even when assisted by lever operation, and I had several nasty moments, apart from the fact that irregular stopping power made cut-off points useless. Then it began to rain – of all the devilish ideas nature could produce, just at the moment when I had to overtake the third Lorraine – and that was where I made a mistake. There was just space in which to overtake and then slow for the right-angle turn at Mulsanne if all went well. The Lorraine driver gave me plenty of room and only two more laps remained before the finish, so every thousandth of a second gained was vital. Just at that moment the brake pedal went flat down on the floor. Using the lever and gear change I thought I had reduced speed enough – I hadn't. The Bentley slid, was held, slid again, then went "wump" into the guardian sandbank.

Livid with fury I dug like blazes, first with my hands, then with a spade which appeared mysteriously from space, while the official at the corner deliberately turned his back. One of the Lorraine drivers stopped his car and volunteered to help but this could not be allowed by the regs – never will I forget that offer. Well, I couldn't free the car so our race was over. Wonderful as W O Bentley was, I felt sick, so I went for a long walk. Actually I was very much affected by the way every single person who knew anything about racing did their level best to make me feel better. All the Lorraine drivers did and even Wagner was surprisingly understanding, while Jean Chassagne was almost fatherly. It didn't remove the nasty feeling that a driver must not make mistakes like this, but it did make the mistake seem one that everyone had made at one time or other.

There was also a humorous incident, as looking out of my bedroom window next day I was surprised to see our runabout Morris Cowley parked in the centre of the tramlines with one rear tyre flat and the other missing. It took quite a long interrogation before we discovered that Moir and Head had gone for a ride early that morning to relieve their feelings. They had got on the circuit and proceeded to attempt the lap record, with the result that the missing tyre was now high in a tree on Arnage corner. To complete the story, Benjy took Number 7 to a race at Boulogne, the brakes failed again and the poor old car crashed into a tree.

... moments of intense gloom ...

Chapter Seven

Fame results from a mistake

Still feeling rather sore with myself I faced 1927. First, the Essex Motor Club organised a kind of Le Mans for six hours at Brooklands and I was asked to drive a 1500cc Alvis. To make things as different as possible from an ordinary Brooklands race, artificial bends were constructed on the finishing straight. This needed some study since there was an unbanked turn on to the home straight. Not that this circuit bore any resemblance to a road, largely because it was so short and the turns had no natural features, but it did have an interest of its own.

This was the only time I had to practice changing valve springs before a race, since there was an idea that this might be needed on the day. The problem that team control had to consider for this race was both interesting and complicated. Every vehicle was set a minimum distance to cover in six hours by a formula according to the size of its engine and the highest speed recorded for a car with that size of engine. Then there was an extra prize for the car which covered the highest

mileage in the time. As Bentleys and Sunbeams were running, as well as a host of smaller machines, it was obvious that it would be a battle royal from the start, and the difficulty was to keep track of the team's position all the time on the formula. Since all the drivers were friends the amount of leg-pulling before the race reached a new height. Birkin, Clement and Callingham formed the Bentley team while George Duller and Segrave drove the Sunbeams, with Harvey, chief Alvis driver, and Urquart-Dykes being with me on Alvises.

From the very start the Alvis went magnificently, with that encouraging snarl of exhaust which tells that the engine is at its best and happy. We actually played "bears" with the larger cars, much to our satisfaction as you will imagine, and the race order grew more and more interesting for us as time went on. True there was a small scene when we brought the car in for its first refill and I was handed a two-gallon tin with which to do it – an idea my language effectually cancelled for future

Le Mans 1927. Sammy and Dr "Benjy" Benjafield with Bentley No. 3 (Old No. 7) before the race.

refilling. The wail that arose when I punched a hole in the bottom of the tin to make it pour fast would have wakened the dead. For several delightful laps we held on to George Duller's Sunbeam, both of us exchanging rude gestures, but that fun ended when a sudden huge puff of smoke arose from the Sunbeam's engine and George's expression changed instantly to horror. As it happened the damage was slight, for the smoke was caused by oil spraying on to the exhaust because the dipstick had jumped out. We were also highly amused at the extraordinary antics of a Bentley when it was driven by Tim Birkin's brother, until a furious team control called the car in for Tim's more expert handling.

Then a spare wheel carrier broke on the Bentley, so we gained lap after lap until the Alvis was second in race order, leading handsomely on formula; and round a track now filled with frantic men working furiously to repair unexpected troubles we brought the Alvis home to win a highly exciting race.[1]

For Le Mans, Benjy and I were extremely anxious to retrieve our reputations with Bentley and make peace with our 1926 car Number 7, a machine which seemed to have had all it wanted from both of us – but we made friends at last. This time the team had a new 4½-litre driven by Clement and Callingham, a 3-litre with George Duller and d'Erlanger aboard, and the 3-litre "Old Number 7" now numbered 3 with Benjy and me on it. The team was better organised than before and the brakes were more efficient and more durable, apart from which we could adjust them while the car was running,

---

1. Sammy won *The Autocar* Efficiency cup for the greatest distance under handicap – 372 miles against Duller's 386. He had his leg pulled for being the magazine's Sports Editor.

which was a very great advantage. The method of refilling the engine sump while the car was running was also more certain than in the previous year.

Head, now acting as team lap scorer, kept a vast chart which showed the position of every car in the race on every lap. The signalling was by sema-phore, easily read at long distance, while the signal station was no longer in the pit but in a place where it was not surrounded by advertisements, flags and other distractions. This year the Automobile Club de l'Ouest had decided it was safer to make all competitors refill with beastly little five-gallon cans, so we had to develop a new drill to reduce refilling time somehow or other. As usual, each car had to carry ballast representing a full load of passengers – always a nasty problem. W O would have none of those sand-filled bags, the requisite weight being made up of lead in steel tubes, and as the regs did not say the weight had to be carried on the seats, one tube was used to brace the frame in front, with the others tucked away low on the rear floor. The amount of thought bestowed on those cars down to the smallest detail was fantastic.

One small part of our personal equip-ment might seem amusing. During the 1925 race both of us had found it difficult to see clearly when driving fast against heavy rain, and we did not like that one bit. While we were strolling in Paris after that race we talked this over and decided there must be some solution to the diffi-culty, which we found by a miracle. Suddenly, amidst the attractively posed dummy models of a first-class dress shop for women, we saw one figure wearing a curious face shield of talc[1]. There was a

Sammy in sombre mood before the race with No. 3. Note the windscreen opening and the guard in front of the offside headlamp.

1. A transparent mineral material, similar to mica.

1927 Le Mans pre-race publicity photo of the Bentley Boys. Front row left to right: Frank Clement, Leslie Callingham, Baron d'Erlanger, George Duller, Sammy Davis and Dudley Benjafield. Back row: Woolf Barnato, a smiling W O and the Marquis de Casa Maury.

momentary startled pause, then with one voice we both said, "That's the job". Well, it seemed that the mask was to protect feminine complexions in a fast open car! You would never believe how hard it was to obtain them from the shop. We explained to a small, dark and very attractive sales girl that we wanted to try the things on, but she insisted they were for "*Femmes seulement, messieurs*". We insisted and she nearly collapsed with merriment when we put them on; all the other sales girls joined in, even the manageress. Obviously this was a factual example of the Mad English. But when we said we were *courseurs* at Le Mans we got the masks – so was the motor racing visor born.

Benjy and I were not happy because Number 7 was not sure she could trust us and was notably slow in practice. Everything was checked, many things were changed, even the cylinder block was lifted, but not a sign of trouble could we find. Only after days of intense work was the old girl satisfied that we would behave and then, suddenly, the speed came back. We also feverishly practiced refilling to get the hang of the new lever-operated filler caps W O had insisted upon instead of the screw version. We also tested the spring-loaded valve which now kept the radiator overflow pipe sealed unless steam pressure developed, so preventing loss of water each

time the brakes were applied, consequently reducing refilling time.

Vigorous argument arose about a tame magpie, Marco,[1] who would lurk under Number 7. They say magpies are unlucky in England but, fortunately, lucky in France. One evening someone suggested that we might sample a new appetiser, non-alcoholic but a rather pleasant beverage suitable for children – we were of course on the wagon. Well we sampled the damned stuff and that evening we all felt unaccountably irritable; definite assertion was countered by flat contradiction as tempers rose and W O sent us all to bed.[2] We opened the communicating doors and continued arguing. Next morning we felt frightful, but it all wore off when we encountered the originator of the damned drink and told him what we thought.

So at long last we came to The Day and drove up to the grandstands for the start. It was a good start too for the team, since Clement got away first magnificently, and Benjy followed him off while most of the rival drivers were

Fifty years on - Sammy aged 90, seated in a Bentley similar to Old No. 7.

---

1. Benjy states that it was a raven in The Bentleys at Le Mans, but in *A Racing Motorist*, photograph p39, shows "Marco", a strange looking (tame and tailless) magpie.
2. Benjy had a totally opposite view as he himself sent them to bed! The "damned stuff" was an aperitif called "Amer Picon".

The White House drama.
(Artist untraced)

struggling to get their cars' hoods up. Immediately it was obvious that the Ariès Chassagne and Laly were driving was mighty fast, and from what we knew of Jean it was unlikely to give trouble. Our cars came into the pits after 214 miles, down went the hoods and the refilling went as smoothly as a clockwork mouse. Callingham, George and I took over and we retained our positions right up in the front. Number 7 was now feeling really good as I worked up to speed, thoroughly enjoying the drive and feeling on top of the world. Callingham led with the 4½-litre, strictly in accordance with instructions, George came next with his 3-litre, then my car. As dusk deepened into darkness we were signalled to increase the distance between the cars, which we did, and a happier run you could not imagine. At the pit, Head accurately put down the number of each car on the chart as it passed, the timekeeper told control when each of our cars was due, and the signal stayed at "OK" lap after lap after lap. Then suddenly the long hands of the watches reached the appointed time and – no cars. A horrible, sick, sinking feeling

came over everyone – it was unbelievable. One machine might be overdue, but not all three in one round.

What had happened was that a French driver had oversped on the very fast White House turn, slid his car wildly, turned at right angles to the course and crashed into the side of a shed. Being injured he could not move the car, nearly all of which now projected and covered virtually half the road, and it was a blind curve. Also taking the turn very fast, Callingham came upon the wrecked car at the most awkward moment. One wild but essential swerve and the 4½ hit the bank, drove its front axle back, also turned at right angles and went over. There were now two cars lying across the road. Into these, also at high speed came George with his 3-litre. His car struck the overturned 4½, mounted right up on it and crumpled its front beyond hope. Fortunately unhurt though bruised, both drivers got out and made for the far bank.

Now the godlets took a hand. I was coming down to that curve flat out when right in the headlamp beams I saw little specks on the road just before the curve. A warning bell rang like mad in my brain as I had seen specks like

In at the pit, the deranged front end of No. 3 is clearly seen. The bar across the front was of lead and equated to the weight of two passengers. W O looks gloomily from the pit, whilst Benjy fills up at the back.

that before[1] and round the next corner there had been an overturned car. The specks were wood ripped from the chestnut paling bordering the circuit and that could indicate another overturned car. Instead of taking the curve at full speed I shut the throttle. Every action from then on was automatically controlled by my brain, from experience. There was no time to think or be frightened. I saw in front of me what seemed to be an incredible wall of overturned vehicles. There was no possibility of stopping in time, my only hope was to skid sideways into the pile. I rammed the handbrake on hard, the car skidded broadside on into the pile with a terrific sickening crash and all its lights went out.

In the sudden subsequent silence I remember thinking, "Good God, we've done it again, this is the end of my driving for this team". Then I saw Callingham and George and the full force of the catastrophe burst on me. Simultaneously came the feeling there were other cars coming. Frantically I restarted the engine and reversed out of the tangle to the sound of much riven metal. Then I saw at last that the road

was not completely blocked. There was just enough room between the two heaps of crashed cars to get through and I did.

The feel of the car was awful and it was exceedingly difficult to see without lights, but I made it to the pit. Inspection revealed that one headlamp was pulped, as was a side lamp. The right front wing was a mess and its supports horribly bent, as was the front crosstube of the frame, and one wheel was egg shaped. The dumb-iron of the frame was bent even more and the axle did not look happy. But there was just a possibility the car could be driven provided W O did not know about the bent frame. After a good deal of smith's work and securing a torch to represent the headlight I got away. I can't say the car felt nice but at all events it could be driven, so I gave a "thumbs up" to the pit, to their infinite relief. Obviously we could only finish with luck, but we might finish.

Now mark how good it is to have a really stout-hearted co-driver. I knew exactly what damage the car had

1. 1924 French Grand Prix.

received and knew also what might happen – Benjy naturally did not. But he took on the car for the next spell without even an inspection and certainly without an inner quaver – definitely that was courage. Things fell off and Benjy tied them on again. The battery on the running board came loose and was secured with a cocoon of cord. The brakes came on one, four, two, three, instead of all together, but my intrepid partner carried on. Spell after spell we struggled with that car, always reporting it to be safely driveable lest we were told to retire. Gradually we even achieved some speed when the eccentricities of control had been mastered. Believe it or not, when the race was three-quarters over the chart showed that only Jean with the Ariès was ahead; only one car to overtake – it seemed impossible. And then suddenly control reckoned that if Number 7 could go faster there was a chance of a more startling result.

Neither Benjy nor I liked that "faster" signal, we were mighty content as we were, but you do not disobey control orders, so faster we drove. It was a nightmare run all the same, principally because of the resulting swerves when the brakes had to be used hard. During my spell everything depended on overtaking Jean's Ariès twice, for there was just one lap between us, though it did not seem really possible. So I will never forget the elation when I saw the Ariès in front and knew I was gaining. Then occurred something for which we all admired Jean beyond measure. The road from the grandstands to Pontlieue was narrow and twisty. Whoever got there first was entitled to use all the road. I came up on the Ariès's tail just at the worst spot, a little worried because I would have to wait until after Pontlieue to overtake when every fraction of a second counted. Jean cut, pulled right to the side and waved to me to pass. There you have the spirit of the great French drivers who made racing history from the beginning. To cap it all, on the final spell with the finish in sight Benjy overtook the Ariès that vital second time. And then he too did something wonderful: pulling into the pit he insisted I took the car for the final three laps to victory. I was very near to weeping when the old car came up the straight to the grandstands and I saw Faroux waving the yellow flag which meant we had won. Never has there

Benjy with his left hand on Chassagne's shoulder, and Sammy behind, holding the windscreen of winning Bentley No. 3.

been anything so incredible and the relief was stupendous. The team had not been let down by its drivers – particularly me.

The aftermath of that drama was altogether astonishing, so much so that Benjy and I had to pinch ourselves to make sure we were awake. You see, both of us had only one feeling: devout gratitude that we had managed to get away with it and had not blotted our copybook, or rather I had not blotted it. The sneaking feeling remained that I ought to have spun the car more, so actually avoiding hitting the wrecked ones. The great satisfaction, apart from the normal joy resulting from a win, was that we would be asked to drive again – maybe. But it seemed that the world had gone slightly mad. We became "famous", whatever that may mean and, which was not good, credit was given to us as drivers and not to the car which really won the race. I cannot quite believe it, even today, nor the legend that arose from the affair.

Dinners, festivities and celebrations ensued out of all proportion to the win. There was one very pleasant incident when the head of my firm, Sir Edward Iliffe, gave a dinner at the Savoy in our honour. After speeches he suddenly said there was a lady outside who he thought had every right to be present, thereby giving Benjy and I kittens lest the surprise should prove too devastating. Then the big doors were flung open and with a roar Number 7, pushed vigorously by the mechanics, entered the dining room. Sir Edward was dead right, the "lady" most qualified to be present had arrived. Mind you, our triumphant procession round Le Mans after the race, with the car covered in flowers and amid the enthusiastic greetings of the French, was the high spot of the whole affair. The amount of champagne we both had to drink at various places proved too

The triumphal entry of Davis and Benjafield on Bentley No. 3 (old No. 7) for her Savoy Banquet, Friday 24 June 1927.

Bentley Drivers Club Savoy Hotel dinner menu, Friday 24 June, 1927. See Appendices, Savoy Hotel, p184.

much for us when we subsequently had to be present at the ACO's official banquet that evening.

Number 7 was Benjy's property, though he had to give it back to the firm before every race and the car was subsequently sold. I have never unravelled the truth, but Benjy told me that the man who bought it fitted a saloon body and painted it yellow, whereupon the old girl, mortally offended, took him into a lamp post and broke his neck.

Later in 1927 I drove a Bugatti in the British Grand Prix with George Eyston. It did not prove an interesting run, firstly because it was staged at Brooklands over a course with artificial corners, and secondly because the circuit was limited to little over two miles, which to anyone accustomed to think in terms of a twenty-mile lap seemed slightly ridiculous for a Grand Prix. Then there was no public enthusiasm, a very poor crowd, so none of the atmosphere the continental events possessed. Finally the Bugatti, though a first-class machine for the job, was delivered too late to be properly prepared. Rival to the Bugattis were the fine little Delages driven by Benoist, Bourlier and Chiron, fast little machines with better brakes and cornering ability than any of the others.

We had trouble all the time, first with oiled plugs then with the brakes and, worst of all, with the supercharger because its vanes overheated, lengthened, and jammed on their casing. Quite apart from that it was extremely irritating to follow Benoist into a turn only to find that the Bugatti simply would not take it at the same speed. This was made the harder to bear by Benoist's friendly but humorous gestures as he watched my car in the mirror of his. Then in my spell the engine pulled up all standing, so that I had to jump on the starting handle to free those infernal super-

charger vanes time after time. Sitting on the handle worked occasionally but gave more food for humour to Benoist, who alleged he thought I found that a better place from which to get a close view of the race, and suggested having the handle padded! Finally I could not get the damned thing clear so ran to the pit for tools, only to find George had run off to find me. Returning to the car I had one more go under George's advice, the engine came free and we struggled on right back at the tail, to finish almost after everyone else had packed up – not our day out.

In June 1928 I drove in the Alvis team at Le Mans with a new type car having front-wheel drive, this being then the source of almost fierce technical argument. Here again the natural obstinacy of those whose job it is to design components and force anything but willing directors to sanction sufficient money for development was obvious. Smith-Clarke, who designed the cars, was properly obstinate and intensely enthusiastic, not to be diverted from his chosen path unless a new direction was argued out and proved better beyond doubt. It is doubtful whether finance entered into his calculations at all, while he far preferred developing something new to the maintenance of proven designs which could be produced in quantity.

He had decided that no shock absorbers were necessary with the special form of suspension he favoured, all four wheels having independent suspension, an idea then in its infancy. I was not so sure about this, neither was my co-driver Urquart-Dykes, nor were the drivers of the second car, Harvey and Purdy, but no amount of argument availed. The fact that in practice my car put a hind wheel up after a bump and did not put it down again in no way interested our

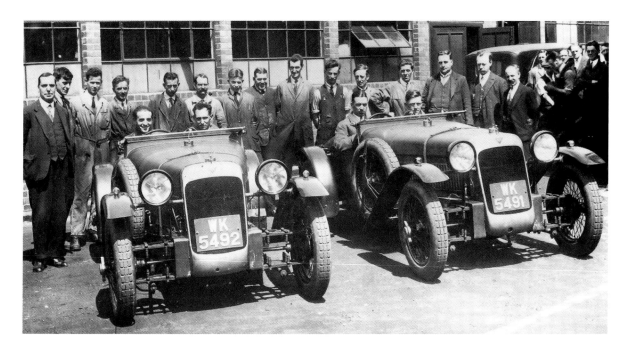

designer team chief, though chief mechanic Tattersall nearly had a fit. Teething trouble is inseparable from new designs, whether it be for normal or racing cars, so it was not surprising we had our fill of them, or that much time was spent in the Bollée works at Le Mans having alterations and improvements made in one big rush. We drivers also had numerous and interesting discussions as to whether a front-drive car cornered better if you

made the engine pull the car round more than was necessary with rear-drive. One of Harvey's experiments during practice resulted in a world record slide over a probable 200 yards without him turning a hair.

In the race itself the car went well, better than we had expected in fact, our chief aim being to win the 1500cc car class against the Aston-Martins and a host of small French cars driven with great abandon. Head and Palmer, who

The two Alvis 1½-litre cars prepared for the 1928 Le Mans outside the works with their original number plates. The front suspension details are clearly seen showing the spring clip dampers and the ends of the front-wheel drive-shafts. Davis and Harvey are in the driving seats.

Le Mans, 1928. 1½-litre Alvis at the Fourche, Pontlieu, driven by Harvey and Purdy. Davis and Urquart-Dykes shared another Alvis, car No. 28. This photo clearly shows the tightness of the bend.

The unveiling of the Diosi sculpture to Louis Zborowski at Le Mans on 16 June 1928. According to Henri Delgove, all manner of dignitaries attended including a director of Daimler-Benz and W F Bradley. The discourse was delivered in French by Clive Gallop.

was Iliffe's chief cashier and an ex-tank corps major, kept the chart excellently all the twenty-four hours. The signals were good and the pit work went according to plan. Every now and again an avalanche of the big cars would roar by, the spearhead of the race being three green 4½-litre Bentleys and a straight-eight Stutz, the whirlwind of their passage making the Alvis quite unsteady. Trouble there was aplenty, with both the Lagondas being in collision early on. Next morning the pace told on the leaders as I saw Clement balefully regarding a cloud of steam coming from his stationary Bentley. Then Tim Birkin worked hard to clear a jammed rear brake from the cocoon of cord wound round the drum from a burst tyre.

Fortunately for us the Astons were not having all the luck they deserved, Bertelli, their designer, being forced onto the grass when overtaking and hitting that very same ditch our Sunbeam had encountered in 1925 – this time the car's rear axle broke. What did upset Harvey and myself was that two laps short of the distance which had to be covered before the car could be refilled, the Alvis showed unmistakable signs of being short of fuel. Now we had tested the consumption with extreme accuracy so this was a shock. However, both of us managed to survive until the car could be refilled. It was subsequently found that the trouble was with the fuel tank being saddle shaped, so it did not feed the last gallon to the carburettors. In addition, we had more tyre trouble than expected, which wasted valuable time.

But the upshot was that Harvey's car won the class and mine came home just astern, so we were satisfied.[1]

1. Harvey finished 6th, Sammy 9th and both beat the 1500cc record.

Chapter Eight

Various gifts from the goddess of luck

In 1928 the RAC announced that the Tourist Trophy race was to be revived, not, as I hoped, in the Isle of Man, but on the new course close to Belfast[1]. Now Reid Railton of Thomson & Taylor at Brooklands had developed a new type Riley[2] with a really beautiful two-seater body, a car much lower than usual and one of the most comfortable I had ever tested. Thomson & Taylor had their own way of doing things. Taylor, who controlled the practical side of the work, was an altogether delightful character, as obstinate as ever a man could be but a first class craftsman. Reid was the brains of the outfit, quiet but with a nice humour, very neatly exerted if one of those know-alls happened to be laying down what he thought to be the laws of design. The firm made a fine job looking after some of the best racing cars running at the track, especially when you allowed for the always tricky financial situation of most racing car owners and the astronomic cost of racing. We had a test run in the Essex Club's six-hour race and the car ran darned well. That the copper oil pipe on one crank throw came adrift proved how essential this practical test was if we were to accomplish anything in the Tourist Trophy, for which this type of Riley was intended.

So in August came the race. Chris Staniland, Clive Gallop and I were the drivers, and never have cars been more carefully prepared and tested than these three little red machines. We could carry mechanics too, which made the race more interesting and which allowed me to have Head as a companion once more.

We had a wonderful run, with the Riley handling well and easily holding the speed we wanted. Sheer bad luck put Staniland's car out, a spring on the quick-action oil filler cap breaking, whereupon the filler lid opened, the crankcase drain tap opening with it and automatically discharging all the engine oil. We were out of luck anyhow, as coming fast round Ballystockart curve Head and I were horrified to see Clive's

1. Ards – Sammy was an RAC delegate.
2. The racing "Nine".

The Essex Club 6 hours race at Brooklands in 1928. The "berry boys" Sammy and L V Head in a Reid Railton Riley 9 team car, which retired.

car in front of us crash into a bank in clouds of dust, but relieved next time round to see him with his mechanic "Chick" unhurt.

The Ards circuit was thirteen and a fraction miles in distance, full of interest as a good road circuit should be. Moreover, there was intense enthusiasm for the race from a vast crowd of spectators. Head and I were thoroughly enjoying all this when it began to rain. For some unexplained reason the road surface seemed converted to ice. Car after car spun – it was quite extraordinary. No sooner had we realised this hazard than we came to Harvey's Alvis spinning wildly just round a corner, the situation being made worse by the fact that a Lea-Francis, which we were about to overtake, slid far and wide as its driver braked to avoid the Alvis. I had to accelerate for all the car was worth to avoid the Lea-Francis, the Riley spun and we went down, bonk, into a ditch. Alas, there was a nasty great rock in that ditch. Head and I tried every trick we knew to straighten out the consequent damage to the steering

gear, but we failed. On the boat going back home, as a morose chief from another team said, "Racing would be fine if it wasn't for the drivers".

Come 1929 and we really had a race to remember – the Brooklands Double Twelve. I was driving a 4½-litre Bentley with Sir Ronald Gunter. Birkin and Holder, Clement and Cook also had 4½s, with Barnato and Benjy driving a six-cylinder[1]. The race itself was for two periods of twelve hours on Brooklands track, the cars being impounded for the intervening night. It was run on the formula setting schedule speeds according to engine size. This was one of the oddly named Junior Car Club's best ideas and was well organised.

The course took in the finishing straight so that there was a very fast curve from the Byfleet banking onto this straight, then another from it onto the last part of the Home banking. Not a true road race, I grant you, but very interesting for all that from the driver's point of view. As usual, the cars were

1. The first Speed Six.

excellently prepared under chief mechanic Clark, while the control was made simpler by a most complicated chart which showed the exact position of each car in the race, not on speed but on formula, a masterpiece of mathematical science.

We now had a special spring-loaded valve in the can with which to refill the spare oil tank. The fuel filler caps also had lever action, screw threads having been abandoned as too slow of operation. Though oil was still poured into the crankcase until it overflowed from a levelling tap, that tap did not close when the filler lid was shut. The object of this was to avoid overfilling by giving the oil time to achieve the right level. When the driver got into the car and pushed forward the clutch pedal the tap closed, a most useful idea of W O's. Once more Head and I practiced every operation we might have to perform until we perfected our time and motion drill, a spare engine being provided so that we could practice a change of vital parts. One incident was amusing. The new Studebaker team asked for some information about the refilling drill. I therefore rehearsed them as required without actually using oil or petrol to save the mess. A mechanic practiced opening the radiator cap, pouring imaginary water from a can then shutting the cap. It just shows how difficult it is to think during a first race, for when that car came to its pit for a refill the mechanic did just that. He poured imaginary water until a howl of invective from his team chief brought him to his senses.

It was another great race, our principal rivals on formula being Alfa Romeos driven by Ramponi, Ivanowski and Kaye Don, supercharged 1500cc cars with plenty of speed. The difficulty was to match their speed, which meant we were almost flat out as our formula speed was much higher, yet we had to

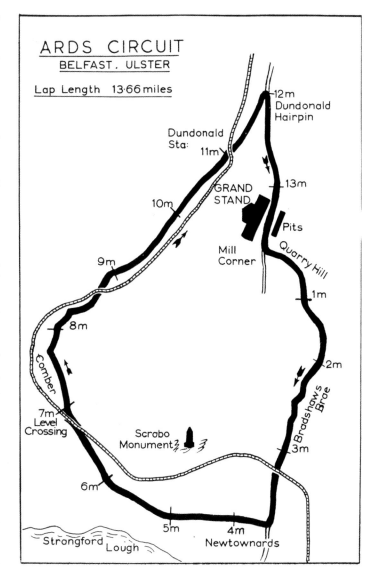

drive no faster than was absolutely necessary, creating a headache for our team control despite its mathematical geniuses. At first the six-cylinder Bentley led in real style, until to our horror the big car came in to its pit in bad trouble with its dynamo drive. That gave the Alfas the lead and resulted in all of us seeing the "faster" signal. There is something inspiring about orders which really allow one to drive with verve, controlled maybe, but verve for all that. Head and I found it inspiring at

In 1928 Sammy borrowed this 1899 Benz to take part in the second modern re-enactment of the 1896 London to Brighton Run. It rekindled his interest in pioneer vehicles and led to him buying his Bollée. Sammy claimed he took part in the first Run in 1927 but research indicates this was unlikely. He may have reported on it, adding sketches, for The Autocar, *November 18th issue.*

all events as the big car went up to full speed all the way round. The speed was so much higher than anyone had bargained for that trouble was inevitably rife and the track seemed to be covered with cars in obvious disrepair.

Our refills were encouraging, Gunter, my co-driver, holding schedule, and everything seemed just right. At that point one of the Alfas fell out, but our satisfaction at a rival's calamity was immediately extinguished because Clement's car ran a big end. Worse was to follow when Birkin came in to refill and the mechanic started pouring fuel into the tank before the engine was quite stopped. Suddenly there was a flash of flame from the exhaust pipe. Instantly all the fuel caught fire and with his overalls alight the mechanic

ran down the track. It was a horrible sight until he was caught and the flames extinguished; by wonderful luck his injuries were not as bad as we feared. A new man took his place and the car was driven away after considerable delay. That emphasised the value of the team rule that engines should be switched off before the car was stopped so as to coast in when it was about to be refilled. The signal for the end of the first twelve hours was given by the firing of a maroon. Of the fifty-two cars which had started only thirty-five remained operational and that showed how high speed had told.

My car was close on Ramponi's Alfa, which led, Ivanowski being just astern of us with the second Alfa. When the signal was given for the start on the following morning there was no thunderous roar of cars speeding away. Instead, the starting line sounded like a blacksmith's shop as mechanics strove to remedy defects or effect repairs. The Bentleys had been thickly wrapped in rugs for the night, so we did get away quickly to cruise for several laps until the engine oil was sufficiently warm. Then the battle continued with unabated fury, the speed being even higher than before.

There were plenty of worries and it rained, which was to the advantage of the Alfas since our big car's higher speed made it trickier to handle on the turns; Ramponi took every advantage of that. When the track dried we could go up to real speed again, urged thereto by another "faster" signal from control. Almost at once, though, the oil pressure became erratic, sometimes high, sometimes ominously low, with each downward swing of the gauge needle making one feel like heart failure. By a miracle the engine went on holding its speed, though oil streaks appeared along the side of the bonnet, making the situation more uncomfortable.

By the twentieth hour of the race our position was desperate. Birkin's machine was seen stationary at the end of the track so we now had no support. Ramponi was fully aware that his car was leading and that he could win. We knew we were gaining slowly on formula, and then the Alfa's battery broke loose. After a sensational and truly Italian-style appeal to the Almighty to do something, Ramponi got down to it himself and, with every rope, strap or cord he could beg, borrow or steal, he secured the battery again and restarted. But then, while Gunter was driving, our Bentley was overdue. A rear tyre had burst into a mass of cord and the car was creeping slowly to the pit.

Again we were behind the Alfa, but because I had more experience W O told me to take over and increase speed at all cost. The subsequent run was fantastically exciting, Ramponi being a rival worth having. Every time the big Bentley overtook his car he tucked the Alfa into its slipstream, thereby gaining speed. Each time he did this I went to the top of the banking to shake him off, and we both enjoyed every minute of the fight. Just as we thought we had gained first place, we were signalled to come into the pit. Furiously we did so, to find that the officials thought the bonnet was coming loose whereas it was secured by a big strap. My language was vivid as we returned to the fray.

I expected an "all out" signal, as the situation required, and was puzzled that it did not appear. But the reason was typical of W O, who had noticed that one of the car's rear tyres had a white streak all round it, indicating a very worn tread, so he blankly refused to sanction the signal in the circumstances. Nonetheless we discovered the streak ourselves and later on I considerably exceeded the scheduled speed ordered. It seemed ages while the hands of the clock, which we could see on the Club House in the paddock, crept round the final hour. And all the time that damned oil gauge needle kept wavering between normal and zero. Head and I were as covered with oil and dirt as was the car. Ramponi and his mechanic might have been Africans for the same reason, but neither of us let up for a moment. The Bentley was now flat out and our cornering was right on the edge, for Head and I had decided to imagine we had seen that "all out" signal which we were sure was necessary. The clock hands reached 24 hours and the blasted thing was fast – no "finish" signal appeared! Five minutes later, just when Head's language was beyond the limit, the chequered flag bravely fluttered and the race was over.

вяя

Le Mans circuit, France, 1929-31. and Phoenix Park circuit, Dublin.

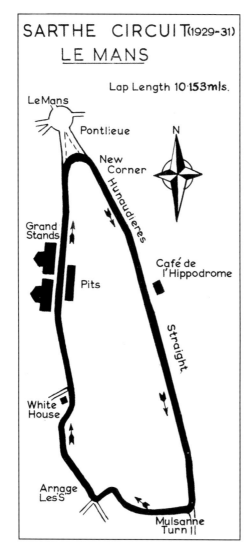

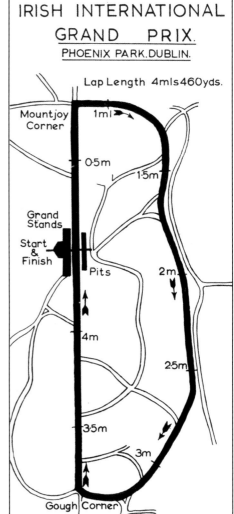

It was quite some time before the result was announced. The Alfa had covered 1,824 miles at 76mph, the Bentley 1,953 miles at 81.39, resulting in a win for the Alfa by 0.003mph – the smallest formula handicap margin ever. What a race!

For Le Mans in 1929 a great friend of mine, Leon Cushman and I, had a straight-eight front-wheel drive Alvis, a quite new model, chock full of teething trouble as it turned out. A second car was driven by Cyril Paul of Brooklands fame and Urquart-Dykes. That adventure was a fine kettle of fish and in first practice our car's engine ran a big end

with calamitous results. Tattersall and Cook repaired this through their miraculous ability to do good work whilst asleep on their feet. But the darned oil circulation system failed again after we had spent every minute available running the new bearings in, and another big end went. "Tat" and Cook were eager to do all the work once more, but Leon and I knew well that an engine repaired like that just before a long race could not last, so we did not start. The remaining car got under way but developed serious overheating in next to no time and had to be with-

LE MANS 1927 LE MANS 1928 LE MANS 1929 LE MANS, RUDGE CUP,
3-LITRE 3-LITRE 4½ LITRE 6 CYLINDER SIX HOURS, DUBLIN, 500
CLEMENT DAVIS BENJAFIELD RUBIN BARNATO BIRKIN.

drawn. Mind you, we had some fun for all this calamity.

France had a smallpox scare for which we were all vaccinated by Benjy (who was driving a Bentley), only to find the restrictions were withdrawn by the time the team landed in France. Then the chambermaid at the Hôtel de Paris could not pronounce Mrs Cushman's name, so called her by the number of her room, *"Madame Douze"*. The first French car to arrive was a most disreputable Tracta which, to avoid jokes at its expense, its driver, Vanessa claimed to have won in a raffle. We were rather proud of our pit organisation because we were easily first in action when Briton's Stutz caught fire at its pit during the race and we actually extinguished the fire.

It was some consolation to me that the Bentleys won handsomely, their superiority being such that they were kept running in formation as slowly as possible for the last hour. This did not suit Jack Dunfee one little bit, as anyone who knew that most amusing character would appreciate. After the third "go slower" signal on successive laps he pulled into the Bentley pit and said, "What do you want me to do with the bloody thing – push it?"

But if disaster follows success, just to keep one's head the right size, fortunately success can follow disaster. So, for a race in Phoenix Park, Dublin[1], I had a Lea-Francis; the two other drivers of the team were Jimmy Shaw and W H Green. The machines went well in practice and we felt fairly confident, though the Alfa Romeos driven by my old opponent Ramponi, the Russian Ivanowski and Fronteras were the obvious favourites. As usual there were crises, and almost at the last moment our special plugs for the race had not arrived. Telephoning producing no result and we were getting very worried when Delaney's father, who had driven in the 1903 Paris-Madrid race and was a very tough citizen by any yardstick, announced that he was damned if he would stand this nonsense. Led by him we broke into the supplier's works, opened a case, took the plugs and returned in triumph. Second trouble was that, Head being unable to be with me, I had Jack Hewitson as mechanic and he received a telephone message saying his father had been badly injured in a crash. Jack was packing up to go home when another message made it

1. First Irish Grand Prix, 1929

Bentleys achieved the hat-trick at Le Mans in 1929 and this photo appeared in the booklet for that year. This copy was inscribed by Sammy and needs no further comment except to add 1924 on the left.

clear that the injuries were not serious, so he came with me after all.

We had a good race. My instructions were to try and "out" the Alfas, so we arrived on the first corner in company with the Italian cars and got round it by a miracle. Better still, the Lea-Francis could just hold its rivals on the straights, though we were at maximum revs all the time. It was a glorious ride of the devil-take-the-hindmost type, with all the cars at their limit or even a little beyond. Under a blazing sun and the stress of sliding vehicles, the road became so slippery[1] we might have been dirt track racing. Ramponi actually slid right off the road, went wide on the grass border, in and out of some trees and still returned. Then we saw Fronteras at the pit with his Alfa, working furiously with his mechanic at something which looked serious – one Alfa out. Then both Alfas had to refill, which they did so quickly I could do no more than come right up on the tail of Ramponi as he got back to speed. He took one glance astern, saw the Lea-Francis and drove with increased fury. We arrived together on a most slippery corner with the Alfa sliding beyond control and crashing into railings, fortunately without injury to its crew – two Alfas out!

The Lea-Francis was feeling the stress; both Jack and I were covered with oil, as was the front of the car, and all our spare oil had to be pumped into the engine. The clutch misbehaved and had to be left engaged all the time, the brakes were definitely weaker and there were funny noises neither of us liked. Yet the car kept its speed at every curve and dicey corner. The last Alfa was at full speed and gaining a little every lap. Ivanowski was too experienced to be rattled whatever manoeuvres we executed or however

much we gained here or there. The huge crowd understood what was happening and were cheering us on with real Irish enthusiasm.

The race was near its end but never for one fraction of a second could one relax, although my car was obviously falling to pieces and was being driven regardless of rev-limits in obedience of the "all out" signal. Neither Jack nor I thought the machine could last but it did, the stout-hearted little devil.

Two laps from the finish we actually gained quite a bit, but our hopes were extinguished when the engine cut out. Fuel in the tank was at so low a level that the liquid surged about, cutting off the supply then restoring it, which was infuriating. We could not believe that we could get to the finish on the small quantity we guessed must remain, but we did, finishing a good second to Ivanowski's Alfa, sixty-six seconds behind. Obviously the smaller godlets who look after me were providing the best of luck. I had always believed that the driver of the car which is second and tackling a superior rival had to excel himself, whilst the leader had a relatively calm time; this was full proof of the theory. The curious thing was that I never really believed the Lea-Francis could do so well when faced with the famous Italian cars, thus full credit goes to the little machine. It lasted magnificently and it was not its fault we did not catch Ivanowski over those 276 hard-fought miles. To add to our pleasure Green brought our second car home in third place.

Then I had Head with me for the Tourist Trophy on the Ards circuit and we had another run to remember. I was driving one of those beautiful little Riley Brooklands models, the other two cars of the team being handled by big John Cobb, who loved very large, very fast cars at Brooklands, and Brian Lewis, whose sense

---

1. Due to the melting road surface.

of wit made every moment worthwhile. Brian tried to tempt John into a game to drive big nails into wood with the palm of one hand, which was not everyone's fancy. The reason for this was that the Mercedes-Benz team for this race consisted of Rudolf Caracciola and Otto Merz[1], a real giant of a German who could do just this very thing. Brian's argument was that as John was our team giant, he must beat Merz for the honour of England. John however very wisely and steadfastly refused to compete.

The start of the race was as sensational as ever, the mass of cars making it seem almost impossible that we would survive the first round, since the machines were three or more abreast most of the time. But we did get free in the end and found at once that the Riley was going like a scalded cat. Head and I thoroughly enjoyed every moment of it, the more so because our signal soon showed we were doing well. As the race was run on a handicap, taking engine size into consideration, team control had to be scientific to ensure we knew the position at any moment. Simpler of course was the class battle between cars of equal engine size, for this was just a plain Grand Prix. Then it began to rain.

Head removed my goggles, substituting a visor, but even then it was none too easy to see, while the damned road surface became exceedingly slippery. At once cars seemed to be sliding in all directions and dodging them became a perpetual headache, especially as one had somehow or other to maintain speed. Just as we drifted fast round one curve we saw John Cobb's's car up a bank, bent, but John and Paddy his mechanic were standing up unhurt, thank heaven. Next time round there was Paddy on all fours, crawling about

the centre of the road. We just missed him and spent all the next lap discussing what in the world he thought he was doing, our surmise being that he had hit his head in the crash and was not quite himself. After the race we found that he had lost his treasured set of false teeth and was bent on recovering them.

Meantime the circuit was being bordered by an ominous number of wrecked vehicles. An Arrol-Aster had hit Newtonards town hall, together with two Lea-Francis, and Kidston's big six-cylinder Bentley was down in a dip of the course looking very bent. Ivanowski's Alfa was head-on in a bank and a 4½-litre Bentley crashed and one wheel came off. Then Merz hit a barrier with his Mercedes, badly bending one front wing. He proceeded to clear this by tearing the mudguard off with his hands, though the regs demanded it remain in place. We then came across Dick Watney's Stutz blazing furiously on a slow corner and had just time to roll our extinguisher over to him without stopping. The upshot was that Caracciola's Mercedes won, with Campari's Alfa second, whilst we won our class handsomely, to our great content.

Racing has its surprises, too. In October 1929 the BRDC organised a 500-mile race at Brooklands. This was a pure speed event with no nonsense about artificial corners but a scientific handicap to relate all the different sizes of entered cars. I had not intended to drive since we were right on the date of the Motor Show and that meant oodles of work for the paper, but I did intend to have a look-see. This plan came to nothing as the Bentley team had entered one of the big six-cylinder models with a sketchy two-seater body and short tail; there seemed to be some suggestion that it was a difficult

---

1. Formerly chauffeur to the Archduke Ferdinand, assassinated in Sarajevo, 1914.

machine to handle. The surprise came on the last practice day when W O took me aside and asked, "Will you drive the car?" Naturally I consented, and had a practice run forthwith. The big car certainly had temperament. In effect I asked, "What about it, old thing?" The car replied, "What about it be damned. If people called drivers would leave me alone I could get round this track as fast as any car".

There was only just time to get my helmet and goggles when the race started, with young Clive Dunfee taking the first spell. Certainly that machine was fast, but it wanted watching and required accurate judgement for the line across the Vickers shed curve as well as on the high bankings. If you did not hold the wheel tight the car, as it said, knew the way round. It was an inspiring ride, with the wind howling round one's ears and the sense of being behind almost unlimited power. There was an almighty bump as the car went over the stretch of the track supported by a small bridge across the river Wey, a bump which nearly shook one's teeth out and did my stern end no good at all. The very high speed made the track more interesting and the only cause for worry was whether the tyre treads would stand it. There was one nasty moment when another car in front suddenly swerved up the banking and I

thought I would hit it, but the interloper swerved down again just in time.

Finding everything as it should be I then went faster, having been told to run the race my own way as there had been no time for briefing. The car responded splendidly and we were enjoying ourselves to the full when there was a hell of a bang and something hit my right elbow so hard I thought it was broken. The tread of the rear tyre had come off at one end and swung round like a giant flail – not funny. The wheel change was quick enough so we were soon back in the battle, all the more pleased because I had learned the car was well up with the leaders. This time I watched the white stripe round the offside front tyre with some apprehension when it appeared, showing the tyre was badly worn. A rear tyre burst was bad enough, but a front one might be tricky as it would affect the steering. All was well, though it caused delay, which was unfortunate. Clive Dunfee took over while I rested, then I faced the last spell of all with the knowledge we might win if everything went well.

It didn't of course, for more wheel changes were necessary, the tyre wear being phenomenal. However the car went like a bomb in between these stops, though it needed watching when we got to "all out" speed in the last hour. It was a miracle we came in second on handicap, putting up the highest average of the race at 109.40mph. I was pleased to note Clement won on formula with the 4½-litre Bentley, for my old team-mate was being more and more successful.

Le Mans in 1930 provided a strategical headache for the Bentley team. Tim Birkin had his own three Bentleys, all with 4½-litre supercharged engines, whilst we of the official team had the unsupercharged six-cylinder cars. So strategy was vital, since without it the

" Now for Le Mans."

teams might race each other to disaster. To make the problem worse, Caracciola and Werner were driving a 7-litre super-charged Mercedes, by far the largest-engined car in the race. Now a properly handled machine of this type should win if it is not made to run at too high a speed, in spite of a six-car opposition. On paper the Bentleys had to win, for no one ever remembers engine sizes when thinking about a race in retrospect. Only our teams knew that the supercharged Bentleys were liable to teething trouble on a large scale, especially if they used their full speed. The plan eventually agreed was for Tim to harry the Mercedes into going flat out if possible, with my car in support, then Barnato's as reserve, then Clement's and the other two "blower" Bentleys. That way we might lose two cars getting rid of the Mercedes, but would still have two of ours and two of Tim's in a good position to win.

It's none too easy to ask a driver to handle his car so that it will have little chance of finishing, and it was obvi-ously impossible to tell Tim that his supercharged car was very unlikely to finish. Our team consisted of Barnato and Glen Kidston, Clement and Dick Watney, myself and Clive Dunfee. Clive being in his first road race, we had to take a good deal of trouble coaching him during practice. The rest of the team had experience in plenty and "Babe" Barnato was a magnificent driver, one of the best ever, and curi-ously enough one who never received the credit his skill had so amply earned. The "blower" team had Tim and Chas-sagne, Benjy and Ramponi, Jack Dunfee and Beris Wood. Amusing how rivals in one race can be team-mates in another. Each team had its own tie, that for the "blowers" being given when you drove in the team; ours was awarded only if W O was satisfied you had done exactly what he had ordered. Benjy, being enti-

tled to both, invariably attended special functions wearing the wrong one.

The race fully justified our plan. Tim and I harried the Mercedes, never letting it get away and always giving the impression we had plenty in hand but did not want to overtake. The Mercedes supercharger could be engaged by pushing the throttle pedal to its forward limit, so allowing the engine to run unsupercharged most of the time. When it was engaged you could hear its whine, and that was beautiful music to us, as we knew the more the whine sounded, the less probable it was that the engine would stand up to the load. Just when everything seemed to be going according to plan, Tim's car burst a tyre and he crawled to the pit with a tangle of burst cords and rubber round one rear wheel. Actually there was more than a tyre in trouble and Tim was out of the game. That let me close up on the Mercedes and we had a most exciting two hundred miles together, Caracciola and I thoroughly enjoying every minute of it, though it was more like a Grand Prix than a twenty-four hour race. Just before both cars had to refill a stone cracked one of my goggle lenses, which was awkward but would have been more so in the days of plain glass. The refill was good, the better because this year both could work on the car together. Then Clive went off in style and I strolled to *The Autocar* pit for a cup of good British tea.

When I returned from a rest the worst possible thing had happened to young Clive. Imagine, in a first race on the first difficult corner, he had misjudged the speed and our big car was buried in the protective sandbank. Clive dug hard but could not free it, and neither could I. Admittedly a driver must keep a car on the road, but the first lap with a fast and rather tricky machine requires much more control than most of us can manage, especially in that

Brooklands, 1930. the 500 miles race. A pre-race shot of the 750cc supercharged works Ulster Austin, "Blood Orange".

Sammy and the Earl of March giving an interview after winning the 500 miles race (note hand-held microphone and other apparatus).

state of nerves which besets a novice. Actually I liked Clive very much, and he made no excuse on this occasion, but I do not think he ought to have commenced road racing with a car like the "big six". The tragedy of it was that he was given the wheel of the even faster Brooklands two-seater[1] later on and it took him over the banking to his death. In spite of this setback the team control saved the situation. Barnato increased speed at once to close on the Mercedes. In obedience to signals he overtook the German car, then let it overtake him, then overtook again, thereby keeping his rival at full speed with the inevitable result: the Mercedes slowed, with steam spouting from its radiator vent, to retire, officially with "dynamo trouble". From there on the Bentleys had it all their own way, Barnato leading the team over the line to victory for the third time.

After a rather irritating run in Phoenix Park with an Aston Martin which had not the power to deal with its rivals, and an almost equally irritating drive in the Tourist Trophy with a Lea-Francis which decided to be temperamental, luck, if you call it luck, changed in the Brooklands 500-mile race. This time I was driving a supercharged Austin, a most impudent little car, with more speed than anyone could believe a 750cc engine could develop and an ability to intrude among the larger vehicles with great verve. From start to finish that little car, nicknamed the "Blood Orange" as a result of its vivid colour, surprised even me who knew what it ought to do, and surprised its rivals even more. My co-driver was a friend of long standing, the Earl of March. Another friend, Earl Howe, was driving a single-seater Talbot. This raised the righteous ire of a Socialist party newspaper of the "keep the Red

Flag flying" type, so it headed its race paragraph, "Two Earls and 33 Misters race", then announced that the race was won by the "so-called Earl of March and his menial Mr S C H Davis". I don't suppose the Editor of that unnecessarily red paper could understand, but Freddie March lived a much more useful and certainly more exciting life than most of his "Misters". Like many of us, his financial life was flexible, so much so that he always looked out of an upstairs window to see who was there before opening the front door.

This 500-mile race had an amusing sequel and provided a first-class, really creepy ghost story. The idea was to round off the season by taking records at Brooklands, so a single-seater Austin was prepared for the Class twelve-hour record. Since this involved running after dark at that time of the year, the path the car should follow round the track was marked out with red lanterns. Goodacre, then an Austin apprentice, was my relief driver and off we set, doing fine until darkness fell. I had never driven a car fast without headlamps in pitch darkness, so had a good deal of trouble persuading myself to keep the throttle open; somehow it didn't seem reasonable despite that line of red lights. All was going well and we were up to schedule when, suddenly, something soft and very hairy came across my face, stopped there a fraction of time then went. To say I was in a near panic would be an understatement. The "thing" could not have been a bat or bird, since striking one of them at 90mph would have been like hitting a brick; for the life of me I could not imagine anything like it. Inevitably it seemed as though the underworld was playing tricks, and if hobgoblins and things were going to fool around during a record, it was time to go home. Then the damned "thing" did it again. Well, you can't go in to the depot and explain

1. 8-litre engined.

HRH The Duke of Kent, a regular visitor to Brooklands, talks to Woolf Barnato and Sammy Davis in the Bentley pits, possibly after the end of the 1930 Double Twelve Race where they finished 1st and 2nd in Speed Sixes. They were partnered by Clement and Dunfee.

that hairy ghosts are mucking about, so I had to carry on. Then the engine cut out completely. At the depot, mechanics soon found out the cause. A very large fuel tank had been fitted alongside my seat to reduce the number of stops during the run. The tank was secured in the usual way by broad metal straps bedded down on felt. The strap bolts had come adrift, allowing the tank to play about until the fuel pipe broke. Unknown to me the long strips of felt, still secured at one end, had been waving about in the darkness like an octopus doing Swedish drill. The result was that one of the blasted things had twice flapped across my face. Even so, we got the record.

The French had built a fine concrete-surfaced track with very steep banking for the curves at Montlhéry near Paris. Reigning queen of that track was Gwenda Hawkes, who had taken the lap record and was famous for being able to handle the fastest cars with consummate ease. That she could excel was hardly surprising when it is remembered that she was the sister of Glubb Pasha of the Arab Legion and the

daughter of a Major General. The whole family were natural enthusiasts for anything highly dangerous and exciting. In the summer of 1930 I was asked to partner her in an attempt to take a twenty-four record with a three-wheeled Morgan. Gwenda was of course chief driver and I was the spare. We took turn after turn and we got the record handsomely, but the delicious part of the business was that we started according to schedule, ran some hours and then the engine packed up. Almost anyone else would have cursed heartily and called it a day, but not so Gwenda and her husband Douglas. Remarking "You go and get some rest", Douglas started forwith to change the engine, did so, tested it, and before I knew where I was we were off again on a new attempt – successfully completed. Two other things remain in memory: the fascination of handling a really fast three-wheeler with a whopping big engine, and the hour or two when Gwenda joined me for the rest before the second start. Lounging in deck chairs beneath a perfect night and a sky full of stars we discussed future life, the world, and everything but cars. What a woman she was, just as fresh at the end of it all as she had been at the beginning.

After this I made a damned silly mistake. At Brooklands one afternoon during the 1931 Easter meeting a friend of mine asked me to take his low-chassis Invicta round the "mountain" circuit, a small triangle of the track which skirted the Members Hill and was used for special races. The reason he asked was that he was not satisfied the appointed driver was getting the best from the machine. I accepted and after a lap or two let go, with the flattering result that the car's average speed improved considerably, so I was then asked to drive it in the race. Now I usually spent a good deal of time in the preparation of any car I was to drive, and even more getting accustomed to its handling. There did not seem any reason why this should be a handicap with the Invicta in question, so I consented. In practice I found the machine needed watching, most fast cars do, and with the big 4½-litre engine right forward and a very large fuel tank astern, you had to be more than usually sure of your line for the curves.

It rained hard on the day of the race. First lap, all was well and we overtook a string of rivals. Second lap, the car slid on a right bend, so we went round in what is now called a "controlled drift", but when the car went high up on the banking the tail continued to slide upwards, which was a puzzle, full left lock on the steering failing to do more than keep the machine on its course. Suddenly, like lightning, the tail swung downwards on the banking slope. Since the steering was low geared it took time to pull over to full right lock but the tail continued to slide down. We were heading for railings, behind which was a crowd of specta-tors, so something drastic had to be done. I put the handbrake on hard, with no real response save that we cleared the railings. A telephone pole loomed very solidly: we missed that but I did not see the pole support cable. We struck it and the whole car went right over on its back with a crash. I knew I was damaged but was chiefly interested in getting clear before the car caught fire. This I did with the help of a small man who climbed over the spectator enclosure fence. There was a good deal of blood about so I concentrated on finding out whether it was coming out in spurts or just coming out! In the former case I would have to do some-thing quick, but it was not an artery. Meantime the small man, with the best intentions, was trying to give me a brandy, which I had the sense to refuse.

CAR-ICATURES

Famous Racing Drivers as seen by F. Gordon-Crosby.
No. 20.—"Casque" and "Caput," his former racing mechanic.
("Casque" is Sports Editor of "The Autocar" and "Caput" a colleague on a sister journal.)

Then he thought it was bad for me to look at all that blood and to reassure me said, "It's all right, it's all right, it's only from your nose". My goggles had cut my nose slightly, resulting in the merest trickle. I could not help laughing, and that hurt.

In due time Benjy arrived with an

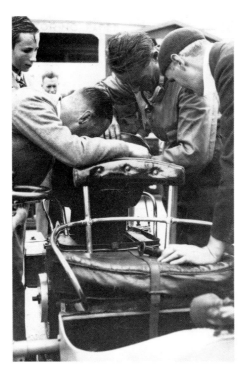

Burrowing into the interior of the newly acquired Bollée. From left: Donald Campbell, Malcolm Campbell, Sammy Davis and L V Head. This was probably before the Daily Sketch "Old Crocks Race" at Brooklands in August 1930.

An original sketch intended for publication. Where and when? Sammy is on crutches, so it was done after Easter 1931.

ambulance and I went off to hospital. The damage was a compound shattered tibia and fibula just below the knee and a clean fracture of the femur just above – as tricky a smash as you could have. Yet the leg was mended marvellously by Dr Bear of Weybridge hospital, a surgeon to whom I owe all the rest of my existence. His repair was near perfect, so much so

that even today it proves vastly intriguing to surgeons busy about other repairs I need. Out of all this two things proved extremely interesting once I had got over the fury of making such a fool of myself. Firstly, during the whole period when the crash was certain there was no time to feel afraid, indeed I seemed to be outside myself watching with interest what my brain was doing automatically. Secondly, I nearly died towards the end of the repair during the year in hospital, something unexpected having gone wrong. To my mother and other people who were watching, I seemed to be suffering considerably. But in actual fact I was, as it were, floating about watching myself disinterestedly, and felt no pain at all. I even heard a doctor tell my mother that he was afraid there was nothing more that could be done, without it seeming to mean anything to me. Obviously if it had continued it would have led to a quiet oblivion, but I did recover and the return to life was very painful.

There was another more amusing incident. One of the doctors said to me, "Is there any chance that you were shot?" Thoroughly puzzled, I said, "Good God no – why?" He replied, "Well, there's what seems to

| Tim | Campari | Howe | Lewis | Campbell | Nash | Gillow | Benjy | G.Poppe |

*"Beelzebub", solo.
Sammy contrasted
it with the modern
Morgan back in
1932.*

be the pointed end of a .303 bullet tucked away just under your knee joint, according to the X-ray". I saw the photo and there was. I was intrigued by this until someone told me they had found a neat round hole in the side of the car next to that leg, exactly the hole a bullet would make. Incidentally, this crash did this model of the Invicta no good at all because people would blame the car. It was not, repeat *not* the car's fault, for a driver must handle a car according to its special peculiarities and I didn't.

The worst part of it all was that my wife Rosamund, who was not well at the time, was very badly affected by the crash and for that it is difficult to disown the blame. This brings up the point: is it right to make one's partner suffer when every race is a torment to her? I don't know the answer, though women have suffered this way ever since men began to be adventurous.

*The Café de l'Hippodrome on the Le
Mans course is a rendezvous wherein
more naughty untruths are told about
cars' performances than any other place
in the world.*

Chapter Nine

Aftermath
of an accident

When the leg was operational again, a process hastened by falling down stairs on crutches having been told not to use these "helps" on them, I freed a stiff knee joint. This was to the fury of the masseuse, who was looking forward to months of work, as I found I could drive once more.

For the time being I turned to team management and found it very interesting indeed. The first effort was as team chief of Aston-Martin in the 1932 Le Mans race, where we won the Rudge-Whitworth cup on formula with the Aston driven by Bertelli and Driscoll. The organisation for control and refilling went exactly as planned, we being the only team, it seemed, who knew where our cars were every single lap. This triumph was all the more pleasing because I had known Bert for years and had wanted him to win.

First drive after I was fit was in the 1933 Le Mans for Aston Martin with Bertelli as co-driver – he was by the way the designer. The team had two machines both of the latest type, but included an earlier model to be driven by "Mort" (Mortimer) Morris-Goodall and Tommy Wisdom's wife "Bill" Wisdom, who thus became the first woman to be included in an official works team. Bill had had plenty of experience driving very fast, very big cars at Brooklands. She was a dear, well able to look after herself and quite without that tendency to the heebie-jeebies which afflicts racing drivers, making team chiefs wish cars would drive themselves. Our second works car was driven by Pat Driscoll and Penn Hughes.

To make things more comfortable we all went, as of one family, to the small but friendly Hôtel des Ifs instead of one of the larger affairs, chiefly because we could relax in its garden untroubled by the noise of other racing cars. Just before practice ended Mort's wife, Vanne Goodall, also arrived. She was a tower of strength, able to deal effectively with any emergency and with a sense of humour second to none. Vanne was a woman with great character and decided charm who in years to follow would become a novelist. One of her children, Jane, became the world expert on chimpanzees, amidst which strange animals she and her husband lived. Her second child, Judy, was an acknowledged expert on making moulds and replicas of parts of prehistoric men or things contrived for museums.

Mort, by the way, was at that time accident prone, which kept us all on our toes with expectation. When we landed at Dieppe he sat on a winch bollard, then saw a small metal button on the quay so pushed it with his toe. It was the switch of the winch, which accelerated to high speed and Mort was flung off, seriously cutting his arm. On another occasion Bertelli and I were sitting in the hotel garden having finished practice early. A vehicle drew up outside and there was a terrific crash as of dozens of large tins falling off a house. Bert said, "I'll bet that's Mort". It was. He had returned from the circuit in the truck on top of the team supply of fuel filling cans and had fallen off when it stopped. He once knocked himself out while boxing, and was hit in the eye by a bumble bee[1] during his first round in practice. Fortunately he never achieved any but minor accidents and was quite safe when racing. We had a really magnificent run in the race and had no trouble at all barring the cycle-type mudguards having to be lashed up when they came loose. We were 7th overall and 2nd on formula with Driscoll's car, which was damned good for a 1500cc car you must admit[2], while Bertelli and I finished 4th. Our third car had engine trouble while Bill was driving which was unfortunate but that led to a humorous incident. Replying to an official in her very limited French, Bill

explained the reason for walking along the course to our pit by the phrase "voiture bang", illustrated by waving both arms in the air. The official instantly thought she had crashed so she was led willy-nilly to the hospital tent, where a much puzzled doctor prodded her all over before announcing that there were no serious results. We also had another trouble as a small but active flycatcher had made a nest in our pit. All the noise of racing exhausts and of people did not deter her from feeding the family. So we cornered off the nest, helped with crumbs and made puzzled visitors keep quiet and walk on tiptoe past the nest, to their extreme bewilderment.

From then onwards most of my energy was devoted to team management, apart from my normal job. Perfecting the drill for refilling, for example, was fascinating since the whole point of it was to ensure the mechanics moved as little as possible; that everything which had to be opened or closed did so in one movement, and that mechanisms were made to do the job whenever possible. Then we had to evolve signals which could not be misread yet were unintelligible to rivals, whilst interpreting every detail of other peoples' signals as well. As information about the speed and probable reliability of opposing cars was valuable, this had to be obtained too. The chart we used was a whole-time job in itself, particularly as it had to be accurate, which is the hardest thing to attain even with experienced chart keepers. In this, Head and Palmer, who looked after the charts, were experts. During the race it was essential to keep the whole picture plainly in mind, no matter what distractions might occur, so that the

1. A wasp according to Sammy in *A Racing Motorist*, p141.
2. But not as good as a Riley Nine, 1091cc, which was first on index.

cars could be controlled to run as slowly as circumstances permitted, yet accelerated just at the right time when opportunity offered. Fuel and oil consumption came into the calculation, since stops at the pit lost time, and above all nothing was to be used which had not been tested and proved beforehand.

The job had all the ingredients of staff control in war, but its value was incalculable since on the circuits we then used no driver could keep the race order position in his head. Each team was entirely different in all respects and each driver equally so. I handled Singer, Aston Martin, MG, ERA, John Cobb's record at Montlhéry in 1934 with that magnificent Napier-Railton, and Alan Hess's record run on the Indianapolis track.

The last named was made more difficult because the car was entered as a standard Austin[1], which meant that any change of anything, even plugs, was checked with eagle eyes by the American observers. It was entirely fascinating as a job even if there were occasional vigorous differences of opinion. In one race on the Isle of Man I felt sure there was a difference between one car allotted to one driver, admittedly skilled, but not so skilful as to put up such high-speed laps in comparison with the other two drivers of the team. Circumstances made it impossible to get more than a solemn declaration from the man in charge of the car preparation that each machine was exactly the same, but the doubt remained. After the race it was proved beyond argument that the car I queried had different gear ratios from the others, so very plain speaking became necessary; favouritism in secret will wreck the morale of any team.

For one race I took an impish delight in running an all-women drivers team which did extremely well. The drivers were Kay Petre, acknowledged queen of Brooklands, Eileen Ellison and Mrs Tolhurst, all of whom obeyed orders without quibbling, greatly to the surprise of rival men drivers.[2]

To cap that, in 1937 I controlled that fine driver Dorothy Stanley Turner at Le Mans when she drove an MG to finish second on formula, to the complete surprise of the officials there. Mind you, I'm not saying that the humorously inclined did not find this ample food for naughty rumours, inseparable from any help given to the opposite sex, but that is all part of the game. Most people are convinced that certain racing drivers hop into bed with any girl that they can catch – artists are regarded in the same way. So I had better explain that with the exception of my original instructress I have never "hopped into bed" with anyone of whom I was not very fond indeed, immoral as even that may seem. True I was caught once when I went to bed early after a particularly exciting race in which my car had done surprisingly well. That time I awoke suddenly to find a quite attractive youngster with almost nothing on who inserted herself in the bed with the astounding remark, "I won you in the raffle". That was all wrong, I admit.

In 1935 I had an even more exciting adventure than usual driving in the Singer team for the Tourist Trophy race on the Ards circuit. Alf Langley, Donald Barnes and Norman Black were driving the other three cars and we were quite happy with our little machines, which were lighter and faster than any previous Singers; they handled beautifully and were excellently prepared. We

1. A90 Atlantic
2. Three Singers, Brooklands relay race, 1934. *Atalanta*, p49, et sec.

106

had a mite of trouble with the gear ratios because it was difficult to get the right top ratio for the straights yet retain the existing indirect ratios for the rest of the circuit, but there is always something to worry about. In the race itself we had a world record dogfight with a bunch of other cars in our 1100cc class, mostly Fiats. Alf Langley, Norman Black and I found ourselves having round after round in such close company that we sometimes took a corner two abreast. The Singers were definitely faster, it is true, but the Fiat drivers knew their stuff so used our slipstreams to achieve higher speed and could not be shaken off.

After some hectic laps it struck me very forcibly that this was highly dangerous, for if one driver overdid things and his car slid, we would all be involved in a pile-up and I had had all I wanted of compound crashes. There

seemed only one remedy, which was to take the engine above the rev-limit ordered for just long enough to get clear, or to let Norman, who was down for the fast work, use my car's slipstream to gain speed. But when I did this, a Fiat used Norman's car's slipstream and overtook as well, so I opened right up and cleared the whole bunch, not altogether happy about what the team chief would say when he heard about this disobedience of orders. As it happened, Stanley Barnes in the pit had realised our difficulties and was about to show an "all out" signal to help. It was a highly exciting, distinctly pleasurable race, largely because the Ards circuit is a real circuit and not obviously artificial. There was a small butcher's shop just round one sharp corner which was "visited" by several competing cars in turn. It always suffered in every race, which brings

In the summer of 1934 the Light Car Club organised a 90-lap relay race at Brooklands. The official Singer team recruited Kay Petre, Mrs S Tolhurst and Eileen Ellison as drivers, and Sammy Davis as manager, here seen pushing Kay's car. They won the Wakefield trophy.

back memories of a time when I came round the turn in company with that very cheerful little expert, Nuvolari. As we passed the rather bent shop Nuvolari and I were very close to the counter, no longer protected by a glass window, and on it was a very tempting leg of mutton. With an impish grin the Italian snatched at the joint with one hand while holding his car in a drift with the other. He didn't get it but the attempt was typical of Nuvolari.

We had no mechanics in the cars this year, they having been eliminated on the score that too many had been injured in crashes, so I lacked the cheerful inspiring company of Head. The refill went well though I had trouble with Quarry Corner afterwards because I had become accustomed to the feel of the machine without a full fuel tank. My car was going well, plenty of rivals were obviously in trouble and we had a healthy lead in the class, but there was just one niggling worry. On the slope of that excitingly interesting series of S bends called Bradshaw's Brae, I suddenly saw Alf Langley's car all crumpled up against a bank at the roadside. Worse still, Norman's was up against another bank a lap or two later, even more damaged, and I could make nothing of it. True it could be driver error, but that did not seem likely knowing the two men, so it might be something wrong with the cars, which was a disturbing thought.

Nine laps from the finish I found out all about it. The car and I started down Bradshaw's Brae, going rather faster than usual because I knew every inch of every corner and enjoyed them. There was a ghost of a shimmy from the front wheels, but that was always there and not strong enough to worry about. Abruptly, on a right turn taken at full speed, the steering wheel ceased to control the machine. There was no time to feel frightened, no time to think –

every action was automatic. I knew the steering had gone so shifted my thighs sideways from under the wheel rim, put one hand on the scuttle, the other on the side of the car and let myself go all limp. We crossed the wide road, then the verge, went right on up the bank, heeling until upside down, turned end for end, then slid down tail first with a real crash. One thousandth of a second before we struck the road verge again, I departed over the tail, hit the ground and rolled.

All this happened so fast that photographs show spectators happily having tea about one foot above the uncontrolled car. Believe it or not, we actually passed right over Alf's Singer, which had crashed at this spot previously. Assisted by artist Brian de Grineau and an official I got to my feet rather dazed, carefully inspected my personal mechanism, found it OK and started to think. My crash helmet had been knocked off by the wreck of Alf's car as we passed over it so all the injury I had was a small abrasion on my head. This infuriated the enthusiastic ambulance crew who had hoped for "the best" as they watched the crash, only to find that sticking plaster was sufficient for repairs, and I had the impression they blamed me. Anyhow I sat on the bank and had tea with the spectators until an official vehicle took me back to the pit.

You can't say life as lived by us wasn't exciting. There was of course a long inquest at the works, because it proved the steering rods were glass-hard instead of normally case-hardened as they should have been, and there was considerable annoyance over it. The full story as told to me sometime afterwards was intriguing. The balls were made from round bar of case-hardening steel. Just before the annual holiday the man concerned with this was asked to make some other fitting in the same machine and of high-carbon steel. This was duly

rough turned when the works closed. The man did not return and his successor, finding a bar of normal size already in the machine, continued to machine ball joints. These were now of high carbon steel which, when case-hardened, became brittle. Be that as it may, I insisted on driving my car again after it had been repaired, and did so at Shelsley Walsh hill-climb with good results. Incidentally the little machine was stripped, lightened and tuned for maximum speed to make the demonstration more effective.

In between all these events I did have one or two races of interest for myself. For example, in April 1937 I drove a standard production model BMW Type 328 sports car at Brooklands to cover over 100 miles in one hour for the first time with a car of this size. The amusing thing was that the sponsors of this run thought there was no need to carry the spare wheel or kit of tools and several other things usually found on any standard car, so I therefore refused to drive it unless all the equipment was actually in place. On another occasion with a supercharged MG at Shelsley Walsh hill-climb, my mechanic and I were listening to the engine and trying to locate a flat-spot in the carburettor. Mistaking what we were after, young Pomeroy (son of Vauxhall Pomeroy), rushed up, unsheathed a sword from its stick, placed the point on the supercharger, the hilt to his ear and said: "It's all right, all right, the blower is going fine," then rushed off leaving both of us speechless.

Barring a run in a racing boat in 1938, that was the sum total of adventure. With racing cars, for reasons which will become apparent, there is nothing out of the ordinary about them, for those

To launch the Type 328 BMW on the British market, the concessionaires, AFN Ltd (Frazer Nash), borrowed a production prototype from the makers and Sammy drove it under RAC observation at Brooklands in April 1937. In one hour he covered 102.226 miles – an outstanding performance with a 2-litre unsupercharged car.

This appears to be a 1½-litre Birmal hydroplane - note the lift from the water. Strange though, given how superstitious Sammy was, that it carries the number 13.

who drive racing cars have usually amassed plenty of exciting experiences, even if they do not always have the luck the godlets gave me. As to the boat race, I had always been interested in the sea, chiefly, I admit, when I could sail, but I had had considerable experience of power-driven boats. So when Percy Pritchard of Birmingham asked me to handle one of his Birmal hydroplane boats in a Royal Motor Yacht Club race, I agreed at once and forthwith spent every possible moment piloting power boats so as to make sure I knew when they were dangerous and when they only seemed to be. The sea is not the nice soft thing so many people appear to imagine, but tricky, even wicked, and needs to be watched every moment. Pritchard and I were to drive two Birmal boats in a six-hour race at Poole, my boat being named *Berylla 2*. It was naturally understood that Pritchard was to win if all went well for us.

The start was sensational, a mass of boats in very close company, streaking at high speed from one marker buoy to another on a not too smooth sea. I could not see a thing owing to the

clouds of spray from the boat ahead and those along aside; *Berylla* felt as though she was leaping from rock to rock. Turning a marker buoy generated even more spray, most of which came into the boat, keeping one working at the steering for dear life and wondering when all of us would turn over. Just when I thought this simply cannot last, someone will hit someone else for sure, the boat ahead went wild and I got past, leaving it in my wake. It was all thoroughly enjoyable and, as you may imagine, utterly unlike driving a fast car.

After some twenty laps of the course I began to look for Pritchard who, I assumed, as he was a more experienced pilot, was well ahead somewhere on the triangular course. Nary a sign of him could I see, though his boat might be in the cloud of spray behind. *Berylla* seemed joyously alive and we gained on each turn, though my inside was protesting about the shocking bangs it was getting and my testicles felt as if they might shake off any moment. Well, it was presently apparent that *Berylla* was leading, and as the next boat was some distance astern I slowed down hoping to find Pritchard and let him take over. But at slower speed the boat banged about even more, so I had to go back to full speed, which resulted in *Berylla* winning the race because Pritchard's craft had been hemmed in by a jostling crowd of rivals and he could not get free. Awkward of course when the owner wants to win and you had said you would give way to him, but there you are, the godlets decided otherwise. Pritchard was certainly disappointed, but he very sportingly refused to blame me in the least.

While on the subject of boats, two incidents in my career on water still stand out. In one we were in a big wherry on the Broads watching a small lug-sailed dinghy nearby, when one of those sudden storms which afflict the Broads arrived. In the hurly-burly of dropping the sail-peak and spilling the wind out of the sail, we did not notice the dinghy going at an alarming speed before the gale. The unfortunate occu-pant had tied the main sheet with one of those knots nothing could undo instantly and the dinghy hit the shore, went right up and was last seen travel-ling at speed in amongst the bushes, undergrowth and trees.

On another occasion we were making Potter Heigham bridge with a view to going under it with the wherry. The navigator had been asked if the water level would allow the boat to go under the bridge and had said yes after studying the tide tables. Our approach was impeccable, we took sail off just at the right moment, took the mast down, started the auxiliary engine, stopped it when the wherry had enough way on it to "coast", and then steered for the bridge centre. From that moment on we could neither slow nor stop. Exactly at that moment the navigator came on deck to announce, "I say, I'm sorry but those were the year before last's tide tables." We got under the bridge with two inches clearance.

"...the most effective and devastating method of removing Shelsley's mud from one's tyres..."

Chapter Ten

Another Kind of Adventure

During all this time car racing was frequent and exciting, but there was plenty of other interest, apart from my normal daily job at Iliffe: the rally to Monte Carlo for example. In my time this was totally different from the Monte of today, a change due entirely to the very different financial circumstances. In the old days the rally was true to its title in that it was a mighty good gamble. The regulations of the organisers designated certain starting points, as widely spaced as possible, the details of which reached intended competitors months before the rally. You had to choose between such places as Stavanger, Norway; Umea, Sweden; Belgrade, Yugoslavia; Athens or John o'Groats. Once the choice was made it could not be altered. During the pleasant months of the year it was beyond human ingenuity to forecast what the weather might be like at any one of these starting points in winter. Experience proved that John o'Groats might be snowed up when Umea in Sweden was snow-free and the Swedish roads not

even iced. The whole point was that the competitor who arrived at the finish within the scheduled time limit, but from the furthest distance, would win, so you had to gamble on the weather.

We usually chose John o'Groats or Umea as starting point, chiefly because the firm whose car we drove considered expense important. Since few people got through from Athens you could not say they were wrong. Mind you, much prestige could be gained if the car simply finished without losing any marks for being late anywhere *en route*. Chance, you see, chose the final victor, since all the cars arriving punctually from the most distant starting place were sorted out by a speed test over the local mountains; that seemed out of character for a "touring" rally intended for quite normal cars. That Monaco put a premium on the number of passengers carried was amusing, it being all too obvious that they were thinking in terms of hotel bills in the principality! Earlier still, by the way, the cars had only to drive to Monte from Paris or some such place, then take part in a

Monte Carlo Rally 1935. Sammy Davis and Charles Brackenbury tower over the diminutive Kay Petre beside their Railton. They had an eventful trip to the Principality from the Baltic coast of northern Sweden.

decorated car competition complete with a battle of flowers, since this ensured all the starters properly finished, but that was before the First World War.

In my time the thing which particularly attracted British manufacturers was a special prize given to the vehicle which was judged to be the most comfortable and best equipped for its journey, provided it had lost no marks *en route*. You can see at once the value of an advertisement which stated that the "So and So" had been given the prize. As time went on the rally became more difficult. In the first of these events in 1911 the cars could be driven almost direct to Monte Carlo from the nearest capital cities, but it must be remembered that the cars of that period were anything but reliable, especially for a long run in severe winter conditions. It was quite easy to select the winner since most, if not all but one of the competitors, would be late at some control. Therefore the number of passengers carried, the comfort and mechanical state of the

cars, added to the distance they had run, made it easy to find a winner. As vehicles improved and competitors acquired experience, the conditions had to be made more severe. Anton Noghes, that most friendly and accomplished organiser, personal friend of all competitors, counteracted all the little tricks we developed by suitable regulations. Two runs I had are characteristic of the whole.

In 1935, with an open four-seater Railton, of all things to drive in a bitter winter, Kay Petre, Charles Brackenbury and I started from Umea. That Kay was included astonished most people, Charles yes, for he was known as exceedingly tough. But Kay, though small, decorative and amusing, could, I knew, stand hours of driving, had lapped Brooklands at 130mph[1] and had the tenacity of a small cinnamon bear; attributes the more unlikely since she could assume an air of extreme fragility. We had an idea we would learn something about winter driving, and we did.

---

1. In a 12-cylinder 10.5-litre Delage.

Unditching gear in action. Moving the lever backwards, then forwards, causes it to travel along the chain, pulling the cable with it. The chain is secured to a tree, the cable to the ditched car

A close-up of the special clamp that holds the cable firmly wherever it is required

The ground anchor to which the chain can be secured if there is no tree available

The enormous advantage of having a member of the crew who was both feminine and ornamental was apparent at once. Whenever we wanted anything we sent Kay to get it. None of us could speak Swedish yet not only did Kay succeed every time but was generally accompanied back to the car by a salesman bearing a parcel. Then at Umea before the start there was a dance and, everybody being in wild spirits, it was a great success, with Kay being in constant demand. To a pleasant Swedish youth who came politely to ask for her as a partner, Charles said on the spur of the moment, "That'll cost you a Krona, my lad". Said in jest, it caught on, but Kay's fury took a lot of appeasing when she found out we were making money hand over fist!

There was some fun too with the gear we used for extracting vehicles from ditches, a Swedish contraption consisting of a cable to secure to the car, a chain to put round the nearest tree, and a lever and claws which could be made to ratchet along the chain pulling the cable with it and thus the car. This most ingenious device was light and efficient but you had to know how it worked. To make sure it did, a feminine crew put their car in a shallow ditch with the brake on and a small tree trunk placed in front of the forward wheels for good measure. Then they connected the unditching gear and started ratcheting. They worked for some time before they realised that the tree selected was not

The Swedish vehicle unditching contraption, which obviously appealed to Sammy's sense of humour and was used in various sketches.

– – – that whenever the unditching gear works properly it brings the tree to the car. And as a preliminary – – –

". . . indulged in the practical criticism of missile weapons when the unditching process did not go according to plan."

Monte Carlo 1931. Winner of the Grand Prix d'Honneur for the best equipped and most comfortable car was this works-prepared Armstrong Siddeley. The drivers were Stafford on the left, Whitlock on the right, and Sammy Davis posing with his wife Rosamund in the middle.

up to the job; the car hadn't moved but the tree had.

We started before an immense and enthusiastic crowd while snow fell heavily, which made the run to Stockholm exceedingly dicey as we had to catch a small ice-breaker ferry, to miss which entailed a wait of half an hour on the wrong side of a river. We could not use chains because they would not stand the speed, so we learned how to handle a car on pure ice or deep snow very quickly indeed. We kept to schedule and caught the small ferry and went over to Denmark on a monstrous big ferry carrying passenger trains for good measure. The snow fell faster, the dazzling white specks made worse by the headlight beams having an hypnotic effect difficult to resist. Kay was driving and we were only just on schedule owing to the ferries and snow and suchlike difficulties. Our estimated time of arrival in Copenhagen was satisfactory, even allowing for the very dark night and the snow. Quite suddenly a car came fast out of a side turning in a village straight across our path — it did

not even have its sidelights on. How Kay avoided a terrific crash was a miracle. To brake was impossible on that snow-covered ice, so she steered hard left, controlling the slide. We hit the other car's overhanging luggage-carrier, spun and stopped.

Inspection revealed one crumpled front mudguard, the right side head-lamp pulped, and worst of all, the front wheels out of track. Somehow or other we got to Copenhagen on time, worked furiously at a garage, then drove fast until we reached another garage for more repairs, and so on, effecting repairs by instalments. We even re-aligned the front wheels, though there was no time to do that job thoroughly. Only when we reached Paris was the car made reasonably handleable; up to that point each of us prayed hard when our driving spell arrived. That made the drive through Hamburg and Hanover on the way to Paris quite exciting, including another near disaster narrowly avoided. With rally expert Donald Healey, we had taken a little-known ferry across a Danish strip of

The 1937 Monte Carlo Rally and the Wolseley which won the Concours de Confort prize. Sammy Davis with navigator George Hill studying their average speed clock.

Close-up of the average speed clock fitted to the Wolseley.

water called the Lille-Baelt instead of going round much further by land. That meant we arrived at an unearthly hour when no cars could be expected. There was a nasty mist and as we drove off we heard a locomotive whistle. Consulting the map we found a level crossing without gates was ahead. The trouble was to make sure where that train was relative to this crossing and ourselves. Our luck held and we got over just before the train. Poor Healey hit it hard, the whole front of his car being wrecked, though neither he nor his crew were seriously hurt.

When we reached Lyon we learned-what had happened on other routes. No one had arrived from Athens, though we heard later that the indomitable Tommy Wisdom and his co-driver, de Belleroche, had dug through drift after drift until they encountered one over a mile in length. Even then they did not give up until they were utterly exhausted and hours late. Rupert Riley's car had skidded over the side of a mountain into a rock which saved the crew. Madame Mareuse had had a head-on collision with another car which was on the wrong side of the road. The Bucharest contingent had not arrived as the roads proved impassable, but the Tallin, Estonia, cars had, though every inch of that route would be called impassable by normal motorists.

We had our fair share of troubles. Firstly we had been unable to gain enough time to have a good sleep away from the car, and cat-naps in it were no substitute. Then Charles was too tired to drive further with any safety, so he had to be packed away with rugs in the back of the car. Kay and I had to reduce our driving spells from three hours to one, each of us sleeping while the other drove. There was no need to navigate once we were on Route National 7, which we both knew intimately. Ability to sleep soundly for an hour while someone else is driving the car fast is an art we both possessed. The last night of the rally is very tiring indeed, and odd things happen when you are very tired. For instance, I suddenly saw in the headlamp beams a haystack walking down the middle of the most famous of French roads in the depths of the night. For a second I was convinced it was the usual illusion caused by extreme fatigue; then we had a phenomenal avoidance because it was a haystack. Some farm-hand, who should have been seen by a psychologist, had put a small haystack on a bullock cart at that unearthly hour for transport somewhere. The hay or straw or whatever it was came right down to the road so nothing could be seen of the cart, or its driver, or the bullock. It had no lights because they would have been dangerous with that load. We decided after that shattering experience to stop and go to sleep at the side of the road for ten minutes, which made a good deal of difference, odd as that may seem.

So at last we came to the warm dawn and Monte Carlo. Charles and I, unshaven wrecks, felt awful, but Kay looked as fresh as ever after a few minutes skilled work with lipstick and comb. We did not win the rally, though, because the final test involved manoeuvring round a figure of eight course which our disarranged steering geometry made impossible at speed. Twenty-four hours after the finale you should have seen Kay, Dior costume, stiletto heels and all; you would have never believed she could have driven so magnificently for all those hours. Where the rally ends and the festivities after it begin is a tale of its own.

In 1937 we tackled the same rally in very different conditions. The crew were George Hill and Alan Hunt, the car a big Wolseley, and our brief was to take the prize for the most comfortable and best equipped product in the rally. To this end the Wolseley had a wash basin, with hot water, soap and towels, a rear seat which could be made into a comfortable bed, a folding table for meals with cups, plates, saucers, food containers, a good heater, extra lights

"Our attire was not quite of the kind you associate with a saloon car even in winter". And to think the car had a heater! The Wolseley on the 1937 Monte Carlo, at Paris.

In this picture are a variety of rally awards. Sammy took particular pride in his Monte Carlo finisher's rally bars. Top row, three silver ashtrays with inset emblems; 2nd row, seven Monte Carlo pendants; 3rd row, five Brighton Run "finishers medals"; 4th row, Monte Carlo plaque 1930, RAC Hastings Rally 193- (?), Monte Carlo plaque 1931; 5th row, 5 plaques - RAC Bournemouth rally 1934, RAC (illegible), RAC London, Brighton and Torquay (illegible) 1939(?), RAC Hastings rally March 1937, RAC Eastbourne rally 1935; 6th row, Monte Carlo plaque 1934, 7 rally bars 1930-1956(?), Overseas Entrants' Section - GB starter, 3 bars 1930, '31 and '34, Monte Carlo plaque 1935.

everywhere and special screen wipers. There was much more room for luggage, extra fuel, a second battery and a radio. The wiring was also rearranged so that any cable could be easily replaced, each having its own fuse. All spares were carried in special boxes, each item being labelled, and there was full-scale provision for the navigator and his maps.

From Umea we faced 2,300 miles through Sweden, Norway, Germany, Holland, Belgium and France to Monaco, most of it in bad weather and snow aplenty. It was a great success.

First of all we slept, ate, and were very comfortable off-duty while the car continued at speed. We were all a little nervous because the Danes had announced that the rally entrants would be escorted by police through Denmark, and that might cause much loss of time against schedule. But when we got to the frontier we were all marshalled in a line and then a large open Mercedes full of police arrived. We were led off at an ungodly speed right through the country, averaging far more than we would ever have dared to do on our own. Hamburg control was

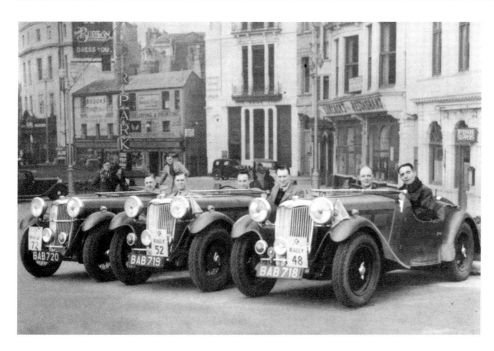

RAC Hastings rally, March 1937. The Singer team with Sammy as passenger in car no. 48.

unpleasantly full of richly uniformed officials with daggers and parabellums[1], one particularly nasty type being extremely rude and very drunk; but the offence was redressed by an excellent motorcycle "pilot" who took us out of the city.

Venlo control had been enlivened by meeting a Norwegian competitor, Countess Blixen-Finecke, who had a large, happy co-driver, a girl, who was christened the Lioness on account of her mane of blonde hair. Their navigation was odd in that when the Countess wanted to note the time, she leaned over her companion, pulled the cord round her neck and raised a huge watch from somewhere near her bra, looked at it and then calmly lowered it back to its place. We finished that rally fit as fiddles and not even tired or with the appearance of having driven all those miles in winter. So it is pleasant to record that the car won the coveted trophy easily.

I drove in seven Montes in all and had innumerable adventures in each.

Everyone else in this game had similar experiences. One novice navigator found France puzzling on his first trip until it was discovered that he thought the "slow down" notice at the entry to each village was its name, and therefore was curious as to why so many villages were called *Ralentir*. On another occasion we needed sleep urgently, sleep in bed by preference, and we had enough time in hand for it. The only place we could find in the next town which offered a bed seemed a mite odd. All the same we slept the sleep of the just for an hour.

A feminine crew came with us and when we went to rouse them a knock elicited two shrill shrieks. It then appeared that they had had the same suspicions as us, and so sat back to back on the bed all the time in order to watch both doors. That we were charged as persons who had "brought their own girl friends" was a bit annoying, but the amount was mighty small for all that; anyhow the red light should have been on.

Loukia Pappou, on her way from

---

1. Luger pistols.

Guest of Honour at the Veteran Car Club's annual dinner at the conclusion of the 1937 London to Brighton Run was Jean Batten CBE, the distinguished New Zealand aviatrix. In 1934 and 1935 she had flown solo from England to Australia and back, the first woman to do so. Here she is obviously enjoying Sammy's company aboard "Beelzebub". It is thought she did not actually travel on the Run.

Athens one time, had struggled through mud and fog on bad roads for six hours, then found her male co-driver had passed out with fatigue. She shook him awake by the hair but he passed out again, so she shot him out onto the road miles from anywhere and went vigorously on by herself. A chambermaid once came screeching with hysteric fright from Tommy Wisdom's room when she took him coffee and rolls. It seems that Tommy was wedged in the wardrobe changing films in his press camera; all the chambermaid saw

Another aviatrix, Amy Johnson CBE, on an RAC rally in 1938, standing with Sammy Davis on her left. On the left is W G McMinnies of Morgan fame who won the French Cyclecar GP in 1913.

being a wardrobe apparently rocking about, growling oaths the while. In Norway, avoiding an out-of-control sledge, Kay and her partner hit the only boundary stone in the country, hidden under the snow, and that bent their Riley's front axle. After frantically walking for miles and banging on cottage doors, they got help and somehow got going again, though none of the helpers could speak English. At the next control mechanics actually succeeded in substituting a Ford front axle for the Riley's and the car finished[1].

Celebrations were always the high spot after the finish. For example, Dorothy Stanley Turner was late on parade for the procession of the cars which had reached Monte, a procession much fancied by the organisers[2]. Forthwith we assembled a court martial, and after appearing to hear the evidence in the form of excuses, sentenced Dorothy to sing six verses of "One More River to Cross" at midnight outside the Casino. Duly escorted by her friends and looking very much like an ornamental feminine slave being led to the arena on a rope, Dorothy sang as ordered, to the immense amusement of Monte's million-aire gambling spectators. We all had hysterics, including the victim, so all the verses were not audible, but she did damned well for all that. Incidentally, the "judges" had thought of ordering her to appear in a shift but no one could find that form of garment in time.

In a way the "Alpine" trial part of the rally was still more trying for the mechanism of a car, since it entailed timed climbs up all the well-known passes in the Alps, with most of the mechanism of the vehicle being officially sealed before the start to ensure it was not changed. A great deal usually wanted changing, so ingenuity was at a premium. Usually, that car-killer the Stelvio Pass eliminated a third of the entry and Alpine storms created an unforeseen hazard. The heights reached played hell with the fuel feed system, so taking it all together we never had a dull moment.

The signs on the political horizon were becoming more and more ominous as we passed 1938, until it was obvious to those of us who had survived 1914-18 that we were in for a return match with the Germans, damned stupid as that seemed.

" . . rne of the subsidiary horrors of the Monte Carlo Rally . . "

"One of the subsidiary horrors of the Monte Carlo Rally", or "You will of course suffer greatly crossing the narrow seas in winter. You will discover, too " (leading to another sketch). This is an instance where Sammy sometimes made use of alternative wording to describe the same scene. In this case the first description probably appeared in The Autocar and the second in More Sketches by Casque.

---

1. 1933 Rally. Sadly the car did not finish and Kay was taken ill. See *Rallies & Trials* p49, Bibliography.
2. This was the 1939 rally.

Chapter Eleven

A Very Different War

As 1939 grew older I knew war was coming. The trouble was to see how I could get into it. The Navy now knew my real age, so did the RAF – only the army remained. But first I became an air-raid warden as something to do if I could not convince the forces to accept me. Months of uncertainty continued and it was an exasperating experience. No one on my beat in Walton-on-Thames would take the thing seriously. I tried to interest them in the simpler preparations such as air-raid shelters, fire precautions, food stores and the like. They were extremely polite and friendly but they did not do anything, the general idea being that the "professionals" would look after everything. Professionals my foot, there were not enough of us to do even the easier jobs. Occasionally a visit to make sure how many people were likely to be in any house, how many were invalids or crippled and how many could contrive shelters easily generated bad tempers born of latent fright. However, we persevered and I have vivid memories of cycling like

mad with tin helmet, respirator, haversack and all the rest of the uniform equipment, whistle and rattle included, to the warden's post expecting war any moment and knowing for certain it would be nasty. I knew my bomber crews well, so felt Walton was just the place which a harassed crew might use for a target they could afterwards claim was London. I had, you see, a mighty poor opinion of bombing accuracy. I constructed a really beautiful dugout for the family which immediately filled with water, so I had a professional brick building made in its place.

On 29th July 1933 Rosamund had presented me with a small but vigorous son, Colin Charles Houghton, and for that I am extremely grateful to her. She had suffered several previous miscarriages, and this made me feel even more nervous about the result this time, though Rosamund faced it with courage. Proud as I was of this small person, his birth had worried me badly, for some unpleasant trouble had made the delivery difficult and I cannot bear hurting anyone feminine, least of all a wife. In the end the baby came into the world as a result of a Caesarean operation, and grew apace. Colin is a son of whom I am exceedingly proud, and he is a friend as well, which is not too common. Before he was of any real age, Kay Petre was terrified by him balancing on one leg upon the arm of a chair on which she was sitting. Her verdict that, "This son of yours has no appreciation of danger" summed up her feelings. Later still, his fearlessness was even more apparent during the enthusiastic cycling phase of his life. From the start I am pleased to record his road sense was good, even allowing for the vigour of this enterprise.

Though for some time Rosamund and I were happy, our marriage did not last. Whilst she did everything she could to make it work, the trouble was that she knew too little about the world, whilst I knew too much. In wartime one is a different person in almost every way in contrast with one's peacetime personality. It was my fault, but I could not live the kind of life expected, so we never quite made a real home of our own. Gradually our association became more that of a brother and sister, and worrying, since Rosamund was very ill indeed at times, although thank heaven she recovered. So it had to end. The one thing I find wonderful is that we can still meet happily, and that she seems contented and at peace, leaving only the pleasant memories. My regret is that I should have ruined part of her life, without ever intending to do so for one moment.

During all these years life had changed considerably of course, just as it always does. My beloved mother died, the shock to me being all the worse because I was not given the news, therefore walked into her bedroom and found her there, looking fragile and peaceful, but dead. Emmie Kate had returned from the States but,

alas, did not altogether agree with my wife, and as I recorded before, all my early friends were dead as well. True there were new friends with whom I had adventures, quite as good as those of the early days, but losing any friends leaves a gap which cannot be filled.

For the moment life was inexorably controlled by events not of one's own choosing. Fortune was with us in that the delay before the war started proved invaluable for training, planning and preparing for what was now certain to come. When at last it came I had wangled into the reserve, not by telling untruths but by not telling the entire truth. Once more, though, the idea that I might have a combatant role was met with polite but firm suggestions that I would be of much better value on the engineering side of the Army. So I found myself an Ordnance Mechanical Engineer at Tidworth workshops in next to no time; it was all highly interesting. I won't say the shops struck me as running on modern lines, but I soon learned that Ordnance had to repair anything and everything, so it was not a matter of planning a good production system. With the aid of an excellent man, Tindall, and his subordinate, Penny, we did however modernise the repair of Ford engines in a more satisfactory manner.

No sooner had I settled down to the routine than the inevitable upheaval occurred. The OME side of Ordnance was converted into a separate corps – the Royal Electrical & Mechanical Engineers, or REME. That it was right is beyond question, yet any drastic change in an army unit invariably produces momentary inefficiency plus considerable "fed-up-ness" and some juggling for high position. When it was over we really got down to work with enthusiasm. In this a regular soldier, Lt. Col. Apps, and a temporary soldier, Lt. Col. Collingwood, both to become great friends of mine, energetically assisted. We had our moments of course, including the time when some Australians being attached to us lost their complete and vastly expensive tool kits almost as soon as they arrived. Deeply suspicious because I had never known the 1914 Aussies to lose anything, but often to acquire much, I thought this might be some financial gain transaction, only to be amazed at finding that the tools really had been removed by quite ordinary Britons. Later there was a question of sheep disappearing, which might have had something to do with our colonial cousins, but as half a carcass, with many pairs of Army plimsolls added, was discovered early one morning piled in front of the door of a civilian fitter, the affair had not the professional finish I expected. Then the Ordnance section had to employ women, and very enthusiastic they were too, but naturally not fully conversant with vehicle or gun parts. True they were taken round and shown what was in the store bins together with the label thereof, but it happened that the bin which should have held Ford crankshafts contained only the V-shaped wooden retaining blocks for them. With exact logic the girl issued these for every indent for Ford cranks.

Naturally the prospect of an air-raid loomed large, Tidworth being a nice big blob on the map such as any half-witted German navigator could recognise. So we had a group of machine guns on the roof, manned when necessary by most enthusiastic Home Guards from the works personnel. Unfortunately, while I was there we only had two raids and in each the blighters would not come near enough but jettisoned their bombs happily in the surrounding countryside. Never have I heard such beautiful language from any other gun crews. This had a sequel in that it suddenly appeared we were responsible for removing any unexploded missiles, a job I cannot say I found popular.

All this was followed by a move distinctly in the right direction, for Col. Collingwood took me with him to the Ashford workshops in Kent which was a real REME show from the start and was also much nearer to the war. There we had quite a few nice raids, in one of which a Messerschmitt decided to fly low beneath the top of a tower on which was a Home Guard. Without hesitation the latter threw empty bottles of beer at the machine, and it would have been magnificent if only he had brought it down. Much of our activities concerned tanks, with which we never had a dull moment. The driving of a tank whose controls one did not know from the station to the works on the blackest night ever, testing the finished product and without lights, was full of fun. On one occasion the cheerful chief tester Dick Kinchin and I took a Covenanter out for a final test. The governor was put out of action so we had a lively maximum on a very temperamental tank. All went well until we started down a nice slope with fast S bend after fast S bend. Exactly at the wrong moment all the compressed air on which the machine depended for steering and brakes vanished. Dick and I took one look at each other then disappeared inside the armour and shut the lid for good measure. One happy thing about a tank is that you are more likely to hurt than be hurt if the tons of metal get out of control, and there was nothing I could do with the steering or brakes to slow the machine, much less stop it. We felt the bump as the tank went off the road over the grass verge, another much worse bump as it carved its way through a bank and hedge, more sundry bangs and bumps as we ricocheted off such trees as we could not destroy, then a quiet peaceful run,

B. & W. Fisk-Moore   Canterbury

Back Row—PRESTON, CHAPMAN, PEARCE, LAW, KIRKBY, HORRIDGE.
Sitting—GAYAH, ALLEWAY, TAYLOR, MAJOR DAVIS, MENZIES, TOCHER, PELLOWE.

obviously on very nice ground, and finally a stop. Dick was jut about to open the lid when he paused to listen. It seemed to both of us that someone who was not quite happy was talking hard outside. We were on the cherished tennis court of a retired Indian Army Colonel and he was furious.

Air-raids became common as time went on, the result being that every single person in the works seemed to have acquired some weapon, not excluding the civilian artificers, just as an example of how stupid it is to annoy

Major Davis seated amidst his men of the 53rd Infantry Troops Workshop, REME. On his left is Sgt Major Menzies, who was in charge of the instrument shop. On his right is ASM J Bramwell Taylor, who wrote to the Veteran Car Club at the time of Sammy's death. He said, "...we respected him for his intimate approach to his Warrant Officers and men alike, and loved him for his eccentricities and dogged spirit. Having broken most bones in his body did not prevent him from limping along on route marches. His life in the field was spartan, a hiker's tent being his only abode, although, I may add, beautifully arrayed with his personal flags. Many a man became an expert marksman under his tuition". Sammy was later mentioned in despatches.

the ordinary Britons, particularly during their tea break. This was dangerous of course, but not half as dangerous as some buddies of mine were in the local Home Guard. Nearly all of them survivors from the '14 war, these elderly stalwarts thoroughly enjoyed themselves, hiding booby traps, fougasses and mines all over the place. All of them were operational so it was essential to tread warily when out for a stroll.

One fine day I was allowed another step towards the desired goal; I was given a mobile workshop intended for France. With exceeding joy I set about moulding that unit the way I wanted, including in the tariff as much shooting as possible and what the unit regarded as near hell, shaped as a six miles in the hour march with full equipment, just to show that we oldsters were as good as anyone. But when the moment came at last to go to France with 12 Corps, an unexpected snag cropped up. A chit of a girl who was an RAMC doctor spent an hour or so checking my chassis with unusual care, then said there was nothing wrong with it – I was quite remarkably fit. But all the same, she did not think I ought to go to the war considering my age – damn it, she was thinking of my official age and not the real one [around 57!]. I was livid and rode my specially tuned twin-cylinder motorcycle furiously to Corps HQ, skidded it around with plenty of noise on their gravel path and demanded the Principal Medical Officer. Inwardly amused, that worthy repeated the examination of my bits and pieces, enquired the origin of a good many scars, gave me a cup of tea and said I was fit. Afterwards he sent a report which in effect meant, "This officer is absolutely convinced he is completely fit or is quite mad. I have examined him with care and find he is genuinely fit". And so we went to the war.

Preparatory exercises as part of the

Corps were fun. We practiced the intricacies of landing on a beach in Dorset, complicated by pouring rain. We had to sleep out and, having made sure the men had some kind of shelter, I was left with the prospect of getting myself very wet. Earnest search of the neighbourhood discovered some Rolls-Royce type pigsties, walled with white tiles and even provided with electric light, though that was not operating. I spent a very comfortable dry night in that sty and I often wonder what the owner would have thought had he known. Then, just before we embarked, there was a pleasant incident. Suddenly, in the middle of the night, there appeared the one thing we had prayed for, namely an aircraft flying very low and quite straight. Every gun we had opened fire, supported by most of the rifles, and every unit nearby joined in. I thoroughly enjoyed myself with a machine gun, firing tracer, except when a very hot empty cartridge fell down the neck of my pyjamas. The aircraft, hit by anti-aircraft fire, exploded, but we found out a little later that it was one of the first V1 flying bombs.

For the rest, the sojourn in France was immensely satisfactory. This was quite different from the '14 war; we were constantly on the move and there were no damned trenches. The populace threw fruit and flowers at us as we advanced and it was all like a Henty war story, just as I had read when very young. Moreover, moving on all the time was like exploring a forest containing dangerous animals liable to pounce at any moment. This was excellent education since there was no defined front line and Germans cropped up anywhere at any moment. During that run through Holland to Arnhem, German troops seemed to be both sides of us, the allies being in a narrow strip.

Anything might happen and a "recce"

of future positions for the workshop sometimes involved a little long-range shooting. I had some fun as a result of the battle to wipe out a pocket of Germans which was almost enclosed in the Falaise gap. The American armour then made a fast, wide sweep forward, liberating Le Mans in the process. I was allowed to go there in my jeep with Sgt. Propert and Cpl. Cooper for company, and it was a joyous adventure. We were armed to the teeth and had to proceed warily every kilometre of the way. Sometimes a notice stated that the road and verges were clear, sometimes that they had not been searched for mines, plenty of which were about, as we discovered when we nearly backed onto the pressure plate of one. We knew all about high explosives, formed to resemble cowpats by the way, and that did not ease the journey either. We arrived at Le Mans to receive a terrific welcome. My great friend Berthie was immensely pleased and entirely astonished at this unexpected arrival of a driver armed to the teeth; so off we went to the principal café in the square. The floor there had been removed in part to get at hidden stores of excellent wine, with which we celebrated in company with all and sundry. Another driver, the giant Hémery, arrived laden with pistols and quantities of ammunition to add to the fun. It was a very great moment, so great and so exciting that when we left we deliberately travelled by a route running across the Falaise gap, quite prepared to tackle the entire German army But the godlets looked after us, the Germans having surrendered the day before – or what was left of them.

A funny incident resulted from a signal asking us to get a roll-top desk for HQ, giving a map grid reference for a suitable one. What was not stated was that the house containing the desk had been a Luftwaffe HQ and was no

distance at all from a rather exciting scuffle going on between us and the Germans. My Sgt. Major and I took our jeep as near to the house as we could and then proceeded to get on with the job. We had to inspect every inch of the ground and every part of the house very carefully indeed, as we had a high opinion of German efficiency with booby traps. Naturally a camera on a mantelpiece was ignored as being too obvious, but the desk itself was suspect. So we attached a long wire to each drawer handle, went outside and pulled; nothing happened save that the drawers came out. Only the top drawer did not respond, all it did was open a little. I felt very carefully inside the drawer and, before I knew what was happening, I touched what seemed to be a trigger and there was a click which almost stopped my heart. With extreme care we felt about in the interior of that drawer only to suddenly realise that the suspect trigger served to release the roll-top of the desk. We then pulled the desk over by remote control, inspected it further and were able to carry it out at last. This reminded me of the German miniature tank.

At that time I had been transferred to the REME staff of 12 Corps and was out on a recce with a friend. We came

Major S C H Davis REME. (Royal Electrical & Mechanical Engineers) standing at the side of his jeep "Fifi". Naturally it was fast.

A tank transporter in Germany prior to crossing the Rhine.

how to make the thing innocuous. We volunteered to do this as though disarming booby traps was just another everyday job, but ruled that all the others must go right away in case the thing exploded. They did this willingly, whereupon we loaded the tank into the three-tonner and departed at speed.

The story that I tried to blow up my C.O., Col. Dick Girdlestone, is pure invention, and originated from the fact that one day when I was out with him I offered him some tobacco. We had just crossed a river on a most unsafe craft which the Sappers had made from anything handy and had powered with a stolen motorcycle engine. Now it happened that I used as a tobacco-pouch the bag intended to contain the charge for a 25-pounder gun. By pure chance Dick filled his pipe with tobacco from a low level in the bag where, unknown to me, some of the original cordite charge remained!

We advanced with vigour, the high spot of the whole affair being the crossing of the Rhine into Germany on the heels of their now disjointed army. Once in Germany, by the way, every house seemed to bear an immense white flag, while every German woman strongly asserted she had had no truck whatsoever with the Nazis; it was curious how unanimous this was. To me there was an obvious difference between the regular German Army, who fought darned well and behaved, as a whole, according to the book, and the over-uniformed, unpleasant Nazi units, who seemed to be just ordinary thugs with no opinion of their own regular troops. Finally we were right up on Lüneburg Heath close by Hamburg when the cease-fire sounded and the war was over. The curious effect was that all we wanted was to sleep and sleep and sleep.

Hamburg was very different from the city of Monte Carlo rally days. There did

across a miniature tank, beautifully camouflaged, a very peach of a toy to possess. The tank was actually meant to be loaded with explosives, then propelled and steered by electric power fed through long cables. The thing proved to be free from traps, but the trouble was we could not get it into the jeep, while to leave it meant another unit was sure to take it away. So we put one end of a piece of insulated signal wire through a hole in the tank's side armour, burying the other end in the ground in such fashion that the wire was particularly obvious, and then we left at full speed to collect a three-tonner. The ruse succeeded beyond our hopes, for when we returned the tank was still there, but all round it was a ring of soldiery thinking hard about not seem to be one single house which was not wrecked or cracked by bombs, albeit the fields for miles round were a sea of craters from near misses. My curious sense of humour was energised by the discovery that several of the submarine repair pens were still fully operational and untouched. We annexed the house belonging to the General commanding Hamburg, who was in the local "cooler", and did quite well for ourselves. One day the General, who belonged to an older, more aristocratic Germany, requested an interview. This we took to be a complaint about his conditions of imprisonment. Far from it, he wanted to hand someone the key of his personal wine cellar and gave the names of the wines he thought would suit us. Of course we had those wines tasted by a commandeered ex-member of the Wehrmacht – but they were not poisonous.

Then came the great day when all of us who were not regulars had to fill in the inevitable form giving particulars of ourselves from which the order of demobilisation could be compiled; for the life of me I could not remember what age I had given on my original papers, so I hazarded a guess. The guess was wrong and all hell broke loose. Informed tartly that I had no business to be there at all, I was returned from Germany to England with strict instructions to produce a birth certificate immediately. That was none too easy, for in the days when I was born birth registration was conducted on leisurely lines whenever anyone had the time and remembered to do it. So I had to search long before I could find the thing at Somerset House. When I found it I discovered the date and year of my birth differed from what my mother had told me. However, the powers that be had kittens when they saw it, though in sober fact there was nothing they could do about it. I had had my war just as I wanted, and though in the circumstances I did not expect any medals, I got them too. Subsequently I had trouble with the passport office, due I'm sure to liaison between one outraged civil service department and another.

One thing which stood out a mile about that war was that Montgomery was an inspiration, a general totally different from those of the '14 war, impish if you like, not given to following tradition, but a man who made one know we were going to win. I shall never forget his talk to our section of the Corps. We were drawn up in beautiful order as requisite when he arrived. Then he stood on the bonnet of a jeep and just beckoned to the men. Puzzled but intrigued, they broke ranks and gathered round him. When he had finished talking, every single man knew that we would win, though we should have to work like blazes and face every kind of hardship to earn the win – and I believed it implicitly too. What a change from scenes in that other war where generals on horseback with a retinue of aides, and attendants flying pennants, ambled about on main roads ignoring the fighting men around them.

While I was in Hamburg I came across a German general who spoke fluent English and found he could not understand why they had lost, though Hitler was an easy excuse, possibly justified. But he left me quite certain we would have a third, and in his opinion final round, in years to come.

Chapter Twelve

After the War

The aftermath of this war was not the same as that of the previous one. Friends had gone but nothing like so many. My French colleague Robert Benoist, driver in so many races, had been murdered at Buchenwald by the Nazis for working with the Maquis underground resistance. Others I had known at Brooklands had died in action with the RAF, but most of a generation had not disappeared in the way we remembered all too well. There was nothing for it save to carry on as vigorously as possible whatever might befall.

Much had changed, as it always does after a major war. The Autocar was organised in a less carefree way and news was important, far more so than before. Naturally this led to profound alterations. Harold Lafone retired and the HQ was now Dorset House, London, with Coventry taking second place as Harry Swindley had gone as well. In the background, but definitely in control, was Geoffrey Smith, a friend of mine from motorcycling days. Some day Geoffrey will receive the credit he

Casque by Casque

entirely deserves, for he introduced a drive and enthusiasm the paper had never had before. As always in such circumstances he was not popular with many, and perhaps he was more worried by this than circumstances justified. Consequently he tended to be on the defensive but, I repeat, he made the paper.

Then "high authority" did something strange, suddenly appointing a famous daily paper journalist of the older days as editor, thereby implying criticism which was undeserved. Unfortunately Massac Buist was not at his best and the result was near chaos; a motor paper like the venerable *Autocar* could not immediately be changed to run on daily newspaper lines, whatever one might hope. One thing Massac did which stuck was to do away with obscurity, insisting that every writing member of the staff put his name to what he wrote. It was speedily apparent that Massac was not well, and the fact showed plainly in what he wrote himself. So his reign soon terminated and Geoffrey was able at last to re-organise, with A A Appleby[1] as Editor. For some reason not quite clear to me I was appointed Sports Editor, though I never had any real editing to do at any time and continued to write a special section under the pen-name of "Casque", choosing this French term for a crash-helmet because I was one of the first, along with de Hane Segrave, to use one when racing[2].

They were good days though. Geoffrey himself took part in several Monte Carlo rallies, usually in company with another great friend of mine, A K Stevenson of the Scottish RAC, the two having much in common. Geoffrey enlivened the Monte considerably by playing on his ukelele, of which few would have thought him capable, while the car was running a frolic. I had one amusing experience with Geoffrey while he was editor. Gordon Crosby, the established *Autocar* artist since our days together in Coventry, had a care-free light-heartedness about expense sheets which drove other people to distraction. After one pre-war Paris motor show Geoffrey had asked me to look at Crosby's version of his expenses, which were decidedly extreme by any standard, so Crosby was summoned to explain things. Geoffrey recited each item and its cost, then asked our artist whether he did not think the amount far too high. Crosby laughed heartily, then replied, "You're a funny man", and departed. As Geoffrey said, "What can I do with a bloke like that?"

Taking it by and large, Iliffe had changed radically, but mostly for the better, even if the original family atmosphere was not quite so obvious. At all events, Arthur Bourne as editorial director got *The Autocar* back on the rails after the rather disturbing incident

of Massac Buist, and incidentally got very little credit for his pains.

It was curious how many of the men now concerned with cars had begun with motorcycles: Appleby, Arthur Bourne, who had been editor of *The Motorcycle*, and Geoffrey Smith who made the journal what it is; all of which was to the good. Provided you are enthusiastic, experience with motorcycles is the very root of car driving. At least one more of the friends of early days was now with the paper in the shape of Montague Tombs, having become Coventry editor after a spell with an aircraft paper, *The Aero*. He was doing well, having grown up with many elder statesmen in the industry and being also a personal friend to them.

We had a very bad blow when Gordon Crosby died in 1943 after a period of profound depression caused partly by the death of his son during the war, but mostly by the knowledge he had that dread disease, cancer. Since Monty, Crosby and I had been very close friends ever since we had started in the writing and painting business, both of us were depressed beyond measure at his death. At least, as there was so much work, we had

"Crosby," by Casque.

less time than ever to brood, and that was a godsend.

One result of the increased rush that affected our lives was that another friend, H S Linfield (later to become Editor), Monty and I tried to make the testing of new cars more accurate. Obviously you cannot get down to the full merit or demerit of a new design with runs lasting three days at most, since durability, reliability, plus efficiency are more important than speed and handling ability. Anyhow, we contrived a gadget to ensure that recorded speeds were reasonably accurate at all events, since speedometers were optimistic as a rule. Firstly, a specially calibrated electrically powered motor to supply a speedometer was mounted on a frame having one wheel of an effective diameter at a given tyre pressure known to the speedometer manufacturer. Then the whole thing was arranged to be towed behind any car, the speedometer itself being carried within the vehicle. We had great fun with this but it is doubtful whether some manufacturers were equally enthusiastic. In all, we must have tested almost every car made, acquiring interesting experience as a result, though the machines likely to develop serious trouble were now few and far between. It was a most interesting life as you will imagine, not least of the fun being that Linfield was extremely serious and equally thorough when car testing and furthermore was absolutely determined to attain first-class driving skills. Watching him develop these, which he did in full measure, was even more interesting than driving the actual cars. The old firm was still very avuncular, since it actually put up with my unconventional way of doing things, just as they had looked after me magnificently when I was in hospital.

So adventures continued. The most striking of these, because it was so

unusual, was the Rallye Gastronomique. As its name implies, this was a cheerful run around France from famous vineyard to famous vineyard in order to enjoy the best wines that could be produced, in circumstances unrivalled for hospitality. Naturally my great friend Charles Faroux was the organiser of the whole affair under the Club des Sans Club, aided by the Automobile Club de l'Ouest. I was a *Commissaire Sportif*, which translated into jockey language would be a steward. It was all magnificent, I had a Rolls-Royce-built Bentley, and another steward who was French as a companion. The evening before the run to the start at Dijon was spent at the Bar des Coureurs in Paris, where sooner or later you met everyone connected with racing. Wine tasting commenced early. On the way to Dijon we were thumbed by a youngster in an unfamiliar air force uniform who turned out to have come from Holland entirely by begging lifts. What a Dutch airman in full uniform was doing in France in peacetime we never discovered.

Being a shade early as befits a Bentley able to average 50mph, we sat in the centre of Dijon watching the world go by. First arrived a gaggle of youngsters, two youths and two girls on bicycles, all in shorts and wearing heavy pullovers inscribed with the name of a cycling club. It was a scorching hot day and they were British of course. They were succeeded by a group of bronzed girls on bicycles, loaded to the brim with tents, cooking gear and baggage, wearing much shorter shorts (before the mini skirt by the way), and they were French of course. There followed an ancient Austin with a GB plate which circulated the wrong way round the square to the shrill whistling of outraged Agents of Police. Afterwards came a spidery contraption swerving about erratically, carrying a mass of baggage and being pedalled with phlegmatic vigour by a Frenchman and his wife. All this, with the usual colourful crowd of strollers and a really jolly woman artist painting hard while exchanging rapier-like quips with all and sundry. It was so good to watch that we eventually reported our arrival with some reluctance.

At the château of one vineyard we were all decorated with neck ribbons holding inscribed corkscrews, after which we had the meal of a lifetime at the Hospice de Beaune by candlelight, the priceless tapestries on the walls glowing with colour as the candles flickered. A vineyard choir sang the traditional songs of ancient France; this was an old masters' painting come to life. Mouton Rothschild showed us letters from kings and mile upon mile of dark cellars. Château d'Yquem gave us lunch enlivened by a wine judging competition and a most interesting talk about the part English kings of French descent played in the history of Bordeaux. In that city the youngest general in the French army gave a reception, making everyone feel that it was for him alone. In an ancient dark room we had another feast by candle-light while a whole ox roasted on a spit nearby. The high spot of that evening was a wine tasting and judging, in which an English woman tied with a female French expert, to the consterna-tion of the organisers. The problem was solved only by each taking one glass more; the English girl merely said she did not like the wine and the French woman announced it was corked, so she won. The Automobile Club de l'Ouest gave us champagne, as did mayors in various cities and even villages. We were taken over Henry the Second of England's castle and as a finale to the rally were introduced to the initiation ceremony of the *Compagnons du Sacavin* at Angers, with bottled wine lying in the streams

running across the floor of a cavern. Initiates were required to rap three times on the head of a huge cask, then recite appropriate verses from Rabelais, with one hand extended over a bowl of wine which must then be finished in one draught to the joyful music of trum-pets. An investiture followed with a miniature wine barrel attached to a ribbon and an admonishment to "Forswear milk, lemonade and the like but to drink only the best of wine".

The grim end of Henri of Guise seemed the more real from having visited the scene of the assassination in the Château of Blois. The ducal owner of the Château de Brissac, rather bored with the huge collection of historic weapons and armour on the walls, made my day by remarking, "Oh, those, if you want their story ask the visitors, they know far more about them than I do". But he relented later to tell me that when he and his sisters were very young, they used to play hide-and-seek dressed in medieval armour. In the huge Château de Cheverny we had the final prize-giving, everyone receiving something. At the banquet, in full dress, we were greeted by huntsmen in uniform sounding traditional French hunting tunes on their long circular horns. We dined in a long gallery, every inch of its walls covered with boars' heads or antlers. It was a magnificent finale. The emphasis may seem to be laid on wine, and we did consume much more than usual, but not a single soul was affected adversely during the entire run because wine properly used in company with excellent food is innocuous. Mind you, each day's drive was very long, so everyone had plenty of fresh air and, counting the visits to historic châteaux, plenty of exercise; a great friend, Jo Ashfield, drove the whole distance without relief.

Gradually of course all the long-estab-lished races, trials and rallies came

An electric mantel clock presented to Sammy by the staff of The Autocar *on his retirement in 1950. The clock is still in working order.*

back, but the expense of competing was very much greater. New events were organised in such numbers that the national and international calendars became fantastically long and unduly complicated. Then it was not so very long after the war that my existence changed radically once more. I had arrived at the official age limit, so I retired with a pension and a really wonderful send-off from the firm I had been with for so long; a strange experience which left a slightly lost feeling, very difficult to define.

There was plenty to do as a freelance, what with articles and books, the only difficulty being that so many people wanted articles about new models of cars, and wanted them quickly. This was a problem to which I devoted much thought over the years. More and more did I believe that the things which really counted – freedom from trouble, availability of spares and service,

comfort and above all cost – were the factors on which new cars were chosen. Performance and speed in particular seemed to be of secondary importance. But most of these items could not be tested in a very limited time, while the news value of the description faded if the vehicle was not dealt with at once. The result too often was that maximum speed seemed almost the principal feature which was deemed to count, in fact glamourized and often exaggerated. After some of this, therefore, I decided to cut out car testing altogether.

There remained though the fascinating sideline of teaching novices to drive, though the novices selected were hand picked. There is nothing more interesting than to watch a novice gradually acquire confidence and commence to handle a car properly – properly, that is, as I saw it. No two persons are alike: some are overconfident, some have no confidence at all and some seem unable to think when first they take hold of a steering wheel. Quite a number of pupils were completely astonished that the initial instruction concentrated on passing the official test, omitting all else, while after the test was passed, then and only then would I admit they could now learn to drive. Not one percent had any genuine knowledge either of the Highway Code or the meaning of most of the signs. Most pupils were obviously dismayed to learn that a full knowledge of both was essential, with a good idea of the law governing motoring as well. All of that had not occurred to them; as they said, they "simply wanted to drive". The worst part of the whole thing was the first few runs, as there was no place where this operation could be carried out privately and a novice confronted by modern traffic density before he, or she, could handle the car could be very dangerous. Curiously enough the women were more efficient than the men. On at least one occasion a pupil who had not only mastered all the manoeuvres necessary to pass the test, and had learned the code almost by heart, seemed to lose all power of thinking and do extraordinarily stupid things when tackling the actual test — stage fright I suppose.

Worst of all, parents occasionally promised their offspring "a new car as soon as you have passed the test", but did not realise that the sort of car was a vital matter. There was a case when a novice passed the test with a Mini and was presented with a fast sports car, the resulting crash being fatal. In one amusing incident I could feel the pupil thinking, "This is all very well but my instructor has never passed the test himself so he can't know how it feels to do so". I therefore arranged to take the test myself. This was not quite as easy as it sounds as my application created intense suspicion that I wanted to write one of those pungently critical articles about examiners and official tests which annoy everyone concerned. The interviewer could not have been more polite or pleasant, but the doubt behind my host's mind was entirely obvious. There followed more fun in that the Chief Examiner himself was instructed to take me out and "not to talk to me save to give orders". Now I happened to be friendly with all the examiners, particularly the Chief, so after a start made as solemn as both of us could manage we talked all the rest of the time and took ten minutes off the test course record.

When the test was over, it being made as rigid as possible, we talked driving for quite some time, both of us being enthusiasts. Later on still, a journalist friend wanted to take the test for an article. It was arranged officially that his real name should not be disclosed to the examiners because he was a well-known writer who had been driving for years and years. Having asked the way

to the driving test HQ, a policeman noticed that he was alone in a vehicle with L plates. Further questioning elicited the fact that he was on the way to take the test. The result can be imagined because he could not produce his own licence or insurance certificate, so the "cooler" loomed large. Only after considerable delay did he manage to prove who he was, so all was well.

Then for a change I helped with a film taken mostly on Pendine sands, in which the much thwarted "hero" took the land speed record. The car used was John Cobb's Napier-Railton, made up with a long tail and other variations which made it a very good substitute for an actual land speed record car of the time. We naturally had differences of opinion relating to details, but on the whole the producer was unexpectedly reasonable. A light-hearted moment arose when I was asked to train the mechanics to make a really fast change of all four wheels. After telling them what I wanted done and how, I said, "Go". Never have I seen such chaos; spokes were knocked out of the car's wheels, only a miracle saved it from falling off the jacks, and one wheel was offered up to the hub the wrong way about. I then realised that the four men concerned were not real mechanics but extras, most convincingly got up to resemble them. They had never changed a wheel in their lives, but they learned.

The actor Nigel Patrick, who had to drive the car, took infinite pains over every detail of a driver's behaviour on such an occasion, going over it time after time until he knew it by heart. I found the technique extremely interesting for the car was photographed running at about 160mph but was shown on the film at twice that speed. This meant that the large crowd of extras had to move at half speed in order to seem to move normally in the actual film, which they did as to the manner born. Another curious difficulty was that the recording of the Napier-Railton's thunderous exhaust was hopeless, sounding more like a motor-cycle than anything. But exactly the right thunder was obtained by recording the exhaust noise of an ancient MG 750 sports car and grafting that into the film.

Taking it all together I had plenty of radio and television work, and though I could never get over the shock of hearing my own voice, found the whole thing very intriguing; especially when a battery of cameras and lights were brought down to the house to work for about two hours and I discovered late in the proceedings they were all plugged into my electric power circuit and on my meter! On one occasion we all had to drive cars in memory of Brooklands days. The cameras were in a huge shed and we all told the producer that if the Napier-Railton engine was started in such circum-stances all hell would break out. Nevertheless it was started and you should have seen the chaos, things even fell off the roof and cameras were blown endways. One of the drivers was Kay Petre, who seemed to be having the row of the century in the wings with her mechanic. Suddenly she was told to go on the set and instantly her furious little face assumed the exact expression of an angel at peace with all mankind. It reminded me that I had a photo showing Kay and me at a café table in Switzerland just after the war. On Kay's face is an unbelievably angelic expres-sion such as is saved for the approach of her very best boy friend. In actual fact she had just seen the waiter bringing a tray full of real cakes and delicacies, which had not been avail-able in England for years.

In 1955 the British Motor Corporation organised a trip for motoring journalists to South Africa, apparently from sheer goodness of heart, but a little to show their overseas organisation in action. For me this was a dream come true. Always since the days of the Jamieson raid and the wars in South Africa I had longed to visit that country. We flew out in a big four-engined aircraft, the controls of which (when I was unoffi-cially allowed to handle them) were much more delicate than I had imag-ined. We landed at Cape Town and had the time of our lives going everywhere and seeing everything. Before one offi-cial lunch we were all warned not to talk about politics in any circumstances. My opposite number at the table was an elderly man with a most interesting face, the kind you want to sketch on first sight, but he seemed to have no conversation which mattered. Driven to desperation at last, I asked if he had been in the second of the Boer wars. With obviously quickening interest he said yes. Then I said, "You must have been shooting at all my uncles, who told me how darned good you all were." From then on, long after the end of the lunch, we chatted over that war: of how he used to walk into a nearby blockhouse to exchange tobacco and rum, pass the time of day with our men, then saunter off to resume shooting when both sides agreed to do so. In a moment of enthusiasm he admitted that he had enjoyed every moment of it and was bored with normal life as lived today. We parted the best of friends, hoping we might meet again some time at Bisley or for any rifle shooting competition in which to enjoy our favourite weapon.

Then there was an hour or more with a Zulu, when, sitting at ease in the burning sun, we managed to master each other's version of English suffi-ciently to talk about things that mattered and agree that if the white man would only go away, you could raid a neighbouring tribe not noted for fighting ability and get women, food, and all you wanted with consummate ease! I remembered this later on when we were taken to see a stockaded village containing Kikuyu, who did not want to be involved in trouble, for their guardian was an enormous Zulu home guard who was obviously on top of the world. Trips with the South African Rifles in Land Rovers, wandering about generally, provided a wonderful view of Africa, even if it did not strictly increase one's knowledge of cars and their service.

One tale told by evening firelight was quite amusing. It was said that a senior official new to African ways nearly had a fit at the sanitation of village huts and demanded action. Accordingly, some beautiful huts, concrete circles with proper thatched roofs, man-high doors and windows, were provided with two miniature huts, one for the stores and the other complete with WC seat and all accessories civilisation demands. The local Chief of Police was sceptical of all this and he was dead right. For a year after these chefs d'oeuvre had been presented to their puzzled new owners, every door had been reduced to crawl-in size, every window was firmly blocked up, and the wife of the headsman was installed in what had been the WC. At least they were comfortable and they had all my support and sympathy if the tale was true.

Somewhere in Africa someone acquired a "Chieftainship" in the best possible way. A relative of my wife's was summoned to headquarters to attend an official royal visit. On the car's roof was a case containing his splendid uniform. When he got to HQ, after a rough ride along bush roads, the case was missing. A native must have found the case somewhere, donned the uniform and acquired authority simply from its splendour – or so I like to think. Quite frankly I am fond of the African in his own country and would do anything to help him if I could. He has a way of life which appeals more and more as our civilisation becomes noisier and noisier and more expensive. I don't see why we should insist on converting him to our ways, or our religions, even if his ideas seem quite wrong to us.

Africa appeals to me also because the animals are animals, not show pieces in ridiculous cages or alleged pets. I spent quite a time sketching my lord the lion in a forest; a sleepier, lazier creature you could not imagine. His coat had a truly beautiful sheen, he was obviously a bundle of fighting muscle and all around him were his wives to do everything he decided should be done. On another occasion I had been enjoying the spectacle of a great fat hippo playing with her baby in a river and looking as though she would not have hurt a mouse. In the strange quiet of the forest she fitted exactly. Abruptly a gaggle of tourists arrived with their guide, making all the noise in the world. They were apparently very annoyed that he could not show them a hippo on demand, saying so mostly in transatlantic accent. Hidden from them in the bush I enjoyed the knowledge that a complete hippo was within twenty feet of them, submerged except for one baleful eye, while her baby had been tucked into the bushes just beyond her.

Again, the wrong kind of tourist caused amusement on another day. We had all been at the Victoria Falls, then had lunch at a nearby hotel. In the bush nearby were numerous dog-faced baboons, animals with which I did not see eye to eye on any subject. Then an elderly American woman decided they were "cute" and that she must have a photo. Taking no notice of warnings, she walked up to a vicious-looking old dog baboon. Instantly the beast grabbed her handbag and made off into the bush. She demanded that we got the bag back. I explained that this was a damned foolish idea as the animals were quite savage; then she demanded their keeper. Nothing would convince her these were wild baboons in the raw and not exhibits in an organised show for the public.

By sheer luck I saw a good deal of country I knew by repute: Mafeking, Ladysmith, Johannesburg, Pretoria, and Bulawayo, together with ridges and kops which had just been names before. It was wonderful, the more so because I was seeing all this with the eyes of a small boy of years long gone by. An old pastor and I spent one morning chatting over it all with mutual interest and considerable increase of knowledge. He knew much about the trek from the south across the Vaal river, then to the Free State beyond, and of the trouble great zeal for religion brings, plus the consequent intolerance brought to humanity. I saw the huge memorial to those tough, obstinate he-men the "Voortrekkers", which has just the right massive character to serve as a perpetual reminder to youth. One thing only seemed strange to me in that the well-executed frescoes of that memorial depicted the massacre of the pioneers by the natives just a thought too much; after all it was the pioneers who won. It all ended too soon and we left by air once more for England.

BMC rounded off the education of all concerned by following up with a trip to Australia in 1956. In another big four-engined aircraft we went off in style to land in Newfoundland in the bitterest cold I ever experienced. Every second of our wait for the aircraft to be refu-elled was spent huddled up as near one of the large stoves as possible, so I cannot say I had more than a fleeting glimpse of either Newfoundland or

Canada. I didn't even have time to visit old family friends, the Gaults, long-time Canadian residents.

Flying is a most efficient business, saving a vast amount of time, but it is a mite hard on a Briton's inside. Firstly I could not persuade my stomach to accept the variation in meals, since no sooner had we had one big meal in the aircraft than we were offered the same again as soon as we landed. Few people own a stomach as obstinately determined to have its meals at regular times according to Greenwich than I do, so the argument was long and difficult. Then we had no sooner recovered from the brief but vigorous cold of Newfoundland's Gander than we were landed in San Francisco, which seemed to be suffering from a heat-wave, and that too had an effect on my stomach, which complained bitterly. It was most interesting to see San Francisco and to note with some amusement that they still assert that the disaster they experienced years ago was due to fire and *not* to any earthquake as history records. On the last leg of the flight across the Pacific to Sydney, Australia, we were right out over that exciting sea when the port engine decided to cut out altogether. It was frightening since I could not remember where the dinghy was stowed, and there was not even the vestige of an island in sight, a shock made ten times worse because the next thing which happened was that *all* the engines ceased to function. It was something to do with changing from one fuel tank to another, then all but one of the engines started up again after we had lost considerable height. We afterwards landed on one of the smallest islands in the Pacific and spent an hour there on solid if barren earth – an immense relief.

Australia was most hospitable and deeply interesting, the more so because its manners and customs were different, and certain out of the way areas reminded me of Victorian days back home. But the Snowy Mountain irrigation system was almost fantastic in its boldness and provision for the future; masses of mountain being moved hither and yon with apparent ease, and tunnels proceeding at a pace which reminded one of drilling wood. We went all over that pleasant land, had a good view of its remote interior and met some native but engaging Aborigines, who seemed to me to be leftovers from pre-historic days. They had serviceable crude weapons but apparently no knowledge of the wheel until Europeans came their way. Of course we saw Australia's unusual animals, tame and wild kangaroos aplenty, and that made one think hard why these beasts developed only on this continent. It certainly seemed beyond doubt that Australia will be made habitable all over, by sheer hard work and engineered irrigation on an enormous scale, provided it is not absorbed by America before the Australians can do things their own way.

We visited the show places, Bondi beach and the like, but this was not as interesting as the wilder parts of the country. Famous beaches all over the world are becoming more and more alike and, thank goodness, you can admire the female in her very latest sunbathing micro garment anywhere. Whatever opinion you may form of Australia one thing is certain, the people are most friendly. If you went there young and enthusiastic, prepared to work like hell, then every possibility in the world is there.

S. C. H. DAVIS

Sammy's logo.

Chapter 12A

(Sammy was superstitious about the number 13 and so marked this chapter 12A in his manuscript)

A Disaster Turned to Happiness

By now life was becoming difficult, my marriage had definitely broken up and it was my fault beyond doubt. My fault, because I simply could not alter my own existence, ideas or friends. In truth the fact remained that a wartime marriage was wrong, for the whole atmosphere of the time is unreal and values easily misjudged. Vanne Goodall, who was having marital trouble of her own, helped all she could and it was comforting to be able to discuss an intimate and serious problem with someone else. But in the end my wife and I parted with all the formalities inevitable when the law deals with such things, though I must say I found everyone, even the opposing side, wonderfully friendly. I was eternally grateful for my son Colin's understanding of the whole trouble.

The sequel was more fantastic than any writer of novels could imagine. I casually met a small, young, dark and very attractive girl, Susanna Aubrey-Hall, who seemed to share my enjoyment of art, interest in people of all kinds and levels, and discussing any abstruse or worldly problem. Both of us had been art school students (though of very different schools), both of us loved driving and enjoyed foreign places. Then a day arrived when it was obvious we felt something about each other, impossible to define, something one had never experienced before and all-powerful – we were passionately in love. So, after what may be termed a "trial run" to make sure this was not a fantasy, we were married and attained a happiness which has lasted and increased all these years.

Now we live in joyous disorder, painting, writing and savouring every moment of life's ups and downs, in what was the coal cellar and a sick bay of a girls' school dormitory before it was converted into flats; a most friendly, very small two-storied house in the ancient city of Guildford, and once more the godlets were benevolent. Naturally we had expected two difficulties: people might be unpleasant about our great difference in age, and we might have trouble with the church, but

everyone was incredibly friendly. As to the church, we both being Roman Catholics, there was no way of getting round its refusal to acknowledge we were married. Both of us maintain that marriage as such is not the prerogative of the church in any case. Our registry office ceremony anyhow had just the right atmosphere. Mrs Stoodley, the wife of the owner of the building, on being informed that we were now married remarked, "We have been expecting that for months," and produced an enormous bouquet of flowers for Susie. We enjoyed a short honeymoon that was altogether wonderful, even though neither of us had any money to speak about, or perhaps because of that.

Then there was Emmie Kate, now resident in the West Country, controlling a large and pleasant collection of relatives. From her came a letter asking what I thought I was doing marrying a chit of a girl and had I taken leave of my senses? Then we learned that her grand-daughter Liz had been ordered to see and report on "Sammy's latest acquisition". She duly arrived, puzzled beyond belief because she did not know whether the acquisition was an old car, a new car, or a woman. Her report was entirely satisfactory, so the next move was an order to come down to Exmouth to see Emmie. We were nervous about this in view of the report that Emmie Kate was very ill, not knowing whether to bring a bottle of the best wine or one of milk. Well, it was quite an evening and we took Emmie out to dinner. She demanded aperitifs, good wine and liqueurs, all of which were strictly forbidden by her doctor. Susie and Emmie took to each other instantly, so much so that their confidences were embarrassing to say the least. The friendship thus begun lasted right up to the time Emmie Kate died some years later.

A problem we had to face together was the necessity to make up our minds about the Church and religion generally. Both of us were Catholics, Susie from birth, myself because the Catholic Church seemed in direct descent from the apostles historically. But neither of us would accept the Church's dicta about many things and we would have

A hand-written note on the back of this photo says "Pit control GP 1948 Silverstone". It was reported as being a golden day, so why are the papers being pinned down with large stones and a log? The event, held by the RAC on 2 October, was heralded as the 500cc National Race and International Grand Prix. The latter was won by Villoresi in a Maserati. Sammy Davis was a Steward.

*Davis the artist
at work.*

*The tiny annexe at
Sutton Lodge,
Guildford, where
Sammy and Susie
lived for many
happy years.*

preferred a simpler form of religious ceremonial. Certainly we would not accept the idea that we were not married. To me the assertion of the Church's power to control marriage is wrong; I cannot agree that the Church has any authority for this control. Taking the thing further because it is important, both of us thought there must be some power, force, or being beyond our knowledge, but creative, simply because we could find no other explanation for the beginning of the Universe which made any sense. It was relatively unimportant whether Christ was man or God. The only thing which mattered was that he must have been immensely strong and marvellously intelligent to preach successfully ideas entirely foreign to his time and circumstances.

We both knew that man has always desired a future life, therefore created a God to his own liking through the centuries, so that the whole belief in future life might be wishful thinking. We did not agree that a desire to try and help people out of trouble was entirely a Christian idea, because we thought it was due to increased intelligence and better education. I had some further difficulties to consider: that most of the Bible was written long after the life of Christ, then translated and retranslated which made me doubt the accuracy of the whole book. In addition the Church might have altered or suppressed unfavourable things in the days when temporal power was all-important. Too many people also chose sections of the Bible they favoured on which to found new religions, whereas reading the whole made the meaning quite different. In fact it seemed to me the Bible was so difficult to understand that it ought not to be read by any but scholars, and if possible, scholars to whom the earliest possible original documents would be available.

I did not like the principal ceremony the Church had evolved; this is best demonstrated by the remark made by an African to whom the ceremony had been explained. He thought it over for a day or so then arrived at the conclusion that Christians were cannibals who ate their God. Minor problems for me are, why was Christ executed in the Roman manner – a rite which had definite meaning in Roman law – when the head Roman official had ceremoniously washed his hands of the whole affair? Also, why does the Christian church use the cross as its principal symbol, whereas everything depends on the resurrection, not the execution? I have written about this at some length, I admit, but for both of us religion is a subject of special interest.

So a marvellously happy life went on. We went to official dinners together, shared the housework, drew, painted and wrote, side by side. It was an understood thing that Susie would be with me whenever I gave a talk to groups of people of all ages. We took to motorcycling together, this time with a 50cc Japanese Honda and, on our first effort to ride tandem, fell off and rolled on the road helpless with laughter, to no small bewilderment of drivers held up by our antics. Major Stoodley and his wife, who owned the rabbit warren of flats in which we lived, were extremely kind to us from the start and our flat was more than friendly as a home.

Both of us have our moments of depression, chiefly about finance, and we have both been ill from time to time, which has a curious effect in that the partner who feels well worries so much about the other that he or she cannot get down to work. Manifestly the small godlets have some hand in our existence – benevolently every time. One day we were both deeply depressed because the typewriter on which the completion of a book

depended broke down from old age. The only alternative was to buy another one second-hand, and that would cost £40 which we had not got. But the very next morning a cheque for £50 arrived unexpectedly. On another occasion of financial stress, just as we were budgeting at low ebb, a record company came to make a disc and next day the BBC also recorded a talk; both provided money.

We enlisted in the Civil Defence because we wanted to be trained for any emergency and could not get into any of the other services together; it was not quite what we expected. We walked into the CDHQ one day on impulse and asked, "Can you use two drivers?" Whereupon we were roped in to Control HQ before we knew where we were, and after struggling with sundry exams were firstly Clerk Two

As Sammy had retired, his presence on his own beside a Morris Minor emblazoned with "Presse Rallye Monte-Carlo" is intriguing. The backdrop was a favoured position for a photograph.

and Staff Officer Operations, and then Sub-Officer and Second Officer, respectively. As Susie said one day when we were shooting at Bisley: "Since no Home Guard is available, Civil Defence is just the job. In fact the joy of our life is that we can do everything together and you cannot want more than that.

We have been to Le Mans together, camping joyously in the site behind the pits amidst people of every nationality. Once we were in charge of a pit for an American who was driving what seemed to be an unprepared car and had no proper pit crew, which entailed thirty-two hours of extremely strenuous work together with much improvisation. A light-hearted incident occurred when I realised that the head mechanic, an Italian, might have been my son Colin's mechanic as well. Colin, by the way, was now a racing driver in his own right, having done well with a Cooper 500 of his own, then with larger famous cars, had won the Targa Florio in 1964 [driving a Porsche] and Le Mans on formula as well. Having found that the mechanic was the one who had helped my son, I introduced Susie to him as my wife. An expression of

extreme bewilderment came over his face. He had, by the way, refused to believe that I was old enough to be Colin's father and now it was obvious he was having trouble over Susie; Colin, you see, is slightly older than Susie. Grasping his difficulty at last I sought to solve it by saying in lame Italian that Susie was my second wife. The phraseology must have been wrong for he laughed and laughed. Then said he, "You English are always so practical, now my wife does not like car racing. If only I could have another wife to come racing, like you have, life would be much more pleasant".

Together, Susie and I had to declare open a road named after me at Le Mans, a surprise which made us both nervous since neither of us had suitable clothes for a formal occasion. Somehow or other we collected fairly reasonable attire for this ceremony, but the godlets would have their fun. I spilled wine down my better trousers and Susie's skirt split from waist to hem just before we met the officials. Being French they never for a second showed any emotion at all at this, so the affair passed off happily.

Le Mans, 18 June 1965. Visiting Rue S C H Davis, named in his honour. In the middle are Susie and Sammy, and second from right Henri Delgove, motoring historian.

We acted as officials for that intriguing affair the London-Sète rally, organised by Col. Geoffrey Portham assisted splendidly by Violette his wife. This was very like the *Rallye Gastronomique* in that all concerned were feasted by famous wine firms. Hospitality was intense and wine tasting formed the chief item in many a day's run; but there was a more serious ingredient of competition. My memory lingers over a marvellous dinner provided by Merciers, for which every single dish had a champagne ingredient. That the accompanying wine was champagne of better and better quality for each successive dish vastly increased the gratification. We went over the Pyrenees to Andorra, which is like no other state in the world and vastly entertaining. A certain sense of irresponsibility about the whole rally helped to make it more enjoyable. For example, we all arrived at Carcassonne looking forward to a nice restful evening and to seeing the

old city later on. At that point it became apparent that the very friendly Frenchman responsible for the hotel booking had done so for the wrong day. When this was brought to his attention in no uncertain manner, he replied with a theatrical shrug of the shoulders that it was "*Un désastre*", an expression meaning there was nothing

Rue S C H Davis in 2006, with Hervé Guyomard, Directeur Circuit Bugatti, Le Mans.

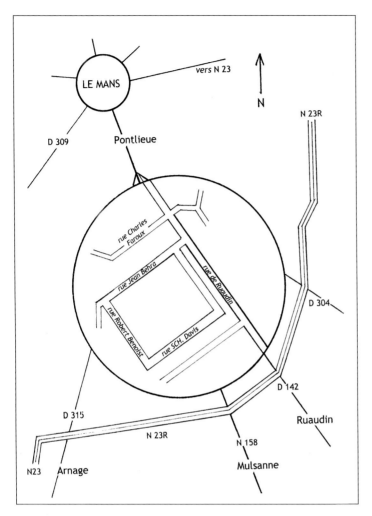

Map of Le Mans clearly showing Rue S C H Davis, right next to Rue Robert Benoist, his old friend who was so cruelly executed by the Nazis. Also nearby is Rue Charles Faroux, commemorating the French motor journalist, another friend of Sammy's.

more to be done. So off he went to a fine five-course dinner, leaving the rest of our folk near to apoplexy.

Somehow the local hoteliers managed to accommodate everyone all the same. Susie and I had a room in what had once been a religious establishment, now a hotel, an affair of bleak stone corridors but comfortable rooms. In the morning there was a need of the loo, but a search of the long corridors revealed no trace of such. In a flash of inspiration I thought of listening and waiting. Three times the distant sound of a waterfall had faded by the time I got near to where I thought it had been. I was just about to give up when a rush

of water sounded quite close so that the place was pinpointed. The door opened and out stepped a Napoleonic veteran in full uniform, suitably moustached and with a musket. He said, *"Bonjour, monsieur"*, and marched off. Afterwards no one would admit that anyone remotely like him had ever stayed in the hotel! At the concours the organiser had left all the relevant papers at his hotel, so Susie drove at full speed there and back to fetch them. A tropical thunderstorm suddenly burst and her drive through sheets of rain and two feet of water remains a high spot in both our memories.

Following the finish at Sète on the Mediterranean, Susie and I were involved in a lunch for the *Marraines* [pen pals] of the '14 war and their soldier friends, both sexes, and now much older. Everyone sang a traditional song, each performance being clapped in a certain way. We not being obviously English to look at were not noticed until we clapped in the wrong place. Whereupon everyone demanded a song from Susie. We explained we were Britons, after which a very pleasant woman was attached to our table to make sure we appreciated all that the company did. We aroused enthusiasm to fever height by timing the hotel's tortoise Sophie over a measured foot. Sophie walked fast between the legs of everyone with consummate ease, devouring black beetles. Lunch came to a stop while diners crowded round exhorting Sophie to more speed, and 0.03mph was greeted by long applause.

Abbeville also figured in our lives as we stopped there twice before catching the boat back to England. On the first occasion the chambermaid bringing early morning coffee could not open the door to our room, which had jammed, so I got out of bed and went to get the tray from her, but she insisted on coming in, which was awkward since I had nothing on. Not noticing a dressing gown nearby I leaped into the bath, which was dry but offered some cover. Not enough it seems, as when we met that girl again next year, she laughed until she wept. The second occasion was July 14th. On a triangle of grass in front of the war memorial bordered with young trees, there assembled all the notables: the prefect, the mayor, the troops, the *anciens combattants* with banners and the band. Just as the ceremony came to the salute, a very small dog called Bobby came out from the café, intent on his usual round of those same trees. His attempt was foiled by his receiving a kick from one of the military. Bobby went back to the centre of the road, there paused in obvious thought, then went down the entire line of waiting official cars, "christening" each in turn, while the furious assembly, rigidly at attention, had to watch this blasphemy helpless to do anything.

Always there was great friendliness. On one occasion we were returning from a rally and happened to be on RN7 at a point where that famous road was at its barest. It was lunchtime, and being as usual very short of money we looked for a small café. None was available so we had to go to a much-badged hotel. In its garden we found meals were less expensive, so we ordered one of simple variety. It was so good that I sent a message congratulating the chef. He, it turned out, was the hotel owner, and he came along, white cap and all, to thank us. In conversation he then found out we knew Charles Bracken-bury. In a flash the bill disappeared, to be replaced by one at half the cost accompanied by an excellent bottle of gift wine. Then, and this was puzzling, we were given a letter which we were asked to take back and post in England to Charles.

We had adventures with those capital machines called "karts", Susie's first drive with one being complicated by the fact she was wearing a very short skirt. Now as she has very attractive legs and was wearing very nice panties, it was obvious she had better not go round the circuit in front of spectators or every male kart driver would be dangerously distracted; so she had to drive up and down a long, solitary runway instead. Susie really could drive, one of her 160mph performances on an E-Type Jaguar which we were loaned making me very proud of her.

The peak of our enjoyment curve in competition came with the annual run of old cars from London to Brighton. It took weeks to prepare that old sinner "Beelzebub", our French 1897 Léon Bollée[1], for this trip with both of us having to work hard and long with due regard to the old devil's temperament.

Susie and Sammy on the Léon Bollée, London to Brighton, c1957.

---

1. Now residing in the Indianapolis Museum, USA

An original 1927 Daily Sketch *programme found amongst Sammy's papers.*

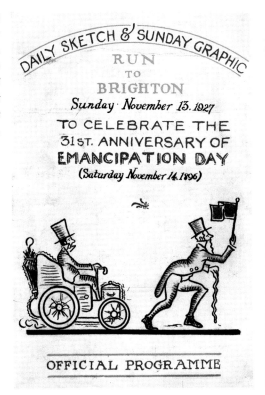

The list of entrants for the Daily Sketch *race, and an advertisment for the event.*

Daily Sketch & Sunday Graphic
OLD CROCKS' RUN TO BRIGHTON

Sunday, November 13th, 1927

❖ ❖ ❖

OFFICIAL LIST OF ENTRANTS

No.	Make	Approx. Date of Mfr.	Entrant.
1.	Panhard	1893	John Bryce, Lanark.
2.	Benz	1893/4	Donald Morrison, Gravesend.
3.	Benz	1894/5	Leonard D. Stears, Surbiton.
4.	Renault	1895	Doran, Taggart & Co., Putney.
5.	Daimler	1896	S. E. Statham, Baker Street, W.
6.	Daimler	1897	Monty Wells, Nottingham.
7.	Benz	1897	Mrs. Mary Miles, S. Croydon.
8.	Daimler	1897	G. H. Pruen, Burnham-on-Sea.
9.	Panhard	1897	G. Levrey, Fitzroy Square, W.
10.	Daimler	1898	D. M. Copley, Birmingham.
11.	Stephens	1898	R. Stephens & Sons, Upper Norwood.
12.	Star	1898	University Motors, Ltd., Hertford Street, W.
13.	Benz	1898	Arthur B. C. Day, Barrow-on-Humber.
14.	Benz	1899	William Vincent, Reading.
15.	Renault	1899	B. J. Smyth-Wood, Victoria.
16.	Darracq	1900	William Vincent, Reading.
17.	Benz	1900	Alfred Hollands, Newbury.
18.	Benz	1900	Dr. F. H. Pearse, Plymouth.
19.	Siddeley	1901	University Motors, Ltd., Piccadilly, W.
20.	Panhard	1901	G. R. Wakeling, Brockenhurst.
21.	Kelicom	1902	F. R. Sheen, Croydon.
22.	De Dion Bouton	1902	Vincent Ballardini, Brighton.
23.	De Dion	1902	Geo. Burtenshaw, Reigate.
24.	Renault	1902	T. F. Morris, Herne Bay.
25.	Clement Talbot	1902	Doran, Taggart & Co., Putney.
26.	Lanchester	1902	T. Hamilton-Adams, Pall Mall, S.W.
27.	De Dion Bouton	1902/4	Arthur Woods, Hythe, Kent.
28.	Oldsmobile	1903	General Motors, Ltd., The Hyde, N.W.
29.	De Dion	1903	A. Spicer & Co., E. Sheen.
30.	De Dion Bouton	1903	E. F. Richardson, Purley.
31.	Renault	1903	William Vincent, Reading.
32.	Cadillac	1903	F. S. Bennett, St. John's Wood.
33.	Sunbeam	1903	W. H. Cocks, Weybridge.
34.	Riley	1903	Victor E. Leverett, North Audley Street, W.
35.	Rover	1903/5	W. E. Watson, S. Kensington.
36.	Wolseley	1904	G. F. Surtees, Lowestoft.
37.	Vauxhall (Single Cylinder)	1904	Percy C. Kidner, W. Hampstead.
38.	Mercedes	1904	J. Polledri, Kingston-on-Thames.
39.	De Dion Bouton	1904	W. J. Baker, Honor Oak Park.
40.	Humber (Beeston)	1905	J. Stringfellow, Wombwell.
41.	Cadillac	1905	General Motors, Ltd., The Hyde, N.W.
42.	Rover (1 cylinder)	1905	Miss G. Dawes, Coventry.
43.	Fiat	1906	J. Stubberfield, Eastbourne.
44.	Renault	1906	G. Eggleton, Watford.
45.	Rover	1906	W. Heckman & Sons, Henley-on-Thames.
46.	10-12 Wolseley Siddeley (2 cylinder)	1906	T. H. L. Salisbury, Bristol.
47.	Rolls-Royce	1906	D. K. Bunn, Newman Street, W.
48.	De Dion Bouton	1906	C. H. Boffin, Middle Barton, Oxon.
49.	Argyll (with Aster Engine)	1906	G. W. Looker, Stanford-le-Hope.
50.	24/30 Panhard	1906	Joseph Walters, Belgravia.
51.	14/20 Renault	1906	T. L. Stopps, Beaconsfield.

Of the many runs with this machine, none had been without incident, which is fair and just since the whole point of the run is to get to Brighton in spite of trouble. Anyone, you see, can drive a car which is entirely reliable over that course. Driving Beelzebub is no easy job, for you have to adjust the throttle and governor, the carburettor air supply, and the ignition, before and after every change of gear or the damned awkward machine refuses to accelerate. In addition, you have to feel carefully for the teeth of the two gears to mesh, and engage them at exactly the right moment, while control of the final-drive belt to avoid slip is delicate. If you put the brakes on hard in Surrey you are not likely to stop before Sussex, which complicates driving though it encourages exact judgement.

Still, the old machine has failed to arrive in time only twice, and on one of those occasions it, and every other Bollée, broke their crankshafts. On the credit side, Beelzebub can attain 40mph and has been certified as averaging 19mph all the way to Brighton. Our finest run was in 1966 and, from the moment we started from Hyde Park at 8.00 in the morning with some 250 other competitors, something seemed to be wrong. We were a gear down from normal on every hill, a fact we thought due to a powerful headwind. But the obvious lack of power persisted although we could find nothing untoward. Twenty miles from the finish the engine developed a very nasty knock and faded out. Susie, who was driving, pulled on to the roadside verge and we investigated. The crankcase drain tap, together with its pipe, had completely gone, leaving a large hole through which all the oil was escaping as soon as it was pumped in. Not liking this the crankpin had unscrewed itself from the crank web, so the connecting rod was now working at the wrong angle. Using

comment suitable to the occasion we set to work. It was a difficult job, out there on the grass verge, which entailed lying under the engine to get at bolts, no two faces of whose hexagon heads were the same. In the process Susie absorbed much oil in her hair. We got the crankpin back in place, bolted the crankcase on again, and now had to seal the hole. Bertram Richards, who was driving our tender car, suggested a cork. One provided from a champagne bottle encouraged us no end and this we secured with a wire.

We managed another five miles and the cork fell out. When we retrieved it and once more screwed the crankpin back, the cork was made more oil-tight with chewing gum. Fortunately a supply was available, and deeply interested spectators volunteered to help chew the stuff until it was flexible enough, some of them without realising that chewing gum with detachable teeth has its difficulties. We managed another five miles, this time in traffic which became denser and denser as we neared Brighton until cars, new cars that is, were three abreast, which was a real handicap to Beelzebub. Then the cork fell out and was lost amid the traffic. We tried whittling wood borrowed from a tree but it did not hold. It was damn near 4pm, which was the time-limit to qualify as a finisher. Obviously we could effect another repair, but if we did we had no hope of arriving in time, especially as the modern traffic was now down to a 4mph crawl with frequent stops. So we decided to push along the pavement as fast as we could, returning to the road only when we saw a policeman. We actually found we were going faster than the pack of modern cars, but of course we became very tired. Fortunately a very strong spectator took a hand at pushing and was so efficient it was all we could do to keep up with him. We finally crossed the finishing line, which had seemed so many miles away,

More Sketches by Casque

For those who like variety, there is the Veteran Run to Brighton, where – – –

– – – trouble – – –

– – – succeeds trouble, – – –

with two minutes to spare.

We were too tired to fully appreciate the subsequent official banquet or the efforts of an American news film team which made us hours late getting Beelzebub from the finish enclosure to our hotel. We had had only a little soup and some rum for sustenance since starting for Hyde Park from Guildford at 4am[1].

That was a run of which to be proud, so I had my finisher's medal gilded in order that Susie could wear it on "state" occasions. She deserved it, having not only driven most of the way but done more than half her share in the repairs. Mighty good she looks with it when wearing her best costume together with high-heeled shoes. On reflection, the trouble could have been caused when Beelzebub was exhibited for some charity, when one of the innumerable small boys always present must have used the drain tap pipe as the most convenient step with which to get up into the seat while we were not looking and his weight had started a crack – that is the technical reasoning. We found out afterwards that when we repainted the old devil, so he could look smart for the run, we had taken off two badges, one British, the other the French "Teuf Teuf" club, which he values above all else, and *we* had forgotten to replace them!

That is a fair sample of the run to Brighton for the very old veteran cars. We arrived once at our hotel dripping water in all directions since it had rained hard all the way. We left two streams of water from the revolving front door to reception, and that did not seem to please the management. When we got to our room we asked for our clothes to be dried and for a bath. Rather haughtily we were told, "The drying room is not open on Sunday and baths are not avail-

1. Sammy was 79 at this time.

able". So we piled our wet clothes in front of the lighted gas fire, which caused a goodly fog, then went off down the corridor until we found a bathroom. We filled the very large bath almost to the brim with the hottest water we could bear, got into it together with a bottle of excellent rum and continued therein until the rum had gone and we felt fine. Meanwhile, the chambermaid had knocked on the locked door and ordered us out. As we took no notice, orders turned to pleading, which had no result either and finally she left us; but whenever we go to that hotel after a Brighton run we are immediately offered a bath and the drying room. Without doubt the "Brighton" is the adventure of the year, and I feel so pleased that I had a hand in getting it restarted by the RAC and in organising the Veteran Car Club in support.

To make life even more pleasant, Colin's attractive wife Eva presented us with the very peach of a grand-daughter, Francesca Victoria Rosamund, in 1965. Colin invited Susie and me down to his villa at Rapallo, Italy, to see the small newcomer and a capital time we had. Francesca, then aged two, was cheerfully friendly throughout, looked most attractive and flirted vigorously. I had been warned that she liked to snatch at anything interesting and pull anything handy. Gurgling with delight she explored my beard and eyebrows as gently as possible, first stroking my eyebrows, which tend to the horny and bushy, then stroking her own diminutive ones in a puzzled kind of way as though wondering why hers were not as abundant. Obviously too, she wanted to convey some thoughts on the matter, and was furious that she could make no noise capable of expressing them – a little pet even allowing for natural bias. She had something of her father's verve with vehicles, for when installed in a four-legged caster-wheeled contraption

– – – and a plague of small boys descends wherever one stops. When, as the last breakdown occurs with but ten miles to go – – –

– – – one is tempted to wonder whether, as horses are barred, the situation might not be saved with the help of some other beast. So, having decided that it is really worth while after all – – –

– – – one can spend the winter putting a coat of paint on the car ready for another year.

[But why a Bugatti?]

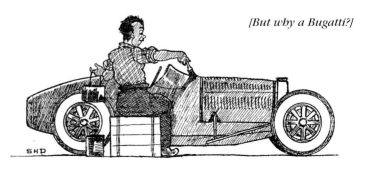

Susie and Sammy at a wedding.

Rosamund, Sammy's first wife, photographed in 1974 when she was 78 years old. She died soon after Sammy in 1981.

in which she could stand up and run, she went down the passage at high speed, either forwards or backwards, bumping off the paintwork, furniture or any obstacle with great delight. Colin proved to be a skilled cook beyond the ordinary. No one, but no one, was allowed near the kitchen, especially during the almost religious ceremony of preparing *coq au vin*.

Another thing which gave me great pleasure was that Rosamund, who also had a flat nearby, appeared to be contented and happy, though she was not as well as I would have liked her to be and was delightfully careless about finance. Introducing one's second wife to one's first is not without unpleasant possibilities but Rosamund was extremely kind to Susie, gave her presents and made her feel entirely welcome, which was a relief. Eva, knowing that we preferred a double bed, had arranged one out of two singles with appropriate bedding. In the middle of the night I felt strangely cold, and half awake I groped about. There were no bedclothes, nor was there any Susie The beds had drifted apart and Susie was sleeping happily on the floor between them.

Memoirs often contain the phrase "The old times were the best", though after 80 years of life I deny this to be true. Of course the adventures of youth, the fashions and the etiquette of years gone by, are remembered with more pleasure than balanced judgement. Life today is every bit as good as it was, better in fact since there is more scope for adventure. I like youngsters skylarking everywhere, possibly their morals are set by fashion rather than a certain knowledge of right and wrong; yet older folk often seem bent on criticising the young in every generation. I am sure the youngsters will do their bit if this country is threatened by a real crisis, even if they claim war is damned foolish and a thing in which they will have no part. I cannot see anything shatteringly wrong about males with long hair provided it is well kept, since it is not so long ago that this was definitely a sign of masculine prowess. I like mini-skirts very much, especially as most of the young wearing them have legs worth seeing. And if on occasions you can see more, that does not mean the owner's morals are weak.

Gunnion Rutherford's dictum, that real trouble arises only when both sides to a dispute are rational from their own point of view and the solution is of vital importance, has always remained in my mind. For that reason I became a policeman during the General Strike of 1926, since it did not involve taking sides in the dispute. Very intriguing it was too, and gave me a wholesome respect for the police. It had its amusing side, as one day I had trouble with two drivers who had narrowly missed each other's cars and were at it hammer and tongs in the knock-for-knock manner. Only by parking them on opposite sides of the road could I calm them down and explain that no damage had been done, therefore there was no need for tempers. I also acquired knowledge that most evidence of eyewitnesses was utterly unreliable, which brought back memories of a lecture on the necessity for accurate observation. During the lecture two men and a girl entered the room. One man pointed a banana at the lecturer, the other dropped four books and the girl sat down. The lecturer fell down behind his desk, then rose and asked everyone to write down what they had seen. Seventy percent had seen a pistol, none had noticed the girl.

As I said earlier, I owe a great debt of gratitude to my parents, to Dr Gunnion Rutherford of Westminster, to Dr Bear and other medicos and surgeons who have effected repairs on me, to a very large number of friends (including

particularly those women who taught me what life was all about), to the Navy and Army for putting up with me, and most of all to Susanna Aubrey-Hall, my wife. That our marriage is so successful may be due to the fact that comradeship is our greatest bond. We had that trial run to make sure that what we felt for each other was not transitory, and our attitude to each other has not changed since marriage.

All these years have made me a Briton, not just Welsh, and no one, repeat no one, could have had a more interesting life. There remains one little niggling doubt. I have had a very minor part in the development of the motor car. To me the car is still a marvellous

The back of this studio portrait is stamped 1975, so Sammy was 88.

Susanna Davis.

I had my time over again, I would choose the science of production, so the doubt cannot be very real.

Now it is a question of waiting to see what death is like, though I hope the wait is long. It is difficult to define thoughts about this for fear does not enter into it, only a profound curiosity and a definite desire to put it off as long as possible provided I do not lose either my wits or my ability to do things; I could not bear to be a cripple in a second childhood. Maybe there is still something of the old pagan in me, a gift from far-off ancestors I never knew, for I would like to die standing up to meet the power, or force, or god which created everything. I hope there is a Valhalla, even if the hope is half humorous, so I could have Susie and all my friends with me again. I cannot possibly imagine myself in a kind of nightgown, sprouting wings which no human shoulder blades could operate.

So there you are.

vehicle full of adventure, but the peace we used to value seems to have gone. Of all things essentially modern I like noise least, and engineering has made life one big noisy rush; could it be that engineering is running away with us? If

And when it comes to spinning yarns, a racing driver should be quite the equal of anybody else in Valhalla.

Sammy died on his 94th birthday, 9 January 1981.
Susie soon followed him to Valhalla on 29 July 1983.

Requiscat in Pace

Epilogue by Peter Heilbron

Colin Charles Houghton Davis

It is intriguing to contemplate the number of well-known racing drivers who beget offspring who follow in their footsteps. In the case of Colin Davis we are forewarned by Kay Petre in Sammy's autobiography when he terrified her as a small boy by balancing on one leg upon the arm of the chair on which she was sitting. "This son of yours has no appreciation of danger," she is stated as saying.

Duncan Ferguson recalls that at a fairly tender age Colin owned a three-wheel sports Morgan which he would "race" round a two-mile circuit embracing Holland Park and Kens-

Father and son on "Beelzebub". Colin acted as mechanic on the Brighton Runs of 1949 and 1950.

Sammy with son Colin and Don Parker, winner of the Daily Telegraph *and other trophies at Aintree in 1954.*

ington and which held the unofficial lap record against a group of sports cars and motorbikes. Certain it is that at the age of 21, and armed with £1000, Colin bought a 500cc Norton-engined F3 Cooper. One can only imagine how Sammy must have felt about this, but if he had any doubts he was surely a proud father when Colin not only finished second in his first race, the annual 100 miles for half-litre cars at Silverstone, but was also third on aggregate in the Yorke Trophy. He came third in the Open Challenge at Brands Hatch shortly after – not bad for a beginner! This was in 1954 and Sammy, incidentally, was President of the 500 Club. The following year, 1955, Colin raced his own 500 throughout and had his first BRSCC win at Brands Hatch on

June 11th. This was a significant date, being the occasion of the terrible Le Mans crash, which both father and son must have ruminated upon. In 1956 a Cooper which was owned by Francis Beart was handed to Colin after a trial where he outran Les Leston, for whom it had been intended. Colin had many successes with it, but needed finance and went to live in Italy. In the process the car was sold but was loaned to Colin with an uprated 600cc engine, and he won the Rome Grand Prix, including the fastest lap at Castelfusano,

He came to the attention of the three Maserati brothers at Modena and was offered an OSCA to drive in the Mille Miglia for 1957 which he wisely turned down, for that was another tragic year, in which the Marquis de Portago, driving a Ferrari, lost his life along with many spectators. Later that year Colin drove an OSCA to victory in the Sicily Gold Cup at Syracuse and followed that with the Esso 6 hours at Vallelunga.

In 1958 he had a win at Monza driving a 1500cc OSCA in the Coppa Shell for sports racing cars. Perhaps one of the biggest highlights in Colin's racing career was achieved that same year when OSCA entered the 1958 Le Mans race with a 749cc machine co-driven by Colin and Alejandro de Tomaso. They finished first of the smaller cars (under 1000cc), eleventh overall, and won the coveted Index of Performance. His father must have been a proud man indeed.

Colin's next triumph was a Grand Prix win at Lago de Ganzirri, Messina, in August 1959 driving a Maserati Cooper-Monaco. There being no Junior Championship at the time (the early 1960s), the Italians set up the "Trofeo Mondiale" which Colin won overall on points, beating Denny Hulme and Jim Clark on the way

Colin had two cracks at F1 racing, the first driving a Cooper-Maserati at Rheims in July 1959, when he had to retire after eight laps with an oil pipeline failure. The second time went better when, driving a Cooper again, he finished eleventh at Monza in September the same year.

In 1964 Colin had a prestigious win with a Porsche in the Targa Florio with co-driver Antonio Pucci. The following year he came second in the Targa Floria, with Gerhard Mitter, again driving for Porsche. Finally, In 1966 he won the Index of Performance for the second time at Le Mans, with Jo Siffert in a Porsche 906/6 Carrera, finishing fourth overall.

Like his father, Colin Davis posted many triumphs. On the way he enjoyed racing a variety of sports and *Gran Turismo* cars, and he also tested early Lamborghinis. It was all in the blood – even down to smoking a pipe!

Colin moved from Italy to South Africa, where he contributed to the local broadcasting network and wrote scripts on a variety of subjects: he and his wife Eva live in Cape Town. His daughter Francesca, whom Sammy

Colin Davis in an OSCA racing along the Mulsanne Straight at Le Mans in 1958. He finished first of the smaller cars (under 1000cc), eleventh overall, and won the Index of Performance.

mentions in his autobiography, is married to a South African doctor and resides in Canada, and, as Sammy said, "So there you are."

Note: Colin Davis has provided an interesting comment about the Italian mechanic mentioned in Chapter 13 when Sammy was in charge of a pit for an American at Le Mans, as follows,

"The Italian mechanic whom S C H met was the head of the Maserati Brothers group. Excellent man, the best of a good lot, Sergio Martelli. He was never my personal mechanic as OSCAs were entered by the Brothers or occasionally by de Tomaso. Sergio had been Tazio Nuvolari's and Guy Moll's mechanic but always as the official bloke from Maserati. He came to the most important races, including my first event for the Brothers, the Coppa d'Oro della Sicilia, the Shell Trophy at Monza, Rome, the Targa and Le Mans, also Pescara. He was not given to paying copious compliments to drivers and an undoubtedly flattering assessment of Yours Truly remains a treasured memory of my lifetime."

Log Book

It has been the Editor's endeavour to translate the Logbook as it was originally written, but with minor editing for the benefit of the reader. Where he encountered any doubts, or failed in his research, he has put a question mark in a bracket.

At the end of the Logbook there is a list of all the passengers Sammy took with him throughout the Period from July 1913 to July 1914. Among them are Aunt and Clayden, whose names regularly appear.

It is the Editor's personal view that Aunt was Emmie Kate, Arthur Clayden's wife, whose smiling face can be seen seated next to Sammy in the Pilot on page 161.

First page of the Log Book, signed S C H Davis. Note that 1912 is altered to 1913.

1913

JULY 1ST, 1913
Douglas 2¾hp
with Clayden
[Journey to French Grand Prix].
Richmond, Southampton non-stop.
70m
Lent to Clayden going well – tappet broke in interior.
Havre, Rouen, Amiens. 90m.

JULY 6TH, 1913
TT Douglas
with Aunt
Grand Prix course, Amiens, Longeau, Domart, Moreuil, Amiens. 30m
Went well, long straight roads very dusty and rough especially after Moreuil.

JULY 9TH, 1913
Douglas 2¾hp
To Excelsior depot. 40m
Missed way and went 10kms too far, belt pulled out, mended it on tram rails so stopping tram till gendarme came along. Pavé bloody ['bloody' scratched out] …worst possible.

JULY 10TH, 1913
Douglas 2¾hp
with Aunt
Dieppe road to watch Schneiders. 20m
Very rough going, carburettor loose also exhaust wire frayed. Schneiders turned at end of road in sensational manner, Thomas bursting tyre on the turn. Picked up Aunt and brought her in, pavé still more awful.

JULY 11TH, 1913
Bollée 20hp
with Clayden
Amiens Tribunes. 20m

[Same day]
Sunbeam 15hp
with Aunt
Amiens, Domart. 10m
Weighing in, hot sun, turned out of press tribunes after conclusion of picnic.

JULY 11TH 1913
with Boilleau, Aunt & Clayden,
Stayed at Domart got very little sleep,
up early next day to watch race at Domart corner.

JULY 12TH 1913
Sunbeam 15hp
with Boilleau
Domart, Amiens. 10m

JULY 13TH 1913
Douglas 2¾hp
with Aunt & Clayden
Amiens Tribunes, Amiens. 10m
Watched motorcycle sidecar and cyclecar race. Marlborough with girl mechanic retired early.

JULY 14TH 1913
Douglas 2¾hp. 100m
Glad to leave Amiens, roads awful in patches but excellent in others. Much troubled by leaking tyre and burst partition in tank but machine very fast when going. Lost way once and found soldier who talked English. Missed boat at Boulogne and caught afternoon boat. Put up at Folkestone in pouring rain,

JULY 15TH 1913
Douglas 2¾hp
Folkestone, Richmond via Tonbridge, Tunbridge Wells, E. Grinstead, Reigate, Epsom, Ewell, Kingston, Ham.
Poured all day, got soaked and had some trouble with leaky tyre and bad shorting by the HT wire. Lost way several times and got covered in mud. One cylinder repeatedly cut out when near Kingston but at finish was OK. Machine taken down for overhaul. Tank repaired. New cams TT, new exhaust lifter wire. 1 new plug. Valves ground, silencer pipes and cylinder cleaned. 1 new compression tap, 2 new gudgeon pin washers, 1 stand clip. 1 change lever cotter pin, two valve cap washers. Carburettor soldered. GB washed out [?].

AUGUST 3RD 1913
Douglas 2¾hp
Brooklands. 20m
Practising. New cam setter with contact in wrong position but afterwards this discovered and machine ran to track very well indeed. Silencer worked loose.

AUGUST 4TH 1913
Pilot 15 hp, [Taxi] 12hp
with Felters [Fetters?] & Aunt
Richmond, London Rd, Westerham, London Rd. 20m
Went to fetch Pilot car but after repair had been effected it was found that the ball races were wrong size. Came home "cussing". Promised car for Monday. Awful Benzole.

AUGUST 5TH 1913
Pilot [& Taxi]
with Aunt & Charles
BARC Meeting Aug. London Rd, St Ermin, Richmond, Esher, Hersham, Brooklands. 36m
Car not ready, borrowed disreputable taxicab in which creaked and groaned to track. Everything much worn got there and back however. Splendid meeting Vauxhall and Talbot best.

AUGUST 10TH 1913
Douglas 2¾hp
PSMC [?] Hill Climb. Richmond, Windsor, Beaconsfield, High Wycombe, Princes Risborough. 70m
Great run against high wind with occasional rain. Bad hill climb no competitors.

AUGUST 11TH 1913
Douglas 2¾hp & Pilot 10hp
with Aunt, Clayden & Leslie
Richmond, Hersham, Weybridge, Brooklands. 26m
Taught Aunt to drive which she did by lapping at a speed of 35. Punctured one tyre and broke back of car when tool drawer came open. Aunt shed underskirt?!!!! Car pulled better with larger jet and accelerates very well but is however no good on Benzole.

AUGUST 12TH 1913
Pilot 10 hp
with Clayden
Richmond, Hammersmith Park, Bayswater, Edgware Rd, Landown [?] Rd.
Returned car to works driving on one wheel with the other loose. Hole in tail lamp oil receiver, brakes won't hold.

JULY 19/20TH [?] 1913
[date out of sequence]
[Itala 35hp with 4-seater body]
with Pope, Albertella [mechanic/
linguist] & Foresti [mechanic]
Record run to Turin. 21hrs, 36m.
London, Newhaven, Dieppe, Versailles,
Fontainebleau, Bourg, Chalon,
Chambery, Modane, Susa, Turin.
Magnificent run view over Mont Cenis,
Pass Fini [?], plug troubles at Chalon,
shackle turned over later, two stops for
horn. Car ran like an express skidding
at all corners, rain and dust made all of
us as dirty as possible. Warmth of Italy
impossible to believe.

JULY 17TH 1913
[date out of sequence]
Germain 15hp
with Roy
Richmond, Paddington, Hut [Hut

Pilot 10-12hp 4-cylinder, 1912-14.

Hotel, Wisley], Weybridge,
Paddington +3 [presumably laps of
Brooklands]. 46m
Had fine run Roy very bucked, he drove
one lap, Raced home to catch train.

AUGUST 15TH 1913
Pilot 10 hp
with Aunt & Clayden
Sevenoaks, Tonbridge, Winchelsea,
Rye. 86m
Picked up at Sevenoaks went along
time fine climbing hills very well,
unequal drive to rear wheels, Clayden
lost pipe. Rye, Dungeness, Rye. Stayed
at Ship as New Inn Winchelsea full.

AUGUST 16TH 1913
Pilot 10hp

PILOT LIGHT CAR
Standard Model, **£150** Complete, ready
10 H.P., 4 Cyl. :: for the road ::

with Aunt & Clayden
Rye, Winchelsea, devious bye-lanes,
Hastings Road, Winchelsea, Rye. 6m
Paddled, ditto afternoon at low tide.
Aunt drove in afternoon, got on well but
made a flat and stopped engine in gear.

AUGUST 17TH 1913
Pilot 10hp
with Aunt & Clayden
Rye, Tonbridge, Sevenoaks,

Westerham, Redhill, Reigate, Epsom, Kingston, Richmond.

Clayden left by train at Sevenoaks. Car ran beautifully climbing Reigate hill at 20mph. Got home 1.30 then proceeded to Pilot depot.

AUGUST 19TH 1913
Itala 40hp
with Pope
York, Thirsk, Sutton Bank.
Itala 35hp & 15hp,
with Rutter
16 climbs of Sutton Bank in 35hp,
1 climb in 15hp.
Itala 35hp
with Albertella
Run home. 26m
Record ascent 2 mins 21 seconds.

Rotary valve Oldham coupling sheared and extra air valve fell off. 10 successive attempts went well. Skidding at corners distance measured to 1 mile.

AUGUST 23RD 1913
Douglas 2¾hp
with Aunt
Esher via Kingston, Kingston via Richmond Park. 20m

Not pulling at all well found [jet?] too large a fit altogether so remedied.

AUGUST 29TH 1913
Pilot 10hp
with Aunt & Clayden
Richmond, Kingston, Ewell, Reigate, Sevenoaks, Tonbridge, Sandhurst, Rye. 80m

Went well got there in 4½ hours going leisurely. Wet roads some rain.

AUGUST 30TH 1913
Pilot 10hp
with Aunt & Clayden
Rye, Camber, Rye. 10m

Dull but not wet, paddled fine fun resolved to bathe. Sands here magnificent.

AUGUST 30TH 1913
Pilot 10hp
with Aunt & Clayden
Rye, Folkestone, Rye. 40m

Still dull and rather cold, roads fine. Aunt drove to Folkestone, getting on well.

SEPTEMBER 1ST 1913
with Aunt & Clayden
Rye, Folkestone, Dover, St Margaret's return. 65m

Tea at Dymchurch. Stormy day threw stones and rambled. Climbed up from beach in fine style skidding hairpin. Magnificent wide road out of Folkestone. Return cold.

SEPTEMBER 2ND 1913
Pilot 10hp
with Aunt & Clayden
Rye, Camber, Rye. 10m

Had magnificent bathe enjoyed ourselves immensely, fine and warm. Played on sands for hours mid next to nothing on.

SEPTEMBER 2ND 1913
Pilot 10hp
with Aunt & Clayden
Rye, Tenterden, Charing, Appledore. 20m

Aunt drove to Charing heaps of flies, much trouble losing way. Tea at Charing, roared back.

SEPTEMBER 3RD 1913
Pilot 10hp, with Aunt & Clayden
Rye, Camber, Rye. 11m

Bathed again cold but ripping. All went well. Car choking a bit, mudguard support touches spring.

[Same day]
Pilot 10hp
with Aunt & Clayden
Rye, Battle, Eastbourne, Beachy Head, Seaford, Lewes, Haywards Heath, Crawley, Reigate, Ewell, Kingston, Richmond. 130m

Cold car choked a lot, road vile. Took carburettor to pieces at Seaford also patched near rear tube. At Reigate changed complete tyre as it was flat. Drove in with side light only so very slow. Car touched 45 on flat. Mudguard support touching spring. Carb alright and car pulling well.

SEPTEMBER 4TH 1913
Pilot 10hp
with Clayden
Richmond, Barnes, Hammersmith, Tudor Street, Baker Street,

London Rd. 46m

Sundry runs of small size.

SEPTEMBER 7TH 1913
TT Douglas
Richmond, Brooklands via Hersham + 5 [laps]. 40m

Much troubled by overheating tried various jets without success. All things alright on road.

SEPTEMBER 11TH 1913
TT Douglas
Richmond, Brooklands via Hersham + 8 [laps of Brooklands]. 47 miles.

Tried new carburettor without making any improvements. Cut away old carburettor for racing and used extra air still without trouble. Found trouble due to no 5 cams [?].

SEPTEMBER 13TH 1913
TT Douglas & Rudge 3½hp
with Parker
Brooklands via Hersham. 2 laps. 32m

Press Race. Had no luck ran second for five miles out of six then top of carburettor fell off. Slowed right down to 10mph.

SEPTEMBER 14TH 1913
TT Douglas
with Aunt
Richmond, Cobham, Hut [Hut Hotel, Wisley]. 40m

Went exceptionally well and climbed all hills except Petersham on top. Had tea at Hut met Wallis and Brewer. Very cold going warmer coming back. Fine little jaunt, met Parker.

SEPTEMBER 20TH 1913
Rudge 3½hp
with Clayden
Boulogne, Colembert, Desvres. 35m

Run round *Coupe de l'auto* course. Machine pulled well on very high gear but engine harsh at high speeds.

SEPTEMBER 21ST 1913
Desvres, Colembert, Boulogne.
Coupe de l'auto.

Watched race from ravitaillement at Colembert. Ballot's Peugeot won, Gaux 2nd, Lee Guinness Sunbeam 3rd, Hancock Vauxhall 4th. Fine race

Guinness, Hancock and Gaux did sensational drive coming past at about 80. Went round course afterwards, pushed Resta's disabled car up hill and found Watson's Vauxhall with broken bevels. [Resta broke back axle in first 25kms and Watson last lap.]

SEPTEMBER 22ND 1913
Rudge 3½hp
with Aunt
Boulogne, Folkestone, Hythe, Ashford, Maidstone, Tonbridge. 50m
Very fine run, gear gave some trouble and single cylinder harsh. Lost way at Maidstone and arrived over awful roads to Tonbridge where it rained. Gear went wrong so put up at Angel. Aunt very sporting and much bumped. Fine little run.

SEPTEMBER 23RD 1913
Humber 3½hp
Tonbridge, Sevenoaks, Westerham, Redhill, Reigate, Esher, Kingston, Richmond. 30.
Very wet roads several small side slips. Gear caused half an hour's trouble and then was not quite right. Left at 12.30 arrived Richmond 2.15. Don't like Humber, engine too harsh, gear hard to handle. Carb not sensitive enough and too many control levers.

OCTOBER 4TH 1913
Douglas 2¾hp
with Aunt
Brooklands via Hersham. 36m
Went well but troubled with mixture.

OCTOBER 9TH 1913
Douglas 2¾hp
with Aunt & Boilleau,
Brookland's via Cobham. 30m
Went to test carburettor but huge crowd to see Pegoud. Collision on track four cars burned. Ran out of petrol near Cobham. [Pegoud flew a Bleriot at Brooklands.]

OCTOBER 11TH 1913
Douglas 2¾hp & Humber 3½hp
with Aunt & Clayden
Brooklands via Cobham and Hut. 30m
Went to see Pegoud. Still huger crowds. Clayden went away, much trouble with

enormous quantity of cars.

OCTOBER 11TH 1913
Douglas 2¾hp
Brooklands via Hersham back to Gray's Inn Rd. 46m
Went down for Sunbeam, Straker and Peugeot records. Sheared keyway on crankshaft.

NOVEMBER 1ST 1913
La Ponette 10hp
with Aunt & Leslie
Tiverton Mansions [first mention], Richmond, Staines, Basingstoke, Salisbury, Chard, Yeovil, Exeter. 190m
Went very well but had to fit gears and much trouble with headlights. 3.5 to 1 top gear too high for hills, springing excellent and speed good for new car.

NOVEMBER 2ND 1913
La Ponette 10hp
with Aunt & Clayden
Exeter, Taunton, Atheleney, Bath, Warminster. 90m
Pulling excellently but reverse out of action also rear footboards knocked up by axle. Took down gearbox at Warminster and fitted new collar to reverse pinion.

NOVEMBER 3RD 1913
With Aunt & Clayden
Warminster, Bulford, Salisbury, Basingstoke, Staines, Richmond, Tiverton Mansions.
More trouble with headlamp generator and many hours lost. New reverse washer working well, no trouble but cold and rather wet.

NOVEMBER 29TH 1913
De Dion 8-10hp [?], Mathis 6-12hp [?], Ford 20hp.
with Aunt, Lafone, Mrs Lafone & Clayden.
Grays Inn Rd, Richmond, Esher, Cobham, Track, Cobham, Grays Inn Rd + 4 [laps]. 52m
Treat runs. De Dion quiet and very slow, decelerator too stiff, straight-through quadrant rotten. Climbed out of track on first, speed 35. Mathis very fast but does not hold road well, big wheel makes steering good. Vertical central

gate excellent. Brakes best yet 2 internal expanding in rear wheels. Throttle spring too light, no diff. Springing bad, cornering good. Speed 40. Thick fog cold and dismal. [The Ford is not mentioned.]

NOVEMBER 30TH 1913
Mathis
De Dion
with Aunt, Leslie, Clayden & Gladys
Grays Inn Rd, Esher, Cobham, Ripley, Guildford, Hindhead, Weybridge, Hersham, 85 miles.
De Dion very slow indeed. Climbed Hindhead mostly on second. Mathis fine, took Charterhouse on second with big skid. Did 40 on flat. Better day, pic-nicked [!] on Hindhead. Cold.

DECEMBER 6TH 1913
La Ponette 10hp, Peugeot 6hp
with Aunt & Clayden. 89m
Very damp, dismal disgusting day. Missed Lafone so went on by ourselves. Ponette very good clutch stop has improved change no end, this now very nice. Climbing on second good. Beat Hupp [Hupmobile presumably] and held 25 Wolseley up Hindhead. Also Peugeot on Petersham after changing to first. Steering had no sense of direction. Peugeot a joke, very noisy howls on all gears but easy to change and very fast on lower gears, top too high.

DECEMBER 7TH 1913
La Ponette 10hp, Peugeot 6hp
with Gladys, Aunt & Clayden
Gray's Inn Rd, Old Kent Rd and Folkestone road to Leeds (castle) by Maidstone. Return Maidstone, Sevenoaks, Reigate, Ewell, Kingston, Richmond, home. 120m
Run to meet Clayden coming from Folkestone. Car very fast but uneasy on mud clung to steering. Change excellent. Climbed Reigate fast on second, good traffic car. Better day, little rain. Stopped for tea at Westerham. Peugeot lamps no good, Ponette's fair, generator good.

DECEMBER 13TH 1913
Ronteix 9hp [Cummikar, successful at Le Mans]

with Aunt
Gray's Inn Rd, Hammersmith,
Richmond, Kingston, Hersham, Track.

Gear box bearing broken so awful
noises. Clutch will not free, foot brake
no good. Engine excellent, difficult to
change gear quietly. Both brakes metal
to metal in rear wheels, notched
quadrant and trigger change. Saw
Hornsted [with 21.5hp Benz] but no
record. Lamps good, generator rotten.
Met Tony, "Baby Nora".

DECEMBER 14TH 1913
Ronteix 9hp
with Aunt
Gray's Inn Rd, Westminster,
Wandsworth, Putney, Kingston,
Ripley, Guildford, Charterhouse,
Hogs Back, Farnham, Oldham,
Sandhurst, Staines, Richmond,
Hammersmith, home. 89m

Not pulling well till flooded with oil,
gear noise worse, now awful. Cleaned

carb outside Farnham engine went well
thereafter. Took many photographs,
enjoyed ourselves. Some sunlight but cold.

DECEMBER 20TH 1913
Armstrong 6-50hp [Armstrong-
Whitworth 50hp 6-cyl.]
with Clayden, Aunt & Leslie
London, Hammersmith, Cobham,
Brooklands, + 6 [laps], Cobham,
Esher, Richmond, Hammersmith,
Gray's Inn Road. 50m

Too noisy and brakes bad. Handbrake
too stiff, footbrake uncertain, gear
change silent but gears cannot be felt.
Only did 49 for lap, 50 for mile,
obviously no pull. Clutch dry plate, good
levers in wrong position, hand control
too stiff. Steering good, self starter good,
Vanden vell [Vandervell?] friction, engine
soft but sweet. Very cold.

DECEMBER 21ST 1913
Armstrong 6-50 hp

with Aunt, Clayden, "Baby" & Leslie
Gray's Inn Rd, Victoria,
Hammersmith, Brentford,
Hounslow, Maidenhead, Henley,
Abingdon, Farringdon, Cricklade,
Cirencester and back. 178m

Got appallingly cold. Stopped at
Abingdon for warm. Still colder coming
back and roads very slippery indeed.
Car bad on hills and difficult to control
owing to poor brakes and bad carb
setting. Rear wheels revolve at touch of
footbrake. Nearly… cycled [?] till
Henley. Stopped for tea and huge warm
at Catherine Wheel. Electric headlamps
good. Got dirt on contact maker which
cleaned at Maidenhead.

DECEMBER 24TH 1913
Wolseley 6hp, Averies [chassis] 10hp
with Clayden
Grays Inn Rd, Hammersmith,
Brentford, Staines, Cobham, Staines,
Brentford, return. 65m

La Ponette. 8hp - 4cyl. 1912

Journey to fetch Averies. Stellite, [Electric & Ordnance Accessories Co. Ltd – Wolseley] 2 speeds, harsh engine, steering rack and pinion excellent. Gears hopeless. Pull fair. Averies chassis much mud thrown up, also oil lights only so very slow progress through thick mud. Ran out of petrol in Staines.

DECEMBER 26TH 1913

[two entries for this date]
**Averies 10hp & Wolseley 6hp
with Aunt & Clayden
Gray's Inn Rd, Embankment, Putney Common, Kingston, Walton, Brooklands, Cobham, Esher, Kingston, Hammersmith, Richmond. 54m**
Very cold, no dash on Averies. Rigged up cappet and pole guards. Petrol tank too low, tool box got in way coming back. Engine pulls well and springing good. Steering excellent and change speed very good (sliding lever). Wind cold, less mud. Lafone started for Exeter.

DECEMBER 25TH 1913

[date out of sequence]
**Averies 10hp & Wolseley [Stellite] 6hp
with Aunt & Clayden
Gray's Inn Rd, Hammersmith, Richmond, Kingston, Esher, Cobham, Hut, return. 63m**
[Entry for 25th changed to 26th]
Very cold, but dry. Averies good Stellite fair. Enjoyable little bumble.

DECEMBER 26TH 1913

**Averies 10hp
with Aunt
Gray's Inn Rd, Hammersmith, Richmond, Staines. 20m**
Howling gale, very cold and uncomfortable. Saw start of Exeter [MCC London-Exeter Trial]. Left chassis at Angel, Staines home by train.

DECEMBER 27TH 1913

**Averies 10 hp & Wolseley 6hp
with Aunt, Clayden & Lafone,
Staines, Hartford Bridge, Staines, Brentford, Hammersmith, Grays Inn, 58m**
Trained to Staines, got chassis out and went to Hartford Bridge to see run. Stiff wind & very cold. Met Clayden and Lafone, tea at Sandhurst. Clayden & self came in later very well to Tudor Street [First mention of Tudor Street, HQ of *The Automobile Engineer*].

DECEMBER 28TH 1913

**Wolseley 6hp
with Aunt
Grays Inn, Hammersmith, Roehampton, Kingston, Esher, Cobham, Hut, Ripley. 64m**
Nice little bumble, Aunt drove from Esher to Ripley and back. Car suffering from Exeter, Steering stiff, engine noise, clutch pedal ditto. [The Wolseley did not officially participate in the trial.]

Armstrong-Whitworth 30-50hp 6-cylinder, 1913-14.

1914

JANUARY 3RD 1914
TT Douglas 2⅔hp & A.C. 10hp
with Aunt & Clayden
Grays Inn Rd, Hammersmith,
Richmond, Esher, Hersham,
Brooklands, Hut, Ripley, Cobham,
return. 54m
Fine sun but cold. Just after Hut con rod broke bike slewed round. Towed by A.C. to White Lion. Here found both pistons and con rods smashed as big end came loose. Returned in A.C.

JANUARY 4TH 1914
A.C. 10hp
with Clayden
Grays Inn, Highgate, Finchley,
Barnet, Hatfield, St Albans, Barnet,
return. 60m
A.C. very slow, change gear fair. Steering strange ["good" crossed out], hill climbing bad. Ran out of petrol. Muddy clay, wings are bad as mud came over. Screen good, brakes good.

JANUARY 4TH 1914
A.C. 10hp
with Aunt & Clayden
Grays Inn Rd, Putney, Richmond,
Sunbury, Watersplash [?] by bye
lanes, Walton, Weybridge,
Portsmouth Road, Hut, Cobham,
Esher, return. 62m
Very slow, steering bad something obviously wrong.

JANUARY 5TH 1914,
A.C. 10hp,
Grays Inn Road, Hammersmith,
Richmond, Kingston. 20m
A.C. works. Returned car. Diff pinion seized and casing turning round badly thus slowing car.

JANUARY 9TH 1914
Humber 10hp
Coventry, Dunchurch, Towcester,
Dunstable, St Albans, Barnet,
Finchley, Gray's Inn.
[How was Coventry reached? No distance recorded]

Roads awful, did trip in 4½hrs, no surface, deep mud, Car fast, smooth, easy to change gear, fair steering, fair lights, excellent brakes.

JANUARY 9TH 1914
Humber 10hp
with Ida & Aunt, Clayden & Leslie.
Grays Inn, Balham. 10m
Very muddy. Drove over curb in dark. Car went well. Slipping on tram lines.

JANUARY 10TH 1914
Humber 10hp & Overland 20hp
with Aunt & Ida, Baby & Brewer,
Clayden & Leslie
Grays Inn, Victoria, Hammersmith,
Richmond, Staines, Basingstoke,
Salisbury, Chard, Yeovil, Exeter. 180m
Overland faster but otherwise not so good. Change bad, Steering good, brakes fair, engine awful. Today very cold. Failed on Chard and Yarcombe. Much trouble with carb air valve. Lunch at Salisbury.

Humber 10hp 4-cylinder, 1914.

JANUARY 11TH 1914

Overland 20hp & Humber 10hp with Aunt, Ida, Baby, Brewer, Clayden & Leslie

Exeter, same way till Staines, Brentford, Hammersmith, Gray's Inn.

Overland very tired, much air valve adjustment. Lunch at Yeovil, tea Andover. Ran out of petrol near Salisbury, waited till Humber returned. Screen lower half broke on Plain, fell out altogether near Hartford Bridge. Much trouble to start at Staines. Eventually Humber had to fetch more petrol from Gray's Inn [it was Sunday]. Top speed will not stay in. Huge Humber headlamps had to light. Overland's Gray & Davis [USA] starter very good. [This was to prove an important test for the Overland, in time for the IAE meeting of Jan 14th. See *Automobile Engineering*, Bibliography]

JANUARY 13TH 1914,

Humber 10hp & Douglas 2¾hp, with Aunt, Billinghurst & Clayden,

Gray's Inn, Hammersmith, Roehampton, Kingston, Horsham, Track + 3 [laps], Cobham, Esher, Roehampton, Hammersmith. 40m

Took repaired Douglas [engine] out and tested Humber, speed 38 against howling gale, two up. 30 or less against wind. Had trouble with special timing on Douglas and replaced old cams (on road). Ignition too far advanced and lever broken. Very cold indeed.

JANUARY 14TH 1914

Humber 10hp with Critchley, Shilson, Biggs, Clayden IAE [Institute of Automobile Engineers] Victoria, Euston, Gray's Inn Rd. 6m

Car running well but fierce clutch. Night of IAE Paper [Clayden read paper *Economics of Design*].

JANUARY 15TH 1914

A.C. 10hp

Ditton, Esher, Cobham, Hut, Guildford, Godalming, Charterhouse, Guildford, Hut, Chobham, Send, Ripley, Hut, Track, Hersham, Esher, Ditton. 65m

Car running well but noisy, brakes want adjusting, engine harsh, second slipped on Charterhouse so took first above bend, and went up well. Change good, Springing poor, Steering (rack and pinion) fair. Wet all day, tried to find special hotel near Splash [?] but failed. Very cold indeed.

JANUARY 16TH 1914,

Humber 10hp. with Aunt

Gray's Inn, Finchley, Barnet, St Albans, Markgate, Dunstable, Stony Stratford, Towcester, Daventry, Dunchurch, Coventry. 90m

Fine but cold day, much mud. Car went very well, (needs little oil). Slow on hills. Very fast for size on level. Clutch improving. Took 4½hrs owing to mud. Do not recommend lunch at Dunstable. Aunt seemed to enjoy run and bucked up no end.

La Licorne 10hp 4-cylinder. Sammy himself is in this picture, believed on a trial in 1912.

JANUARY 24TH 1914
Bayard 10hp & Swift 8hp
with Aunt, Walls [?] & Clayden
Gray's Inn, Brooklands via Hersham
+ 4 [laps], return. 40m
Swift lumpy, two cylinders no good.
Speed 40. Held Bayard on hills. Change
excellent.

JANUARY 25TH 1914
Bayard 10hp
with Leslie
Gray's Inn, Hammersmith,
Hampstead, home. 20m
Helter [skelter?] round. Car hard to
change up.

JANUARY 25TH 1914
Bayard
with Aunt & Clayden
Gray's Inn, Hammersmith, Esher,
Hut, Ripley, Pyrford, Addlestone,
Track, Hersham, Hammersmith,
Gray's Inn. 60m
Tried to find pub but failed. Wandered
all around Ripley [odd as village had
many pubs!]. Car noisy, fair amount of
pull, probably needs decarbonising.

JANUARY 29TH 1914
Sunbeam 15hp
with Boilleau & Lafone
Tudor Street, Finchley, Barnet, St
Albans, Dunstable, Towcester,
Daventry, Coventry. 90m
Fine car, Very smooth and nice, control
levers on wheel too stiff. Change good
steering good. Brakes excellent,
particularly foot brake.

JANUARY 31ST 1914
La Licorne 10hp
Gray's Inn, Hampstead, Brockley,
Watford, A/Clinton, Whiteleafe,
Dashwood, Oxford, Lechlade,
Cirencester, Cheltenham, Gloucester,
Oxford, Wickham, Amersham,
Stanmore, Edgware, Hampstead. 250m
North West London MCC 12 hrs test.
Fine run very muddy very skiddy. Cart
fell on Swift. Singer smashed to pieces.
Took Martin and partner to Oxford.
Picked up injured motorcyclist and
drove him to Cirencester. Much rain and
heaps of mud. Lamps gave trouble,
clutch slipped. Change awful, brakes

good, throttle very bad [and still
managed 250 miles!]

FEBRUARY 1ST 1914
La Licorne 10hp & Decauville 20hp
[Decauville ceased 1909 – 10]
with Aunt, Robert, Clayden,
Leslie & Baby
Gray's Inn, Putney, Kingston, Esher,
Hut, Ripley, Pyrford, Woking Village,
Woking, Pyrford Lock, Wisley, Hut,
Track, Byfleet, Woking, Chobham,
Upper Shepperton, Sunbury. 90m
Gear change awful. Tried to find pub.
Lost Robert. Tea at Track. Found pub at
Shepperton. Came home well,
headlamps excellent.

FEBRUARY 13TH 1914
La Ponette 10hp
with Sandy
London, Dunstable, Daventry,
Dunchurch, Coventry. 90m
Throttle stuck down and tyre punctured at
Towcester. Changed wheel (these
detachable wheels are good). Throttle
sticking, cured by filing rod. Car fast,
steering fair inclined to run off, brakes fair.

FEBRUARY 14TH 1914
La Ponette 20hp
with Sandy & Mont
Coventry, Kenilworth, Stonebridge,
Berkswell. 20m
Colmore Cup. First slipped out twice.
Arrived Stonebridge well. Steering still a
bit weird. After start pulled up to record
Horstman's stop [Horstmann car?]. On
trying to move off found couldn't. Had
to take gear box out. Found striking
shaft and ball race on layshaft broken.
Very mad. Had to leave car and walk in.
(Beer at White Horse good). Towed in
by Humber to Swifts garage. Rotten time.
This car is undoubtedly weak in the gear
box and should not be taken long runs.

FEBRUARY 15TH 1914
Humber 20hp
with Mont & Sandy
Kenilworth, Coventry, Kenilworth.
12m
[The following related to Ponette]
Fetched gear box and worked all day to
repair it. Had to find new bearing, have
striking rod turned up. Found three ball

bearings in grease which with one
found on road makes seven in all. Race
badly split.

FEBRUARY 15TH 1914
Humber 20hp, with Mont & Sandy
Kenilworth, Coventry, Kenilworth.
12m
Went to fetch kit from hotel. Humber in
pieces, had trouble with clutch ball race.

FEBRUARY 16TH 1914
[Ponette]
Brought in gearbox and replaced it in
chassis. Had trouble with various bits
particularly de Dion joints, brakes and
gear lever shafts, about bored [fed up]
with this car. Sandy worked like a
Trojan, no more Ponettes for trials of
importance.

FEBRUARY 20TH 1914
Hillman 10hp
with Osmond
London, Wickham, Oxford. 50m
Gear slipped out. Car with bad period at
high speed. Sprung too stiff. Gear
change fair, steering stiff, brakes fair.
Engine plenty of power and car fast.

FEBRUARY 20TH & 21ST 1914
Hillman 10hp
with Osmond
Oxford, Bicester, Buckingham, Stony
Stratford, Wellingboro, Kettering,
Stamford, Grantham, Newark,
Bawtry, Doncaster and return. 350m
Oxford Clubs trial in awful rain with
fearful wind. Sleet and snow later, gale
and heavy rain, much mud. Generator
broke, tried to mend it with copper
wire, strong rope. Finally after 12 stops
procured another generator. Alright
then, lost way several times especially
at Stamford. Stopped at Bawtry for
huge breakfast, lovely morning,
Saturday... [?] rod came off, U joint
cover also. New generator no trouble.
More rain sleet and mud. First in to
huge meal at Mitre.

FEBRUARY 22ND 1914
Hillman 10hp
with Osmond
Oxford, Faringdon, Swindon,
Devizes, Wells, Glastonbury,

Taunton, Exeter. 120m

More rain mud sleet and wind, hood turned inside out several times. Engine better. Awful skids over Athelney Marsh. Arrived at 7.10, tea at London [?] Taunton.

FEBRUARY 23RD 1914
Hillman 10hp & De Dion 18hp
with Aunt, Sandy, Uncle & Leslie
Exeter, Taunton, Andover,
Basingstoke, Blackwater, Staines,
Richmond, Gray's Inn. 200m

Hillman much better, faster than De Dion uphill, slower on level by perhaps ½mph. Aunt in great spirits. Tea at Basingstoke.

FEBRUARY 27TH 1914
Turner 10hp
with Lafone
Gray's Inn, Euston, Hyde Park,
Shepherds Bush, Hammersmith,
Kingston, Esher, Cobham,
Weybridge. 20m

Car pulled well but seemed overhot, clutch jerky, gears good, steering stiff.

FEBRUARY 28TH 1914
[Turner 10hp]
Weybridge, Cobham, Burford Bridge,
Ranmore Common, Combe Bottom,
Pebblecombe [Hill], Wray Lane
[Reigate], Leatherhead, Cobham,
Brooklands. 72m

Cyclecar Club reliability trial. Failed on Ranmore ditto Combe Bottom, pushed Pebblecombe, pushed Wray Lane [hill]. Stopped to oil universal joint owing to greaser falling off. Car very bad, mixture too rich.

FEBRUARY 28TH 1914
Benz 200hp
with Hornstead
12m

4 times round track once up test hill once round Bluebird [café]. Magnificent, the ride of one's life, touched 130mph. shut off half way up test hill, took corners very fast, absolutely it.

[Same day]
Turner 10hp
Brooklands, Heath, Hersham,
Kingston, Hammersmith, Gray's Inn.
20m

No trouble, no power. Found Jennings with broken Morgan, took friend in to Oxford Street. Gear change bad clutch stop being irregular.

MARCH 6TH 1914
Calthorpe 9hp
London, Luton, Bedford, Kettering,
Leicester, Loughborough, Derby,
Ripley, Chesterfield, Sheffield.
160m

Great gale blowing, cape hood blown up three times. Could get no speed. Tree branches blown down.

MARCH 7TH 1914,
Calthorpe 9hp,
ACU [Auto- cycle Union] 160¼m.

One day trial. Awful hills nearly stuck on Anchor Knoll but climbed others

Calthorpe 9hp 4-cylinder, 1914.

easily. Burst tyre on corner, reversed to get round another. Engine excellent. Climbed Cowdale easily, scenery fine. Steering weird, brakes good, springing fair, gear control excellent. Roads narrow slippery and with bad camber.

MARCH 8TH 1914
Calthorpe 9hp
Sheffield, Chesterfield, Ripley, Nottingham, Melton Mowbray, Oakham, Uppingham, Kettering, Finedon, Chelveston, Eaton Socon, Biggleswade, Stevenage, Hatfield, Barnet, Finchley, London. 180m
Wind bad much rain, steering worse. Ran out of petrol and walked 4½ miles. Picked up by Daimler for remainder. Steering very bad, queer brake noise. Speed good.

MARCH 14TH 1914
Turner 10hp
with Parkes & Cummings
London, Hounslow, High Wycombe, Princes Risborough, Kopp Hill and back. 60m
Violent rainstorms, much mud, roads, partially submerged. Could not use top much going. Clutch slipped at hill, afterwards wheels refused to grip. Brought in Cummings, Sirron having broken gearbox. Climb in pouring rain. Returned to tea at Wycombe. Very wet, car ran fairly. Four seater too much for engine.

MARCH 15TH 1914
Pilot 10hp
with Sandy & Uncle
London, Hammersmith, Kingston, Ewell, Burford Bridge, Ranmore, White Downs, Combe Bottom, Dorking, Pebblecombe, Ewell, Epsom, Hook, Esher, Hersham, Track. 120m
Pouring rain most of time. Tested Pilot over Cyclecar Club route, three up. Climbed Ranmore fairly well. Combe excellently and all other well, Pebblecombe very well but would not restart. Water boiled badly on later hill. Rain very bad near Hook, went through 9" water splash without difficulty. Transmission noisy, engine good, brakes good, good run. Car fast touching 68 without trouble. Rather clanky on high gear if run slow.

MARCH 12TH 1914
[Date out of sequence]
Wilton 10hp
Tudor Street, Baker Street, Hampstead, Highgate. 10m
Overheated on two hills, gear lever would not cross gate. Clutch slipped, steering very stiff, gears very noisy.

MARCH 15TH 1914,
Belsize 15.9hp
Brooklands 20 [laps]. 6m.

MARCH 20TH 1914
GWK 10hp
with Sandy
Whestone through bye roads to Barnet and Finchley. 10m
Test run, car driving badly and running on weak mixture pressure adjusted before start. Condition good not much play anywhere. Upholstery poor. Hand brake re-lined and poor, footbrake good. Could be made a good car.

MARCH 24TH 1914
Douglas 2¾hp
London, Hammersmith, Barnes, 10m
Missing badly, tried various jets without improvement but found trouble in porcelain plug which had points fused intermittently.

MARCH 28TH 1914
Douglas 2¾hp
with Aunt
London, Hammersmith, Roehampton, Kingston, Hersham, Brooklands. 40m
Excellent day bright sunshine. Saw Calthorpe smashed as steering tie rod arm broke. Aunt rode to Barnes on back of machine, much dust and some trouble with nuts.

MARCH 29TH 1914
Douglas 2¾hp
London, Hammersmith, Roehampton, Kingston, Hersham, Brooklands. 40m
TT Sunbeam arrived. Rain all time nothing doing at track.

MARCH 30TH 1914
[Douglas 2¾hp]
London, Hammersmith,

Roehampton, Kingston, Cobham, Hersham, Brooklands +16 [laps], return. 57m
Watched TT Sunbeam, speed 95. Jets changed every other round. Douglas overheating and lubrication giving trouble.

MARCH 31ST 1914
Douglas 2¾hp
Portland Rd, Hammersmith, Roehampton, Kingston, Hersham, Brooklands. 40m
Run for photographs [?], fine at first rain later. Slow running jet choked up much trouble as result.

APRIL 1ST 1914,
Douglas 2¾hp
London, Hammersmith, Roehampton, Kingston, Esher, Hersham, track. 18m
Fine bright day too much dust. Tried advanced ignition, better results.

APRIL 2ND 1914
Douglas 2¾hp
Heath, track + 6 [laps]. 18m
Altered cam timing, still better but overheating.

APRIL 3RD 1914,
Track + 6 [laps].
Still overheating, a little better, perhaps too much carbon deposit.

APRIL 4TH 1914
Peugeot Bébé
with Wallis
Trained up then Edgware, Watford, Rickmansworth, Tring, Aston Clinton and back. 60m
Much rain all the time but relay hill climb run off. Peugeot very noisy and apparently in bits.

APRIL 5TH 1914
Pilot 10hp
with Clayden & Sandy
London, Hammersmith, Roehampton, Kingston, Esher, track. 20m
Car went well, transmission very noisy.

APRIL 6TH 1914
Douglas 2¾hp
Track + 3 [laps], Hersham, Kingston,

Roehampton, Hammersmith, London. 29m

Running much better but overheating still.

APRIL 7TH 1914
Pilot 10hp
Round about town. 6m

Very noisy.

APRIL 8TH 1914
Pilot 10hp
Smiths, Douglas, Oxford Street, Dunlop, Frosts, Bensons. 13m

Collecting accessories and spares for Pilot's run.

APRIL 9TH 1914
Pilot 10hp
London, Hammersmith, Barnes and back. 12m

Took Clayden to Swindleys for Straker.

APRIL 10TH 1914
Pilot 10hp & Straker 15hp,

with Clayden & Sandy
London, Richmond Staines. 18m

Went well, all seemed well, feeling very fit. Bright fairly warm moonlight night.

APRIL 11TH 1914
[On Pilot]
with Sandy
MCC Land's End Trial. Staines. Egham, Blackwater, Basingstoke, Salisbury, Dorchester, Bridport, Lyme Regis, Sidford, Exeter, Ashburton, Dartmeet, Tavistock, Liskeard, Lostwithiel, Truro, Redruth, Penzance, Land's End, Penzance. 295m

Rain at first fine afterwards. Headlamps Willooq Bateen excellent. Car running very well and faster than all competitors' except Mathis. Across Plain went excellently and held road well. Climbed Charmouth excellently and had breakfast at Exeter. Overheated on Holden, failed on hairpin near Two

Bridges because baulked but climbed Lee Tor very well. Radiator too small. Arrived Land's End awful state from dust and had eye trouble Sunday.

APRIL 13TH 1914
[On Pilot]
with Sandy
Penzance, Truro, Dartmeet, Exeter, Sidford, Lyme Regis, Bridport, Dorchester, Blandford, Tarrant Hinton. 192m

Not going so well but got up Dartmeet excellently. Arrived Exeter without trouble but failed first time on Throw Top because discs slipped. Went badly to Dorchester and then forward sliding shaft bearing seized. Walked five miles for bed, Sandy 4 miles more. Pushed car into barn.

APRIL 14TH 1914
[On Pilot]
Tarrant Hinton, Salisbury, Andover, Basingstoke, Egham, Staines,

Peugeot Bébé 6hp 4-cylinder. 1913-14.

Brentford, Hammersmith, home. 98m
Walked out again 5 miles, spent all
morning repairing bearing and tyre
LHR. Got going at 3.00pm, punctured
RHR on Salisbury Plain and belt charred
off after water pipe nearly cut through.
LHR punctured near Basingstoke. Awful
time absolutely done up, car in bits and
selves tired out .

APRIL 15TH 1914
Mitchells garage, Pilot works. 5m
Took blistered machine back.

APRIL 17TH 1914
Douglas 2¾hp
London, Hammersmith, Kingston,
Hersham, Track + 5 [laps]. 55m
Tuning up could not use No: 5 cams,
owing to missing had to change to
ordinary timing. OK then but slow,
advanced ignition another tooth.

APRIL 18TH 1914
Douglas 2¾hp
London Hammersmith, Kingston,
Hersham, track + 1 [lap]. 43m
Jet came unscrewed, stopped first lap,
otherwise quite fastest. Want 2 point
plugs, another carburettor.

APRIL 19TH 1914
Douglas 2¾hp & Pilot 10hp
with Aunt & Clayden
London, Hammersmith, Kingston,
Hersham, track + 5 [laps]. 51m.
Tried lag and lead No: 5 no good,
ordinary lag and lead no good. Normal
best so far, want 31 jet.

APRIL 20TH 1914
Ronteix 10hp
with Cummings,
Putney, Hammersmith, Acton,
Southall, 15m
Saw Sirron 1000 miles car, she appears
good.

APRIL 21ST 1914
Pilot 10hp
with Aunt & Sandy
Gray's Inn, Hyde Park + 5 [lapped
Hyde Park five times?]. 20m
Little bumble round, very pleasant.

APRIL 22ND 1914
With Clayden & Aunt
Gray's Inn, Hammersmith,
Richmond, Kingston, Esher. 30m
Aunt drove, getting on much better.
Troubled by inverselle [indecipherable]
wings.

APRIL 23RD 1914,
Pilot 10hp
Gray's Inn, Hyde Park, Putney. 15m
Saw Cummings, arranged about jacks,
found Sirrons too near weight limit.

[Two Sirrons were entered for the RAC
trials. S G Cummings was a Cummikar
driver.]

APRIL 25TH 1914,
Cummikar 10hp
Essex Club one day trial. 120m
Won silver medal, failing in stopping
and restarting test, otherwise good. Car
hard to handle.

APRIL 26TH 1914
Cummikar 10hp
Gray's Inn, Hammersmith, Kingston,
Brooklands + 4 laps. 52m
Met Hugh on Douglas, spent day at track.

APRIL 27TH 1914
[Cummikar 10hp]
10m
Redelivered [?] Cummikar.

APRIL 28TH 1914
Sirron 10hp
with Hunt
London, Barnet, Hatfield,
Biggleswade, Stamford. 90m
Had to tune up carburettor. Stopped
for Hunt's tools. Took down steering
because too stiff. Clutch slipped, fullers
earth and resin applied. Gears howled,
car gradually improving.

APRIL 29TH 1914
Sirron 10hp
with Hunt
Stamford, Doncaster, Pontefract,
Aberford, Harrogate. 126m
Going better but radiator split, took it
down and soldered. Filled up with
water eight times.

APRIL 30TH 1914
Sirron 10hp
with Hunt
Harrogate, Ripley, Pateley,
Greenhow. 24m
Went up Greenhow well, split radiator
at top, had to take it down and repair.
Raced home to weigh in.

MAY 1ST 1914
Belsize 15hp & Pilot 10hp
with Brewer, Aunt & Uncle
Harrogate, Buroughbridge, Thirsk,
Sutton [Bank]. 60m
[Headed "1,000 miles trials"] Tried Sutton,

La Licorne 14hp 4-cylinder, 1914.

got Pilot up, two up, with 13 tooth sprocket. Sat on tail of racing Belsize.

MAY 2ND 1914
Sirron 10hp
Harrogate, Thirsk, Wass, Whitby, Saltburn, Sutton, Harrogate.
Climbed Wass well but piston head blew in at Sutton, Afterwards con' rod seized.

MAY 3RD 1914
Pilot 10hp
with Aunt & Uncle
Knaresborough, York Filey, Scarborough, Whitby, Pickering, York, Wetherby, Harrogate. 187¼m
Good run climbed Garrowby and Blue Bank without trouble. Broke chain belt on moors. Finished well.

MAY 4TH 1914
Pilot 10hp
Ripon, Leyburn, Borough, Appleby, Kirby Stephen, Aisgill, Bedale, Thirsk, Harrogate. 164½m
[RAC Light Car Trial started – Sammy not entered. See *British Trials Drivers*, Cowbourne, Bibliography] Took Smith's car, made non-stop, running well. Climbed Arkangarthdale and Scarth Nick fast and well, much rain.

MAY 5TH 1914
[Pilot 10hp]
Knaresborough, York, Ripon, Pateley [Bridge], Gargrave, Settle, Aysgarth, Bolton Abbey, Harrogate. 175½m
Failed on Pateley owing to disc but climbed well after adjustment. Tyre pumped up. Came home well, rain all day.

MAY 6TH 1914
Pilot 10hp
Tadcaster, Illely, Colne, Settle, Airton, Pateley, Thirsk, Harrogate. 176m
Climbed Ilkley and Heaton Woods very well, indeed failed on Brownstay [Ridge] owing to slip, got up solo. Burst 2 tyres coming back.

MAY 7TH 1914
Pilot 10hp
Ripon, Thirsk, Sutton, Helmsley, Scarborough, York, Wetherby, Harrogate, 132¼m

Failed Sutton, discs slipping. Got up solo, radiator leaking, frame broken and had to fit new tyre before start. Finished well.

MAY 8TH 1914
Pilot 10hp & Pilot 10hp together, with Aunt & Uncle
Harrogate, Doncaster, Nottingham, Leicester, Coventry. 120m
Good run but both cars four [up?] carb' stopped with mud.

MAY 9TH 1914
[Pilot 10hp]
with Aunt
Coventry, Dunchurch, Towcester, St Albans, London. 90.
More rain but good run no trouble, very cold.

APRIL 24TH 1914
[Date out of sequence]
Pilot 10hp
with Miss Smith
Brighton and various Hills. 20m
Testing trials. Pilot went up Cinder Hill well.

MAY 16TH 1914
Pilot 10hp
with Aunt & Sandy
Gray's Inn, Watford, Tring, Aston Clinton. 35m.
Hill climb day, bright sunny, awful dust clouds of grit, bumpy road.

[Same day]
TT Douglas 2¾hp
with Uncle
Aston, Amersham, Harrow, Hammersmith, Gray's Inn. 35m
Return journey better because of tarred road.

MAY 17TH 1914,
Douglas 2¾hp & Pilot 10hp
with Aunt, Sandy & Uncle
Gray's Inn, Hammersmith, Richmond, Hersham, track + 3 [laps], Cobham, return. 52m
Pilot's discs slipping. Bearing came unscrewed. Climbed test hill with more pressure. Douglas running well.

MAY 18TH 1914
[Pilot 10hp]

with Gladys & Aunt
Gray's Inn, Richmond, Kingston, Hersham, track, Hut, Cobham, Esher, Richmond, Gray's Inn. 62m
Excellent little run in lovely weather. Chain fell off twice.

APRIL 19TH 1914
[Date out of sequence]
Pilot 10hp
Gray's Inn, London Rd, Gray's Inn. 7m
To works to fetch friction gear parts. Chain adjusted. Ran out of petrol.

MAY 23RD & 24TH 1914,
[Pilot 10hp], Douglas 2¾hp,
with Sandy, Aunt & Uncle
Gray's Inn, Barnet, Hendon, Gray's Inn. 30m & 40m
Went to see aerial derby but this was off. Disc slipping [Pilot]. Tried machine, overheating badly, but fast otherwise.

MAY 25TH 1914
Stellite 6hp
with Ganly
Dublin, Dunbar, Dundalk, Castleblaney, Ardec, Slane, Dublin. 133m
Irish Trials. [Irish light car trial. Sammy was not competing] Good run, too much dust. Country awful, food bad, people curious, no hills, bad roads.

MAY 26TH 1914
Stellite 6hp
with Ganly
Dublin, Sally Gap, Arklow, Wicklow, Rathnew, Annamoe, Pollaphuca [reservoir], Terrenure, Dublin. 120m
No hills worth talking about, scenery lovely in Wicklow Mountains. Dust better, roads and food worse. Stellite awful, filled up water four times.

MAY 27TH 1914
Douglas 2¾hp,
Dublin, Ballinascorney [Gap – hill climb], Pollaphuca, Carlow, Ballybuttas, Kildare, Naas, Dublin, 128¼m
Dust abominable, Carburettor choked once but machine excellent. Roads fearful especially Gordon Bennett course.

MAY 28TH 1914
Austin 10hp
with Huet & Murphy
Dublin, Enfield, Kinnegad, Athlone,
Tullamore, Lucan, Dublin. 158¼m
Dust still bad, much rain, car ran out of petrol.

MAY 31ST 1914
Douglas 2¾hp
Gray's Inn, Hammersmith,
Kingston, Hersham, track, Kingston,
Gray's Inn. 42m
Running badly, overheated a bit, must change plugs, SU carburettor fair.

JUNE 1ST 1914
Douglas 2¾hp
Gray's Inn, Hammersmith, Kingston,
Hersham, track. 39m
Brooklands meeting. Excellent

meeting, machine ran well. Brewer's Belsize four smashed pistons. Itala and Theo Schneider made good show.

JUNE 3RD 1914
Walham Green, Oatlands Park,
Gray's Inn Rd, Walham Green. 20m
Fetched remains of tricycle [?] home having been smashed up by taxicab on 1st of June.

JUNE 5TH 1914
Repaired [tricycle].

JUNE 14TH 1914
At Edinburgh 1,000 miles Scottish. [Edinburgh & District Motor Club 6 days Motorcycles & Cyclecars Trial. Sammy was not competing.]

JUNE 15TH 1914
Douglas 2¾hp
Edinburgh, Falkirk, Stiring, Amulree,
Trinafour, Blair Atholl, Dunkeld,
Perth. 156¾m
Roads bad, weather splendid. Had to run on Amulree but got up Trinafour without trouble, subsequent roads and dust awful.

JUNE 16TH 1914
Douglas 2¾hp
Perth, Brechin, Cairn o Mount,
Ballater, Carrbridge, Inverness, 173¾m
Roads frightful, got up Cairn o Mount OK but somewhat hot at top, no gradient, rocks, stones, rut and clonky banks.

JUNE 17TH 1914
Douglas 2¾hp
Inverness, Beauly, Braemore [Lodge],

Overland 20-25hp 4-cylinder, 1912.

Gairloch, Dingwall, Inverness 180½m
Worst roads yet, abominable bumping, no trouble with Kinlochewe Hill at all and got up Abriachan all correct skidding on unrolled stones.

JUNE 18TH 1914
Douglas 2¾hp
Inverness, Garve, Auchnashellach, Applecross, Jeantown [Lochcarron], Kinlochewe, Inverness. 179m
Two stops to cool on Applecross which is most awful hill imaginable, rocks, boulders, gulley hairpins, mist, stones and length combining to make anything but joy. Lost nut off spring fork lever motion.

JUNE 19TH 1914
Douglas 2¾hp
Inverness, Abriachan, Cluani [Inn], Tomdoun, Invergarry, Grantown.

145¾m
Getting sick of this, nearly off five times. Lost nut has had awful effect on forks which are now bound up with rope. Very stiff and sore. Had to deviate for oil. Bored.

JUNE 20TH 1914
Douglas 2¾hp & Ford 20hp
Grantown, Tomintoul, Pitlochery, Kenmore, Stirling, Edinburgh. 185m
Feeling worse, forks very bad, engine funny but got up all hills. Much more bored, very sore and most stiff. 6 miles from home, con' rod belt broke wrecking engine. Came home on Ford.

JUNE 21ST 1914
AC 10hp
with Scott & Pauling
Edinburgh to machine and back. 12m

Towed in Douglas.

JUNE 24TH 1914
Crespelle 20hp racer
with Westall
Walham Green, Gray's Inn, Westalls Garage, Kingston, Baker Street. 20m
Car awful to handle. Clutch very bad, much trouble with clutch joint which had to bind with wire. Choked pilot jet, no tools.

JUNE 25TH 1914
Crespelle 20hp racer
with Westall
London, Southend, Speed trials [Essex Motor Club]. 45m
Could not stop clutch slipping. Worked all day, used four packets fullers earth, four penn'orth resin, much petrol and two saw blades. Lost both races

AC 10hp 4-cylinder, 1914.

through slipping and clutch leather came off. Trained home mad.

JUNE 27TH 1914
Hillman 10hp & Straker 15hp
with Billy, Westall, Whittal [?],
Miss Whit, Rutter
London, Roehampton, Kingston,
Hersham, track, Kingston,
Richmond, Hammersmith, Gray's
Inn. 40m
No reverse, Had to push back Hillman. Straker good. Rutter can't drive and nearly died of fright.

JULY 1ST 1914
Pilot 10hp
with Osmond & Clayden
[Journey to French Grands Prix - there
is no log for the journey to Lyon] 35m
Weeyyy went nolly [left to eh reader's imagination!]. Did 60 in places. Bumps awful, chassis needs overhauling. Course not fast because of Rive-de-Gier and bumps on straight.

[Same day]
with Aunt & Crosbie
Sunbeam depot, Peugeot depot, Les
Sept Chemins, Lyon. 15m
Frightened Crosbie stiff by taking corners fast.

JULY 2ND 1914
with Clayden & Mont
Lyon round the course to Sunbeam
depot. 30m
Mont also scared.

[Same day]
with Uncle
Lyon, Givors, Lyon, Mercedes depot.
25m
Very hot beautiful day. Went to see Mercedes and FIAT.

[Same day]
Indianapolis 30hp Sunbeam,
with Guinness & Van Raalte
[Chassagne, Resta & Guinninness drove the three Sunbeams in the Grand Prix],
Sunbeam depot, Les Esses, Les Sept
Chemins, Givors La Madeleine.
Too many people on course but did eighty in places. Road much cut up.

JULY 4TH 1914
Pilot 10hp
with Uncle, Aunt & Osmond
Lyons, Tribunes then round course,
Lyon. 35m
Magnificent race, well won by Mercedes, Lautenschlager.

JULY 5TH 1914
Pilot 10hp
with Uncle & Aunt
Lyon, Les Sept Chemins, Givors,
Mercedes depot, back and return
once more. 60m
Raging hot, saw Mercedes in pieces. Had dejeuner at café in Givors.

JULY 6TH 1914
Pilot 10hp
with Aunt & Uncle
Lyon,
Villefranche,
Tarrare, Roanne.
70m
Went off route and had difficulty to find it again, much rain. Stayed at a little pub in Roanne.

JULY 7TH 1914
Pilot 10hp
with Aunt & Uncle
Roanne, St
Porcain,
Montlucon,
Chateauroux.
120m
One puncture had to replace tyre and vulcanize tube in three places. Put gaiter on near rear also. One tyre... [/] Started late

JULY 8TH 1914
Pilot 10hp
with Aunt & Uncle
Chateauroux,
Chatellerault,
Chinon, Saumur.
150m
Two more punctures and had to repack rear tyre.

JULY 9TH 1914
Pilot 10hp,
with Aunt & Uncle
Saumar, Angers, Rennes. 160m
Awful trouble, off front burst. Had to pack with rags and drive 35kms. Fitted new tyre at Rennes, also shifted gaiter on near rear.

JULY 10TH 1914
[Last page of log ends here]
Rennes, St Malo. 45 milesm
Another puncture. Chain came off twice. Tried to find St Michel.

Last page of the logbook, showing a list of cars driven in 1913-14.

PASSENGER NAMES IN LOG BOOK WITH DATE OF FIRST ENTRY

Albertella 20/7/13

Aunt 6/7/13. Emmie Kate, Arthur Clayden's wife?

Baby 21/12/14. See "Baby Nora". [Relation?]

Baby Nora 13/12/13

Biggs 14/1/14. The IAE meeting *q.v. The Automobile Engineer* 12/2/14 p55

Billinghurst 13/1/14. Was at the IAE meeting 14/1/14

Billy 27/6/14

Boilleau 12/7/13

Brewer 14/9/13. R A Brewer, went to Exeter. Was at the IAE meeting 14/1/14

Charles 5/8/13

Clayden 1/7/13. Arthur Clayden, Editor of *Automobile Engineer*

Critchley 14/1/14. J S Critchley, Daimler Co. Was at the IAE meeting

Crosbie 1/7/14. Gordon Crosbie, *Automobile Engineer*, official artist

Cummings 14/3/14. S G Cummings. *Motor Racing* p23

Felters [?] 4/8/13. Fetters?

Foresti 20/7/13. G Foresti. OM (*Officine Meccbaniche*) team, Le Mans, 1925-26

Gladys 30/11/13

Guinness 2/7/14. K L "Bill" Guinness

Hornsted 28/2/14. L G Hornsted. Benz 200hp record breaker

Hugh 26/4/14. Sammy's youngest brother

Hunt 28/4/14. F G Hunt? See A B Demaus, Lionel Martin biography p47

Huet 28/5/14

Ida 9/1/14

Jennings 28/2/14. Morgan driver

Lafone 29/11/13. H C Lafone? (Later beacme Joint Editor of *The Autocar* with E J Appleby)

Mrs Lafone 29/11/13

Marlborough 13/7/13

Martin 31/1/14. Lionel Martin of Aston-Martin. See A B Demaus biography p47

Mont 14/2/14

Murphy 28/5/14

Osmond 20/2/14

Parker 13/9/13

Pauling 21/6/14. AC cars - driver?

Pégoud, Adolphe 9/10/13. Blériot test pilot, completed first parachute jump from a plane in 1913 and France's first fighter ace. Killed in August 1915 after six victories

Pope 20/7/13. H R Pope, Chairman of Itala Autos. See 5/7/13 p16

Robert 1/2/14

Roy 17/7/13

Rutter 19/8/13. H Thornton Rutter? (Author of *Modern Motors et al.*)

Sandy 13/2/14

Scott 21/6/14. AC car driver. See *Motor Racing*, p26

Shilson 14/1/14. B W Shilson, Coventry. IAE Hon.Sec for Midlands

Smith 4/5/14. W Smith, Pilot driver

Thomas 10/7/13. René Thomas, French Grand Prix Schneider driver

Tony 13/12/14

Uncle 23/2/14. Dr A T Wood, Ipswich? Owned an Argyll and Wolseley. See Autobiography.

Van Raalte, Noel 2/7/14. Drove for Sunbeam. (Bought first Bentley). See *Antique Automobile*.33-2/51

Wallis 14/9/13. Claude Wallis? See *A Racing Motorist*, p11

Walls 24/1/14

Westall 24/6/14. S C Westall, AC car driver. See *Motor Racing*, p26

Whit, Miss 27/6/14

Whittal 27/6/14

Appendices

Books by Sammy Davis

Atalanta, Women as Racing Drivers,
mid-1950s, G T Foulis & Co. Ltd

Cars, Cars, Cars, Cars,
1967, Hamlyn

Car Driving as an Art, A Guide for Learners and Advanced Drivers,
1952, Iliffe & Sons Ltd

Casque's Sketch Book, Motor Racing in Lighter Vein,
early 1930s, Iliffe & Sons Ltd

Controlling a Racing Car Team,
1951, G T Foulis & Co. Ltd

Expensive Noises,
1950s, Dudley Noble Publications

Great British Drivers,
1957, Hamish Hamilton

The John Cobb Story,
1950s, G T Foulis & Co. Ltd

Memories of Men and Motor Cars,
1965, Seeley, Service & Co. Ltd

Motor Racing,
1932, Iliffe & Sons Ltd

More Sketches by Casque, Racing Rallies & Trials – as they often are,
mid-1930s, Iliffe & Sons Ltd

A Racing Motorist, His Adventures at the Wheel in Peace and War,
1949, Iliffe & Sons Ltd

Rallies & Trials, The Monte Carlo Rally, Alpine Trials, the Rallye Gastronomique, RAC Veteran Car Trials, and other motoring occasions,
1951, Iliffe & Sons Ltd

A selection of Sammy's books.

Promotions

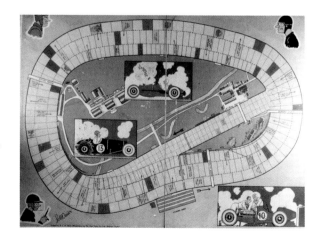

Brooklands Automobile Racing Game
Designed by S C H Davis, 1930s. Made at Harborne, England, by Chad Valley Co. Ltd. (Gordon Crosby painting on the front)

Pratt's High Test Brooklands Race Game.
Sammy Davis cartoons. Copyright Anglo Iranian Oil Co. Ltd, 36 Queen Anne Gate, London SW1

Casque's Stamp Album
Sheet(s) of stamps of well-known racing drivers.*The Autocar 2/5/1930.*

Brooklands Automobile Racing Game.

Bibliography
(Publications consulted by the Editor)

AC and Cobra
John McLellan, 1982, Dalton Watson

Alvis
Kenneth Day, 1981, Gentry Books, pp138-160

The Art of Gordon Crosby,
Peter Garnier, 1978, Hamlyn, pp13-28
Many other references

The Austin,
1905-52, R.J. Wyatt, 1981, David & Charles. p140, p248

The Autocar
27/9/13, p546, Resta/Watson, Course de l'Auto;
11/10/13, p692, The 10hp Pilot; 4/4/14, p648, 200hp
Benz; 4/4/14, p653, Overland; 11/7/14, p53 & pp65-
102, Grand Prix de France. Many other references

The Automobile Engineer
12/2/14, pp49-56, Clayden paper "Economics of Design"

Automobile Quarterly
Vol 17/4, p400. Vol 22/2, p159. Vol 39/3, p42

The Bentleys at Le Mans
J Dudley Benjafield, 1948, Motor Racing Publications
Ltd. pp12-24. See also Appendix I & II pp41-44

Bentley, The Vintage Years
1919-31, Michael Hay, 1986, Dalton Watson

**British Racing Drivers' Club, Silver Jubilee Book
Bouverie Street to Bowling Green Lane**
Arthur C Armstrong, 1946, Hodder & Stoughton

**British Trials Drivers,
Their Cars and Awards 1902-1914**
Donald Cowbourne, 2003, Smith Settle Ltd

Bugatti
H G Conway, 1963, G T Foulis & Co Ltd

The Complete Encylopaedia of Motor Cars
ed. G.N Georgano, 1973, Ebury Press

Encyclopedia of Motor Sports
ed. G.N Georgano, 1971, Ebury Press and Michael Joseph

Fifty Years with Motor Cars
A F C Hillstead, 1960, Faber & Faber Ltd, pp173-174

Green Dust, Ireland's Unique Motor Racing History
Brendan Lynch, 1988, Portobello

Histoire de L'Aéronautique
Charles Dollfus, 1938, L'Illustration, Paris

The History of Brooklands Motor Course
William Boddy, 1957, Grenville Publishing Co. Ltd, p57,
Pegoud. Many other references

Horseless Carriage Gazette
Downey, California. Vol 29, Jan/Feb 1967, pp38-39,
article "Beelzebub the Bollée"

Lionel Martin, a Biography
A B Demaus, 1980, Transport Bookman Publications

Motoring Annual Illustrated & Year Book
1906, Motoring Illustrated, Kenealy

Motoring Entente
Nickols & Karslake, 1956, Cassell & Co Ltd. pp232-233
& plate 38

A Racing History of the Bentley
1921-31, Darell Berthon, 1956, Autobooks

The Racing Zborowskis,
David Wilson, 2002, Vintage Sports Car Club. p42

Sir Henry Segrave,
Cyril Posthumus, 1961, Batsford. p125, p172

Sunbeam Racing Cars, 1910-1930
Anthony S Heal, 1989, Haynes Publishing Group

Tourist Trophy,
Richard Hough, 1957, Hutchison

Transport Pioneers of the Twentieth Century
Interviews conducted by Sir Peter Allen, 1981,
The Transport Trust, Cambridge

TT Pioneers,
Robert Kelly, 1996, The Manx Experience, Douglas,
Isle of Man.

Veteran Car Club Gazette,
Vol. X111 Nos.156/157, Jan–April 1981.

The Vintage Alvis,
Hull & Johnson, 1967, Macdonald & Co. Many
references.

Wheels Take Wings,
Michael Burn & A. Percey Bradley, G T Foulis & Co Ltd.
(1933-34). p145

Racing Events 1921-1938

Ch 5	1921	Brooklands	AC (record breaking)
	1922	Brooklands	Aston Martin (record breaking)
	1924	French GP	Mercedes (riding mechanic)
Ch 6	1925	Brooklands	Sunbeam 350hp
	1925	Le Mans	Sunbeam
	1926	Le Mans	Bentley
Ch 7	1927	Brooklands Essex MC	Alvis
	1927	Le Mans	Bentley
	1927	Brooklands British GP	Bugatti
	1928	Le Mans	Alvis FWD 4-cyl
Ch 8	1928	TT Ards	Riley
	1929	Brooklands Double 12	Bentley
	1929	Le Mans	Alvis FWD 8-cyl
	1929	Phoenix Park	Lea Francis
	1929	TT Ards	Riley
	1929	Brooklands 500-Mile	Bentley
	1930	Le Mans	Bentley
	1930	Brooklands 500-Mile	Austin 7
	1930	Brooklands	Austin 7 (record breaking)
	1930	Montlhéry	Morgan (record breaking)
	1931	Brooklands	Invicta
Ch 9	1932	Le Mans	Aston Martin (team manager)
	1933	Le Mans	Aston Martin
	1935	TT Ards	Singer
	1937	Brooklands	BMW Type 328 (observed run)
	1938	RMYC	Birmal hydroplane (1st, Club race)

Major Racetrack Achievements

Le Mans

2nd, 3 litre Sunbeam, with Jean Chassagne, 1925
1st, 3-litre Bentley, with Dr Dudley Benjafield, 1927
4th, Aston Martin, with Bertelli, 1933

Phoenix Park, Dublin

Saorstat Cup,
2nd, 1½-litre Lea Francis, 1929

Brooklands Automobile Racing Club (BARC)

Brooklands Six-Hour race
1st on formula, 1½-litre Alvis, 2nd on average speed, 1927

500-miles race
2nd, 6½-litre Bentley, with Clive Dunfee, 1929

Junior Car Club Double-Twelve-Hour race
2nd, with Sir Ronald Gunter Bt,1929

British Racing Drivers Club (BRDC)
Gold Star Award of Merit, Road and Track Races, 1929

Junior Car Club Double-Twelve-Hour race.
2nd, 6½-litre Bentley, with Clive Dunfee, 1930

500-miles race
1st, 750cc Austin, with The Earl of March, 1930

Class G flying start
1100cc Riley, Mountain Course, 66.86mph, 1930

British Racing Drivers Club
Gold Star Award of Merit, Brooklands racing, 1930

500-miles race
2nd, 3-litre Talbot, with The Hon Brian Lewis, 1931

RAC observed run
in a Type 328 fully-equipped BMW.
One hour test at 102mph, 1937

Non-racing Achievements

Aston Martin Owners Club
Founding Vice-President 1935.
President, re-formed club, postwar.

Bentley Drivers Club
Honorary member.

British Racing Drivers Club (BRDC)
Founding Committee Member, 1927.
Vice President.

Guild of Motoring Writers
Chairman, 1953

Honorary Citizen of Le Mans
Sammy's Honorary Citizenship of the City of Le Mans probably ranks as the highest accolade he received as will be seen from the short list of recipients. See also Rue S C H Davis in Le Mans; similarly his old friend Robert Benoist and those others who had roads named after them.

Veteran Car Club of Great Britain (VCC)
Joint Founder and first President 1930-34.

Vintage Sports-Car Club (VSCC)
President 1936-37.

Brooklands Automobile Racing Club (BARC)
Committee, 1939.

500 Club
President

City of Le Mans Accolade

Citoyens d'Honneur de la Ville du Mans

Général Patton
Commandant d'armée des États Unis

Albert Bobroch
Journaliste Américain, historien

S C H Davis (1971)
Vainqueur en 1927 (Bentley)

Briggs Cunningham
10 participations

Luigi Chinetti (1982)
Vainqueur en 1932, 1934, 1949

Jacky Ickx (2000)
Vainqueur en 1969, 1975, 1976, 1977, 1981, 1982

Derek Bell (2002)
Vainqueur en 1975, 1981, 1982, 1986, 1987

Donald Panoz (2003)
Constructeur, initiateur et promoteur de l'Américain
Le Mans Série

Savoy Hotel

Signed Savoy Hotel dinner menu, Friday June 24th 1927 (see page 83) (deciphered as far as possible)

Top
1. H (?) Henry Petre

Lefthand column
2. Walter O. Bentley
3. K. Lee Guinness
4. R.C. De(?) Morgan
5. A.R. Buckland
6. R.S. Witchell
7. ?
8. ?
9. F.T(?) Burgess
10. H. Massac Buist
11. T.S(?)Fletcher
12. G.R.N. Minchin
13. S.C.H. Davis

Righthand column
14. Vernon ---------?
15. Montagu Tombs
16. L.T. Delaney
17. Maurice(?) Sampson
18. C.W. Nichols
19. Gordon Crosby
20. Francis (Frank) C. Clement
21. J. Dudley Benjafield

Hippodrog

There was a lovely story about the Hippodrog. We all had English breakfast and suddenly Bertelli and I noticed that people at the other end of the table were staring at something. We looked round and there was the most extraordinary dog you have ever seen. It was a black dog with double-jointed legs, it had luminous eyes, and it didn't look like a dog at all. We tried to attract it to come but it wouldn't. It just looked and went away, so when the girl came out from the hotel we said, "What's that dog you have got?" and she said, "We haven't got a dog!"

The Hippodrog.

When we explained it to some of the other people, they said, "Are you sure you were drinking coffee?" Do you know, it was four years before we could get a photograph of it! It was a very old Belgian barge dog, very thin on its legs and looked as if it was double-jointed, and it had cataracts. It's a wonder it survived so near the course. [Probably 1933 at Café de l'Hippodrome. Sammy had a great liking for dogs and a number of them appear in sketches in this book].

Supplementary Correspondence

A number of letters concerning Sammy Davis, written between 1946 and 1970.

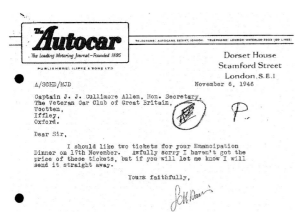

November 6th 1946 from The Autocar *to Capt.
C Allen, Honorary Secretary VCC, Iffley, Oxford
Request two tickets for the Emancipation Dinner.*

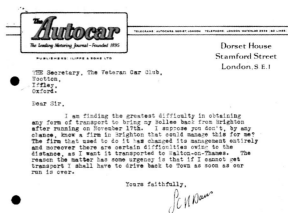

Undated (1946) from The Autocar *to the
Secretary, VCC, Iffley, Oxford
Transport of Bollée from Brighton to Walton-on-
Thames*

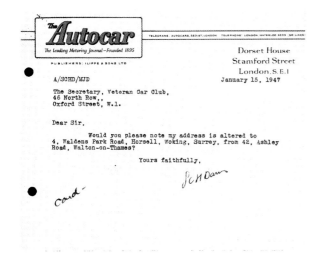

January 15th 1947 from The Autocar *to the
Secretary VCC, Oxford Street, W1
Change of address.*

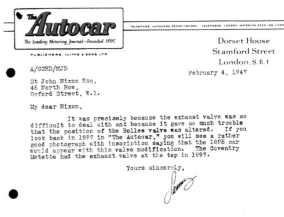

February 4th 1947 from The Autocar *to St John
Nixon, Oxford Street, W1. Dealing with the Bollée
exhaust system.*

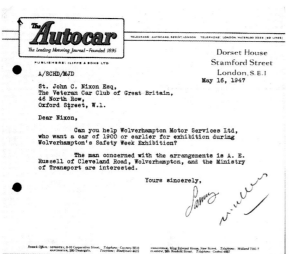

May 16th 1947 from The Autocar *to St John Nixon, VCC, Oxford Street, W1*
Car required for Wolverhampton Safety Week Exhibition.

November 10th 1948 from The Autocar *to Miss Ruxton, VCC, Oxford Street, W1*
Re tickets for the pre-Brighton dinner. [Times were changing! See Nov.1946. Ed.]

March 15th 1949 from The Autocar *to Miss Ruxton, Secretary, VCC, Oxford Street, W1*
Visit to the USA.

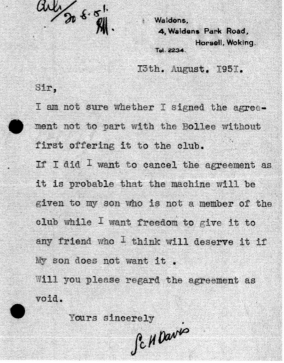

August 13th 1951 from Woking to Secretary VCC
Concerning the Bollée and the acquisition scheme.

*August 24th 1951 from C. Allen, Ifley, Oxford, to
Secretary, VCC, Oxford Street, W.1
Mr Davis free to dispose of the Bollée.*

*February 4th 1960 from Guildford to
Capt. D C Morrison (Secretary VCC)
Various, including query re veteran car safety
and new road regulations.*

*January 26th 1959 from Guildford to
Capt. D C Morrison (Secretary VCC)
Querying women prize-giving at the RAC.*

*November 9th 1960 from Guildford to
Capt. D C Morrison (Secretary VCC)
Argument about early Bollée dates, and
comments on the* Daily Sketch *run. [Sammy drove
on the second run in 1928. Ed.]*

S. C. H. DAVIS
JOURNALIST

Sutton Lodge,
Clandon Road,
Guildford, Surrey.
28th October

My dear Morrison,

No, we did not take tickets for the dinner for a number of reasons. We found that at the end of a run of the type Beelzebub gives us, we were very tired indeed late in the evening. That made getting into dress clothes seem uninviting.

Further, as retired journalists have no expense sheet, it became a mite too costly and we had to economise. There is the Hotel in London, which is ridiculously expensive though convenient, the hotel at Brighton, the garaging etc, and it ran us into £ 22 last year which is more than our budget will stand.

I think you will understand, and I wish it could be solved.

Yours

October 28th (1961?) from Guildford to
Capt. D C Morrison (Secretary VCC)
Relating to Brighton Run costs. Sad reflection on
Sammy's pecuniary state.

THE VETERAN CAR CLUB of GREAT BRITAIN
Hon. Secretary: CAPT. J. J. C. ALLEN, WOOTTEN, IFFLEY, OXFORD

You will be helping the Club by filling in this form and
returning immediately

MEMBERS or ASSOCIATES

1. Full Name........ DAVIS S C H
2. Permanent Address .. 42 ASHLEY RD WALTON ON THAMES
3. Profession or Occupation REME
4. Whether a Full Member or an Associate..... FULL
5. Year, and if possible the month, of first joining the Club. DAY Club was created.

1946 VCC record form
Question 5 – Year, and if possible the month, of
first joining this Club
Answer. Day club was created.

S. C. H. DAVIS

Sutton Lodge,
Clandon Road,
Guildford, Surrey.
TEL. GUILDFORD 60596
1 June   GUI 2DS

My dear Marcus,

Good to hear from you again and hope we can meet for a natter sometime.

Thanks, it was a surprise and I still don't know why they made me a citizen. something to do with that episode in the war suggests itself. But it was really rather wonderful.

Funny world isn't it but you and I had a hell of a good time and the new people don't seem to have a chance. Too many financial difficulties.

Yes I knew Scott and it is sad that he has gone, I had to make a new address book the other day cos the old one was too sad.

Nowadays competition cars are covered with adds and any colour.

Yes an auobiography is written but I alter it every week and it is afterthoughts about things we did and an explanation of how one was made up so as to have an enormously exciting pleasant life but no money

Susanna is going fine as head art-therapist of a big mental hospital and is darned good at it.

I find my "control" is Ok but the chassis not so good, Mind you we are perfectly happy.

Every possible good wish to you all

Yours

June 1st (circa 1967) from Guildford to Marcus
Chambers, one-time BMC Competitions Manager
(ex-VCC)
Discusses this book – altering it every week!

Index to Autobiography